100 PAPERS
WITH CLASSICAL PATTERNS

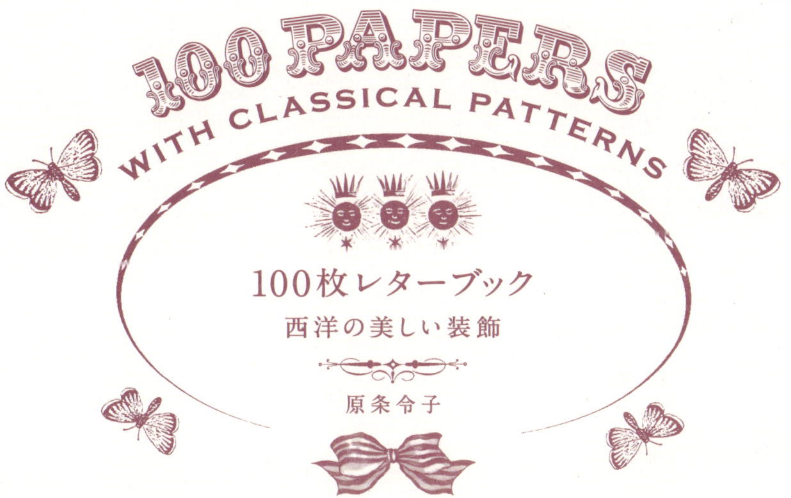

100枚レターブック

西洋の美しい装飾

原条令子

PIE.

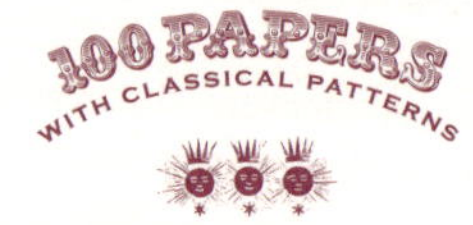

まえがき

本書は、1枚ずつ切り離して使える便せんを104枚収録したレターブックです。☆☆☆☆☆☆☆☆☆☆☆☆☆☆☆☆☆☆☆☆
17-19世紀初頭に使用されていた印刷のための装飾や銅版画を中心としたヨーロッパのクラシックなモチーフをもとに
新たにデザインしました。特に、繊細な描き込みが美しいフランスの画家J・Jグランヴィル（1803-1847年）のイラストは細部が
ユニークで楽しいものがたくさんありますので、色々なところにちりばめてみました（ぜひ探してみてください）。☆☆☆☆☆
印刷には、通常のカラーに加え、金や銀のインクも使用しています。☆☆☆☆☆☆☆☆☆☆☆☆☆☆☆☆☆☆☆☆☆☆☆☆
送る相手や用途に合わせて、デザインを選んだり、ペンの色を変えたりしてお楽しみいただければ嬉しいです。お手紙の他、
ラッピングやクラフトなどいろいろな用途にご活用ください。☆☆☆☆☆☆☆☆☆☆☆☆☆☆☆☆☆☆☆☆☆☆☆☆☆☆

原条令子

Enjoy beautiful patterns printed on 104 removable papers! All patterns such as small flowers, decorative frames and classical motifs
are designed and collaged with using European chalcography & printing ornaments in 17-19 century. J.J.Grandville (1803-1847), a
French caricaturist, is my favorite artist and I tried to introduce many of his unique and marvelous motifs in this project.
Most pages are printed with gold or silver colors so that each copy conveys gorgeous impact for anyone who take it in hand. Also,
papers are carefully selected to go well with each design and various purposes. This is an one-and-only gift book for females who
love writing letters and paper crafting.

Reiko Harajo

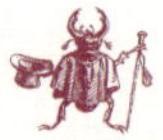

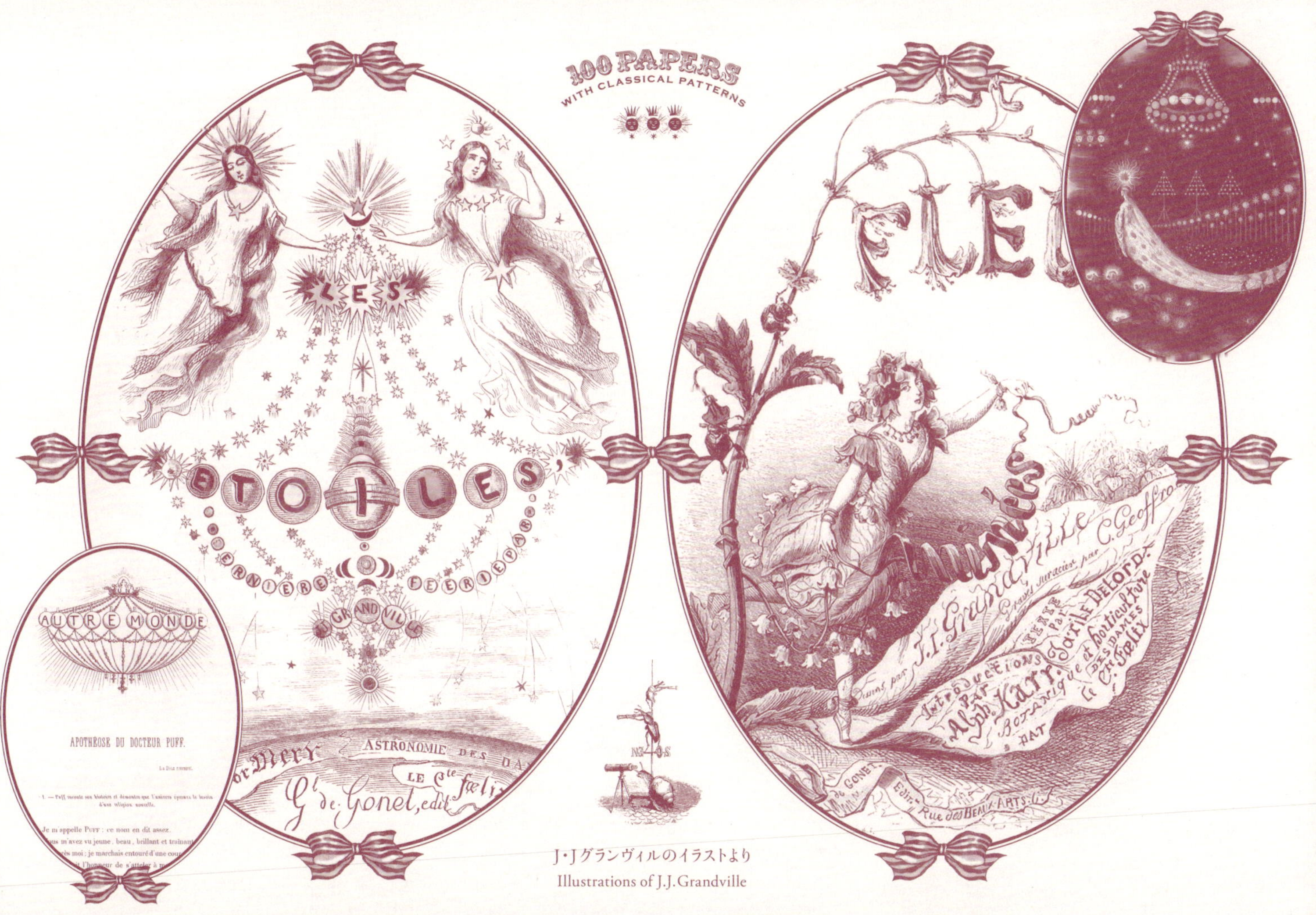

J・Jグランヴィルのイラストより

Illustrations of J.J.Grandville

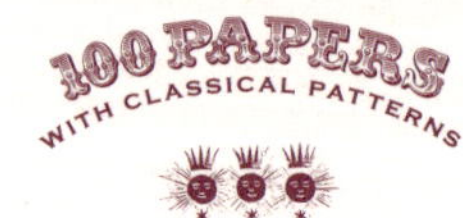

100枚レターブック
西洋の美しい装飾
100 Papers with Classical Patterns

2015年11月13日 初版第1刷発行
2025年 9月 8日　　　第4刷発行

アートディレクション　原条令子
翻訳　山代有紀
編集　根津かやこ

発行人　三芳寛要
発行元　株式会社 パイ インターナショナル
〒170-0005　東京都豊島区南大塚2-32-4
TEL 03-3944-3981　FAX 03-5395-4830
sales@pie.co.jp

PIE International Inc.
2-32-4 Minami-Otsuka, Toshima-ku,
Tokyo 170-0005 JAPAN
TEL +81-3-3944-3981　FAX +81-3-5395-4830
sales@pie.co.jp

印刷・製本　アベイズム株式会社

「100枚レターブック」特設サイトでレターブック
シリーズの取扱店舗一覧、使い方を紹介した
連載などをご覧いただけます。最新情報をお届
けするメルマガもぜひご登録ください。

原条令子　Reiko Harajo

武蔵野美術大学卒業後、広告デザイン会社に入社。
退社後、studio Magic にて横尾忠則氏に師事。
1998年に原条令子デザイン室を設立。『iA/interior
Architecture』(エクスナレッジ)『relife+』(扶桑社)
『Renovation journal』(新建新聞社)などの
アートディレクションや、『おとぎ話の幻想挿絵』
『ジョルジュ・バルビエ』(パイインターナショナル)『海外
ミステリ Gem Collection』『影の縫製機』(長崎出版)
『味写入門』(アスペクト)『書き出し小説』(新潮社)
『遊べる浮世絵』『幻想の花園 図説 美学特殊講義』
(東京書籍)『昭和時代vol.1〜』(中央公論新社)
など、多数のブックデザインを手がける。

She is a graduate of Musashino Art University,
Tokyo, Japan. She began her career as an art
director in Tokyo, Japan, and created/produced
commercial ads. Afterwards, she worked as an art
director at 'studio Magic' in Tokyo, Japan, and
found a mentor in Tadanori Yokoo, one of the
famous Japanese artists who are internationally
recognized. In 1998, she established Reiko Harajo
Design Room, and has been active as an art
director for many major magazines as well as in
designing books since then.

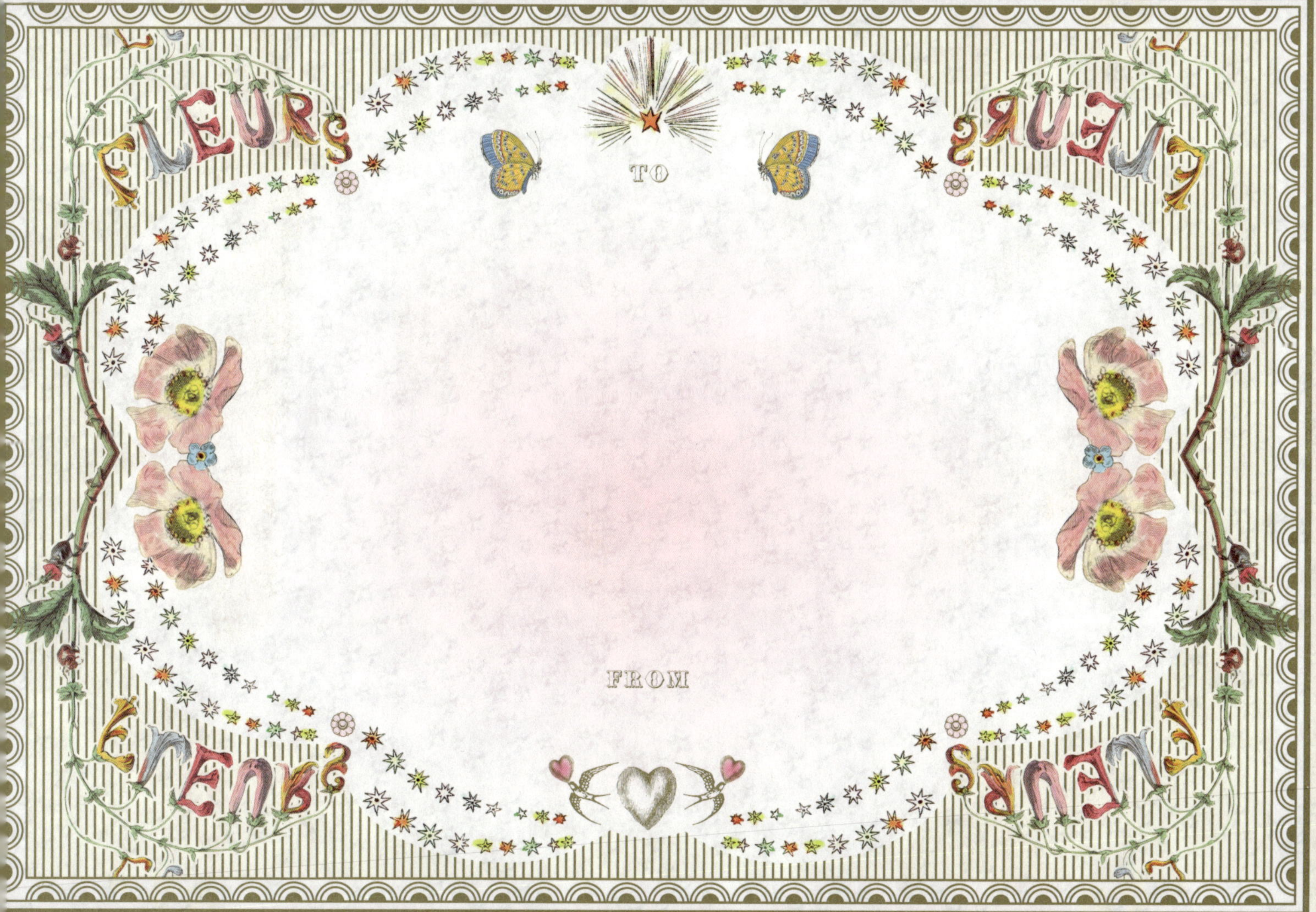

FLEURS
TO
FROM

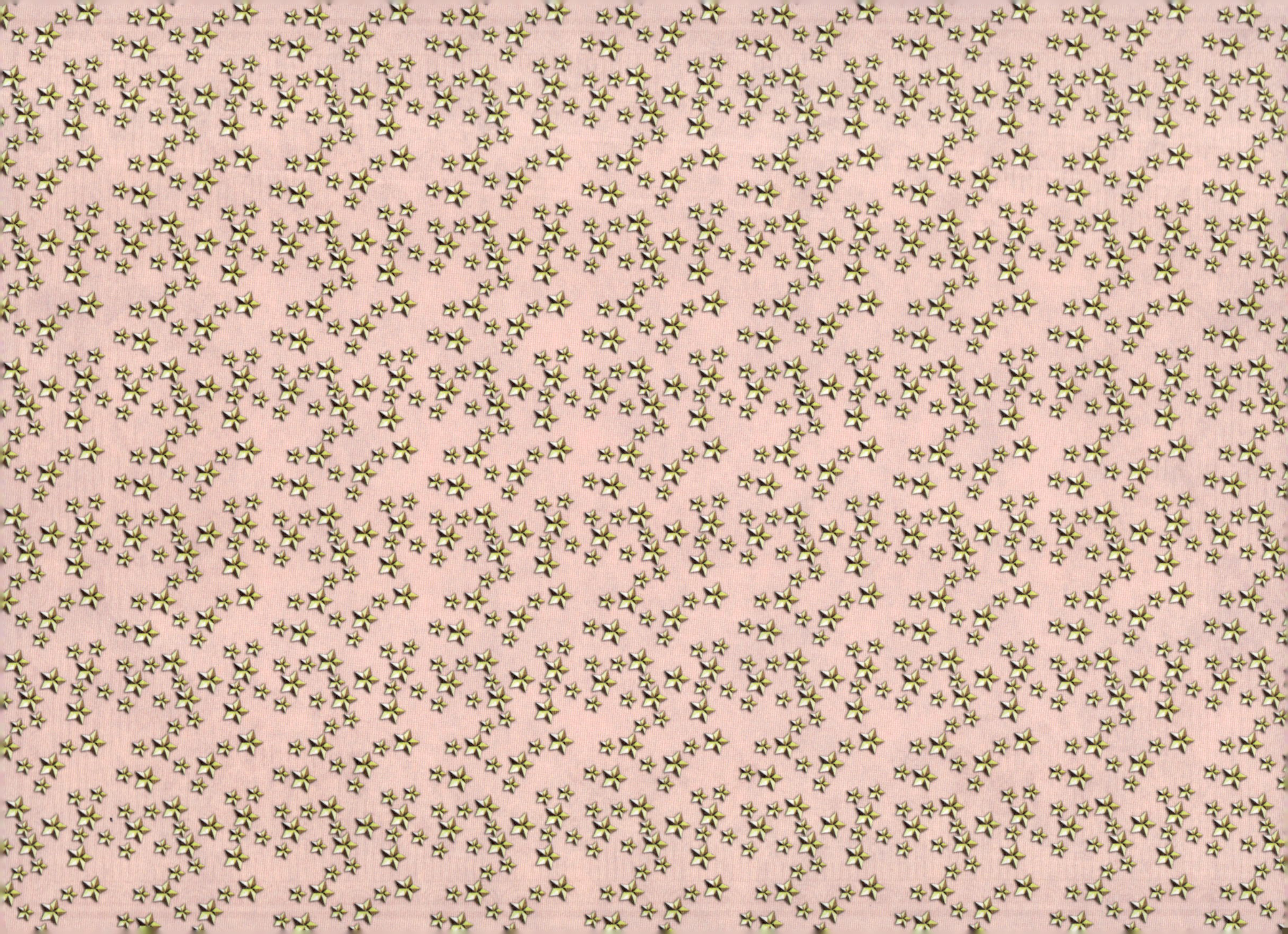

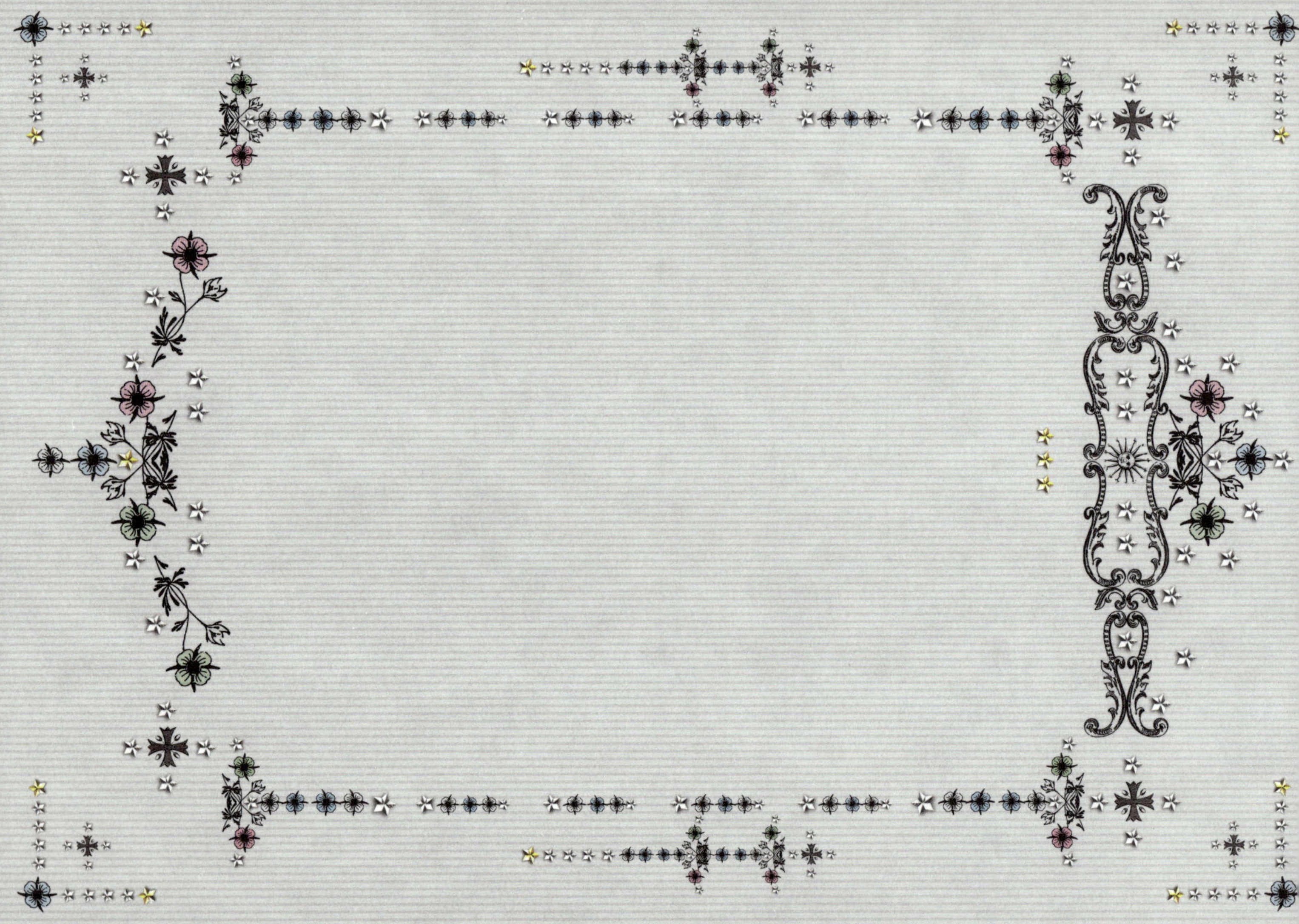

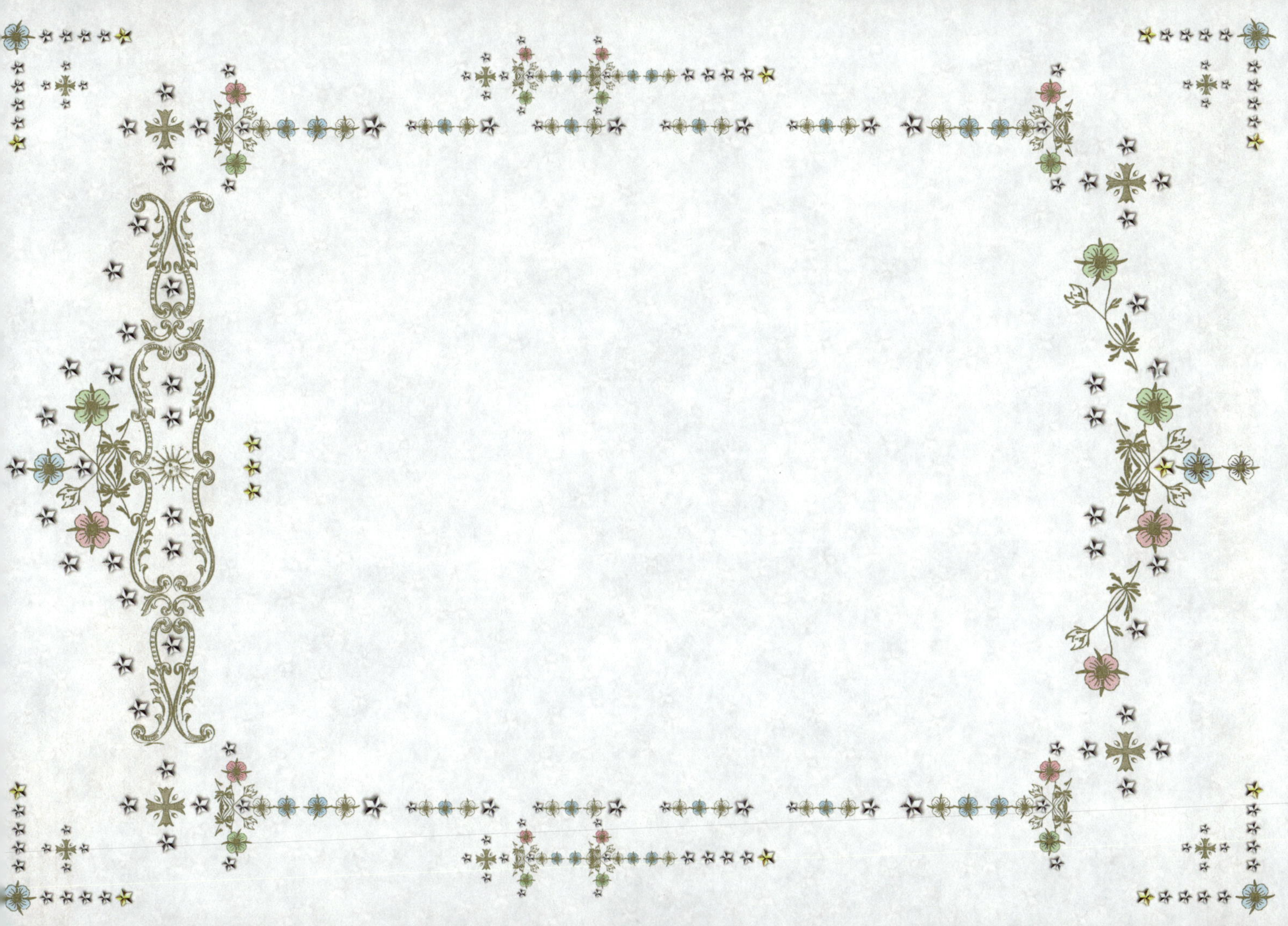

To
From

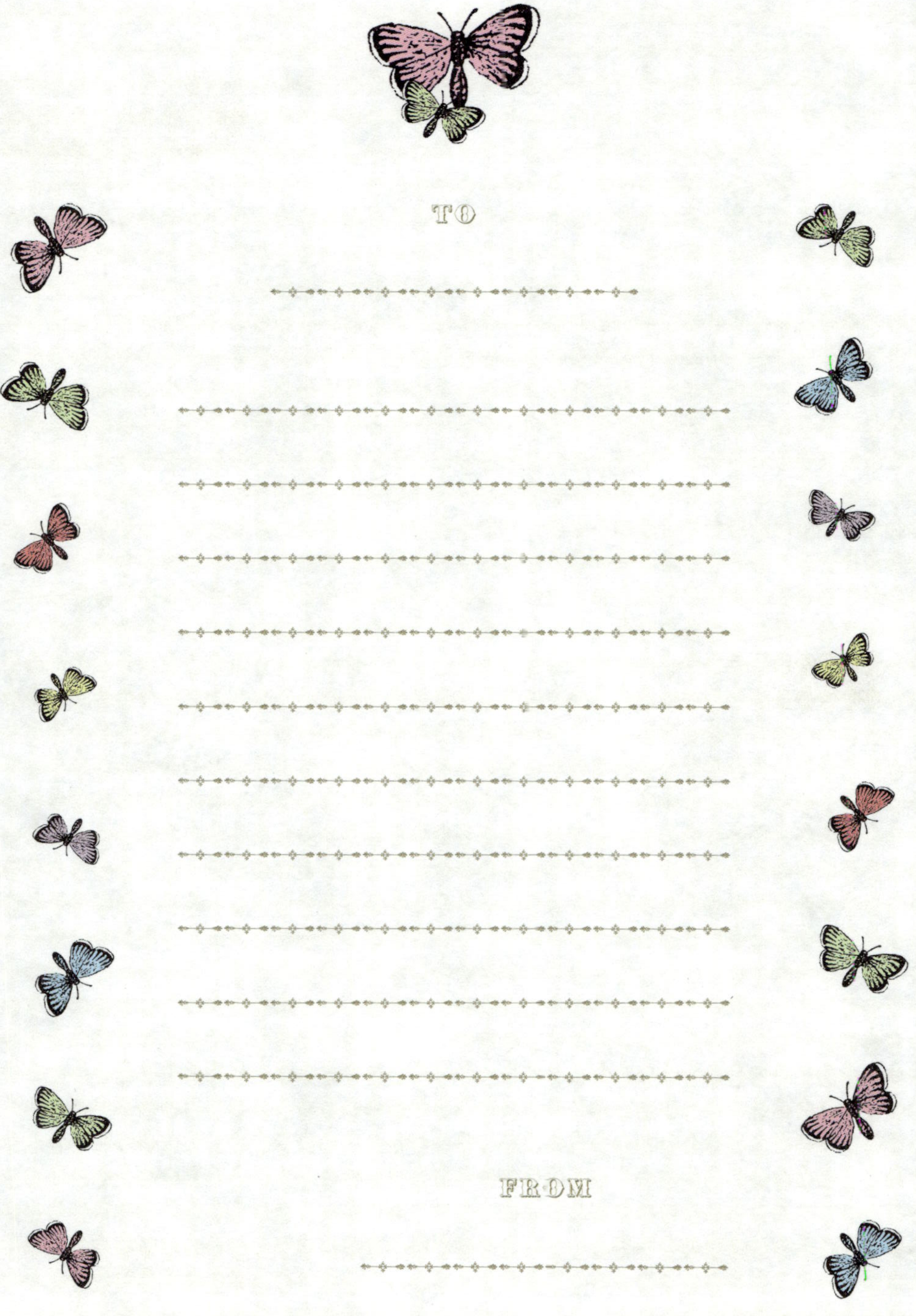

TO
FROM

TO

FROM

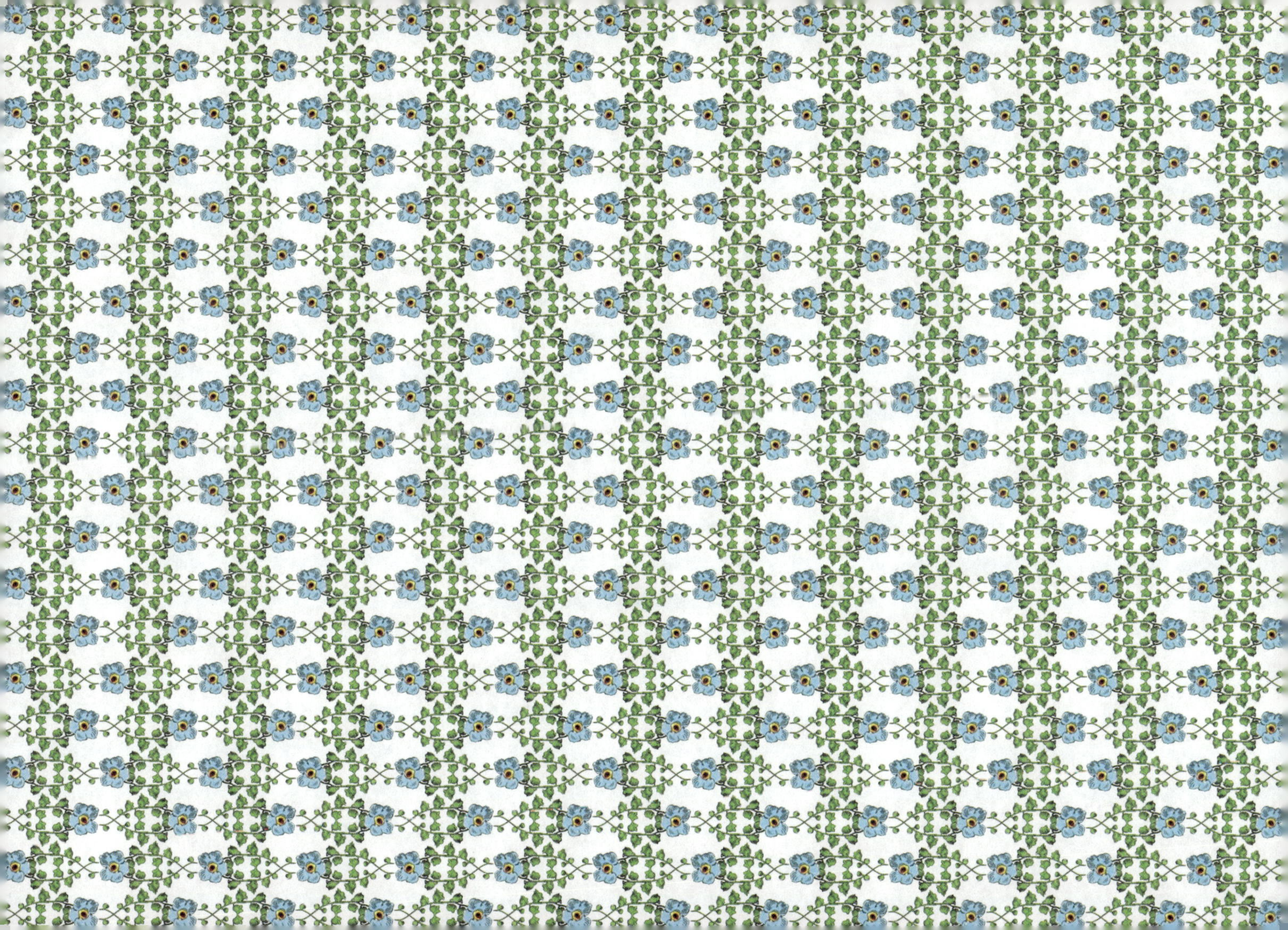

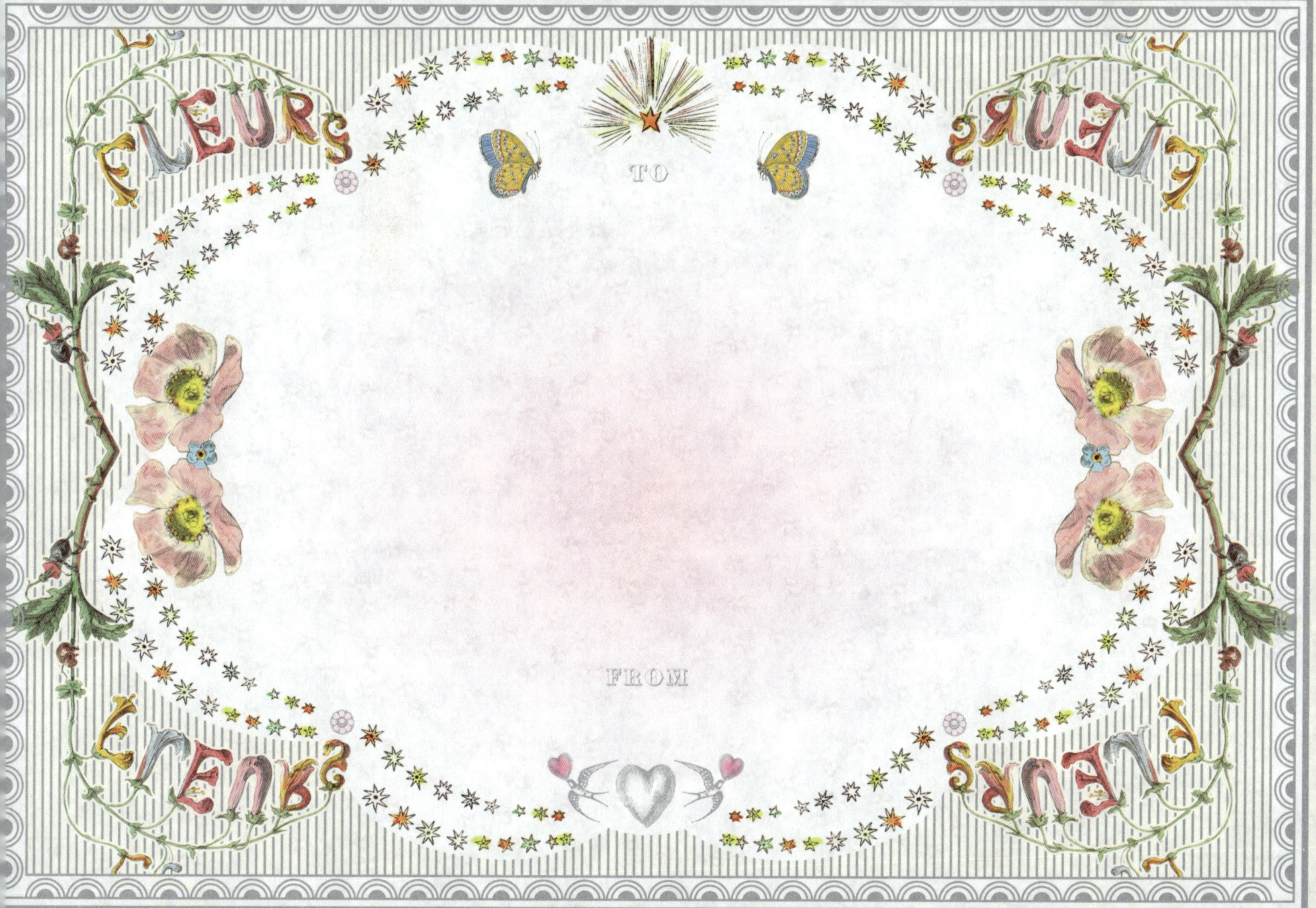

FLEURS
TO
FROM

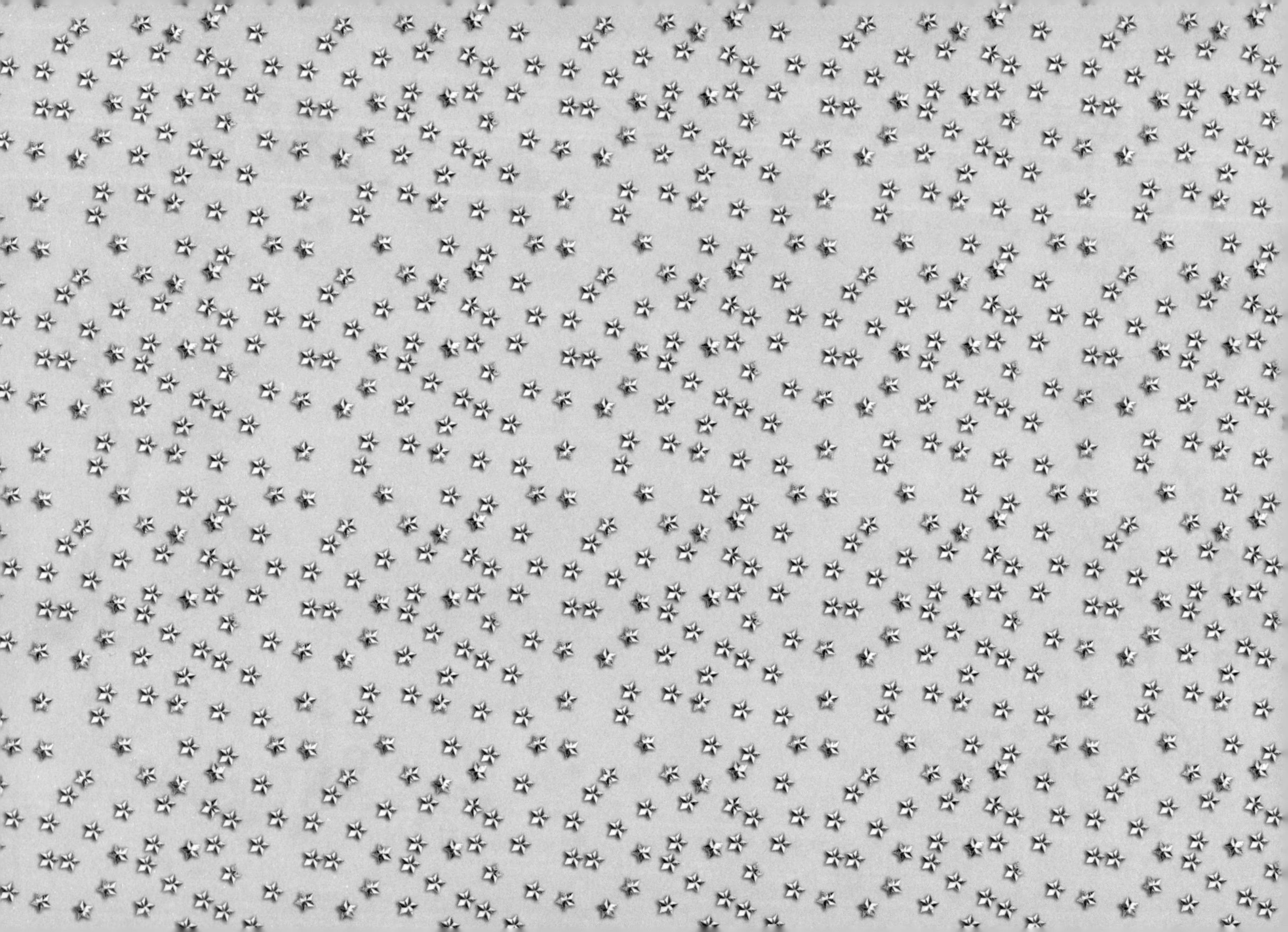

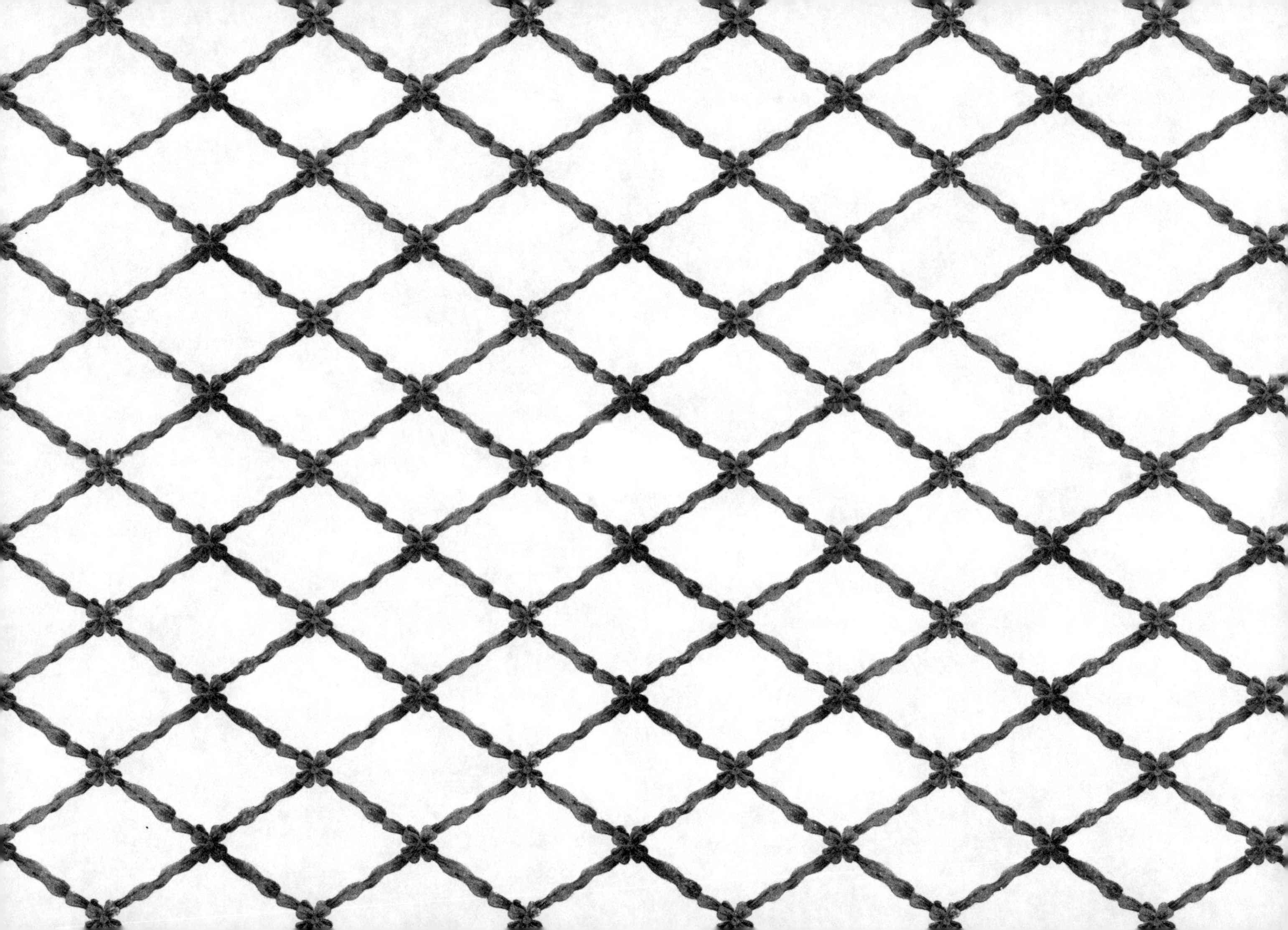

To
From

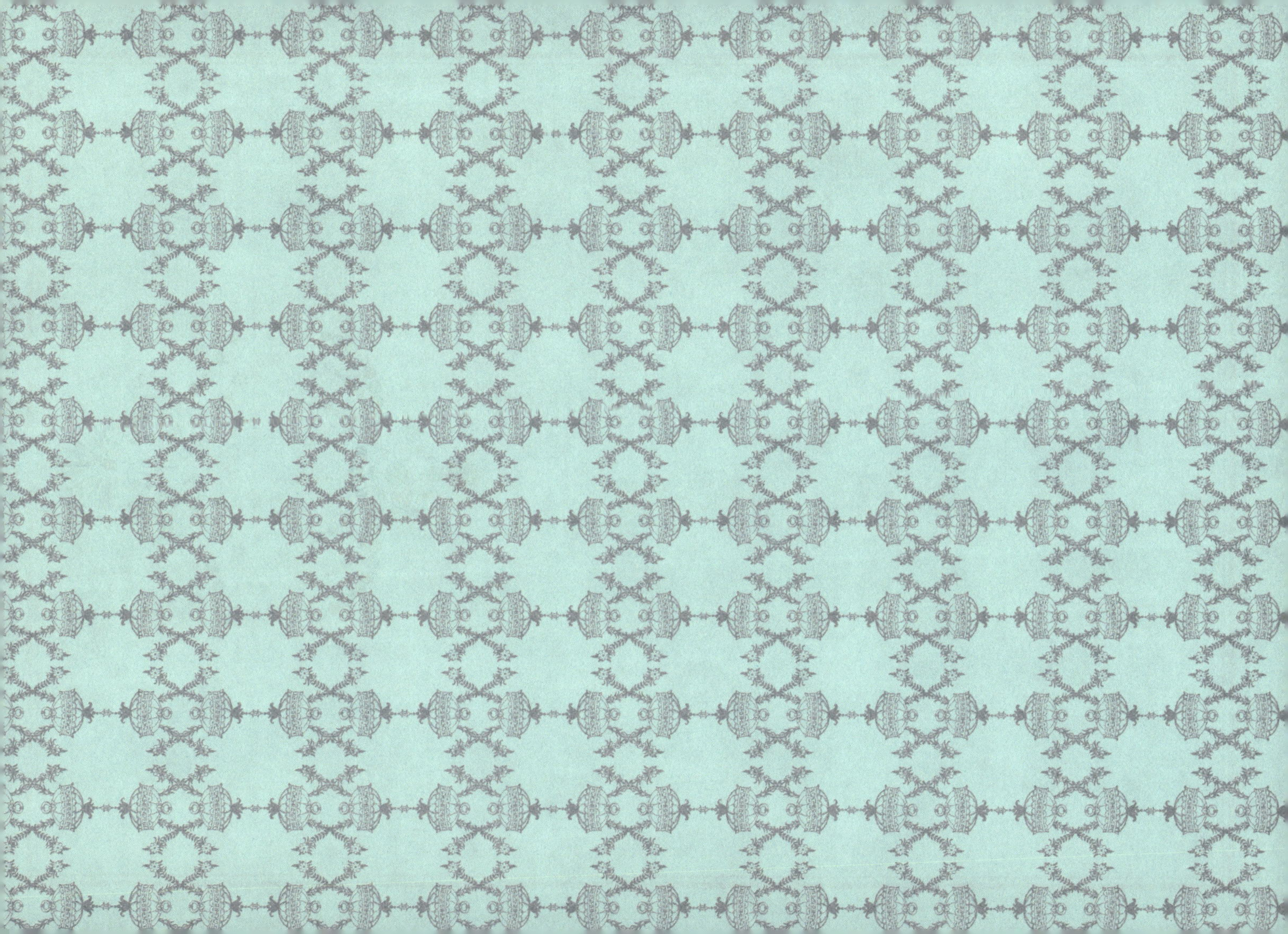

From

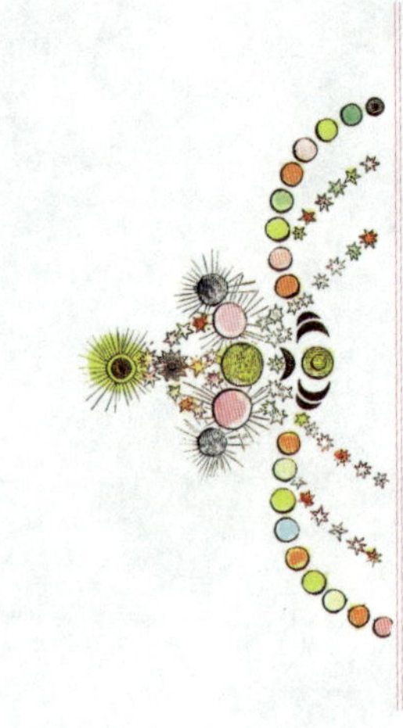

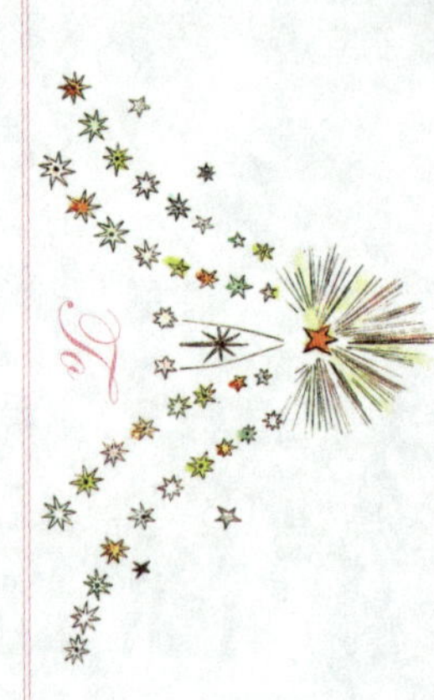

To

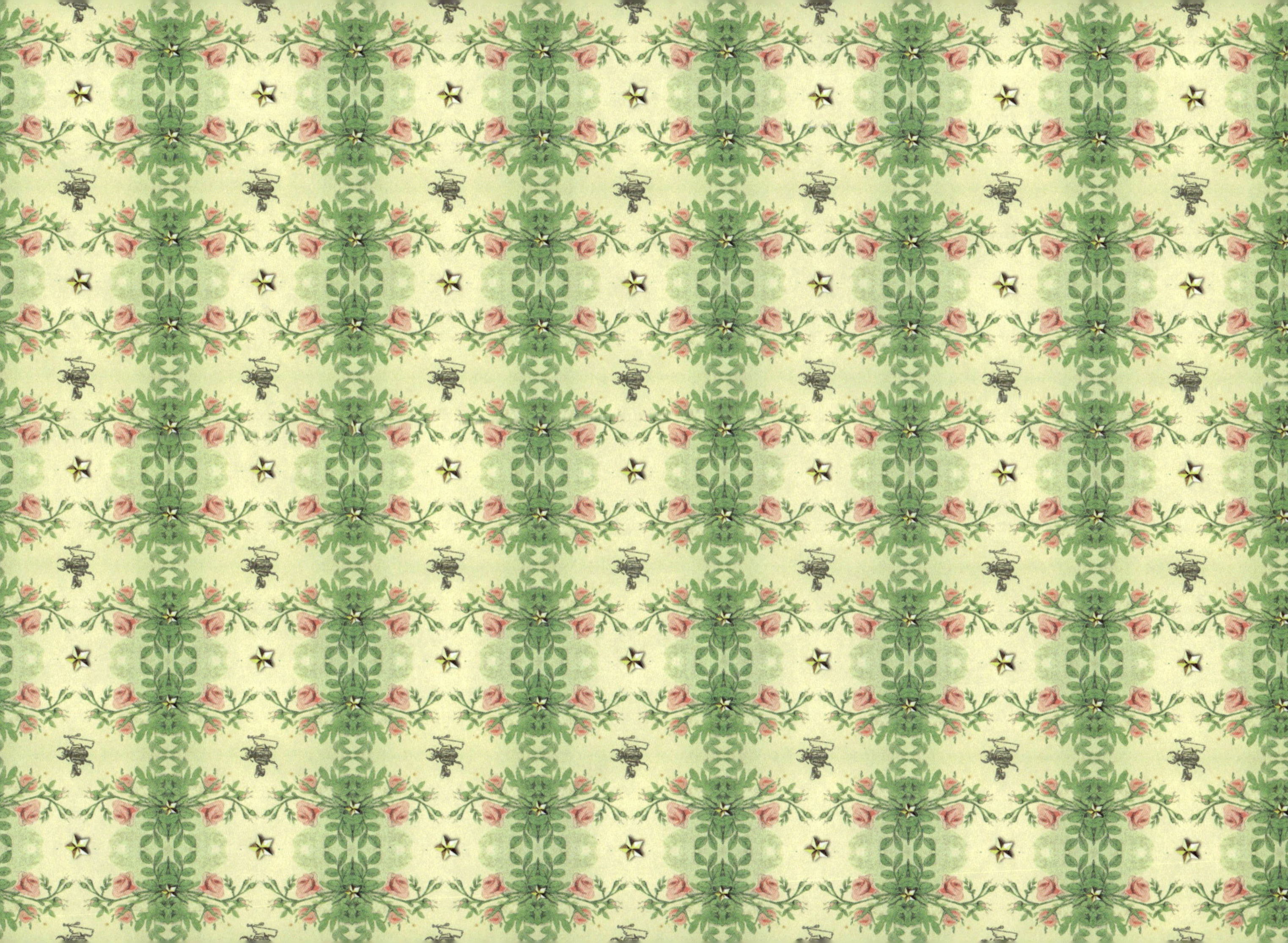

To

From

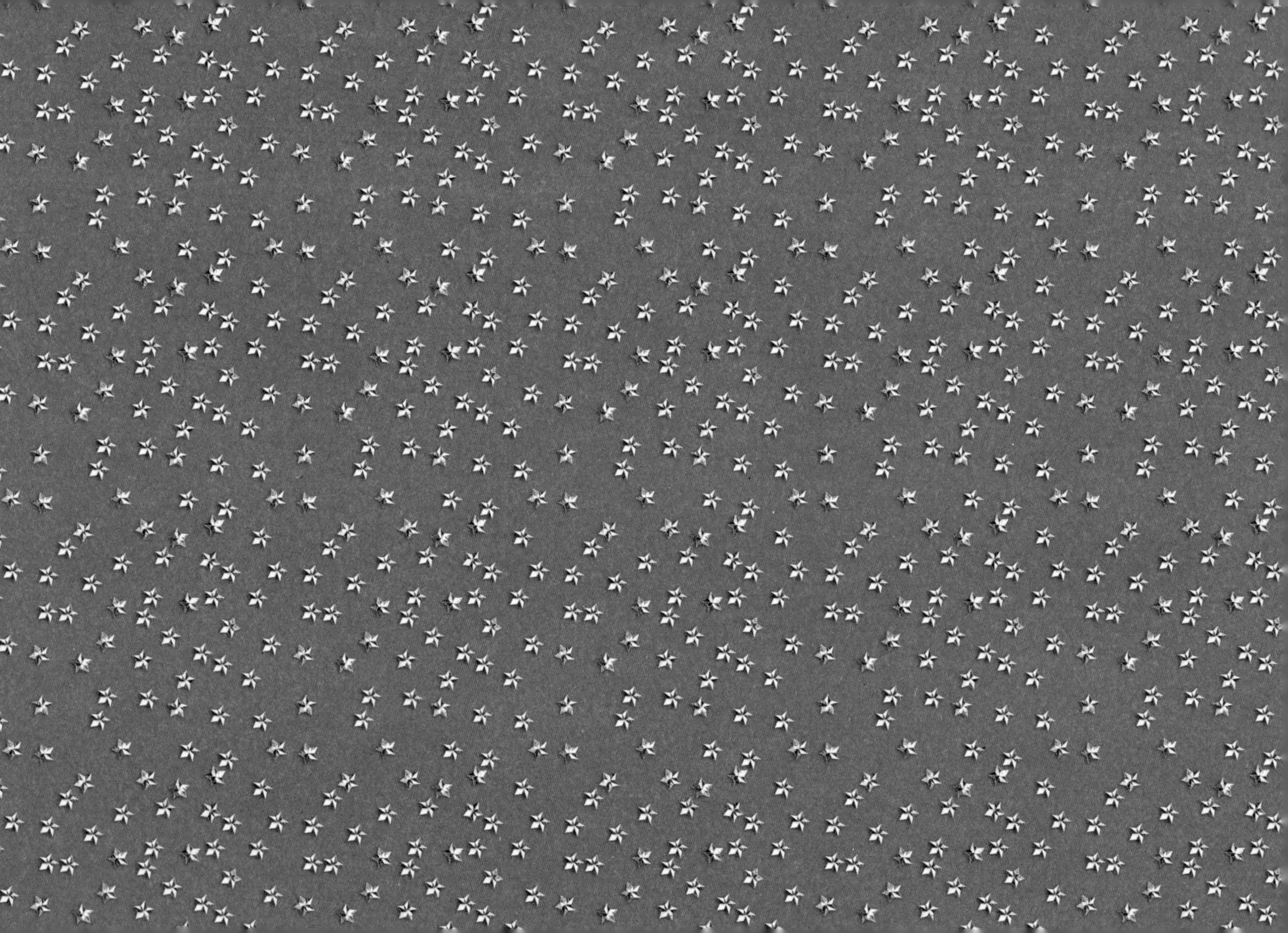

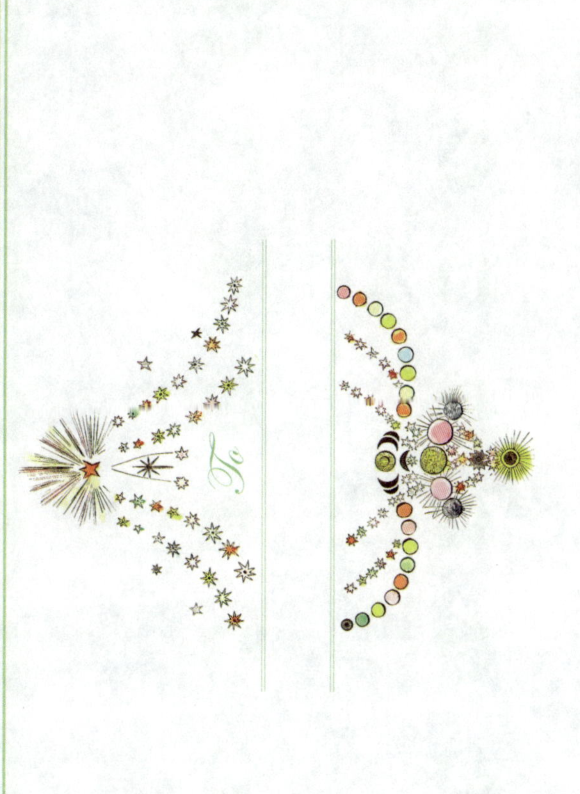
To

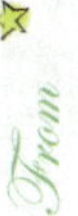
From

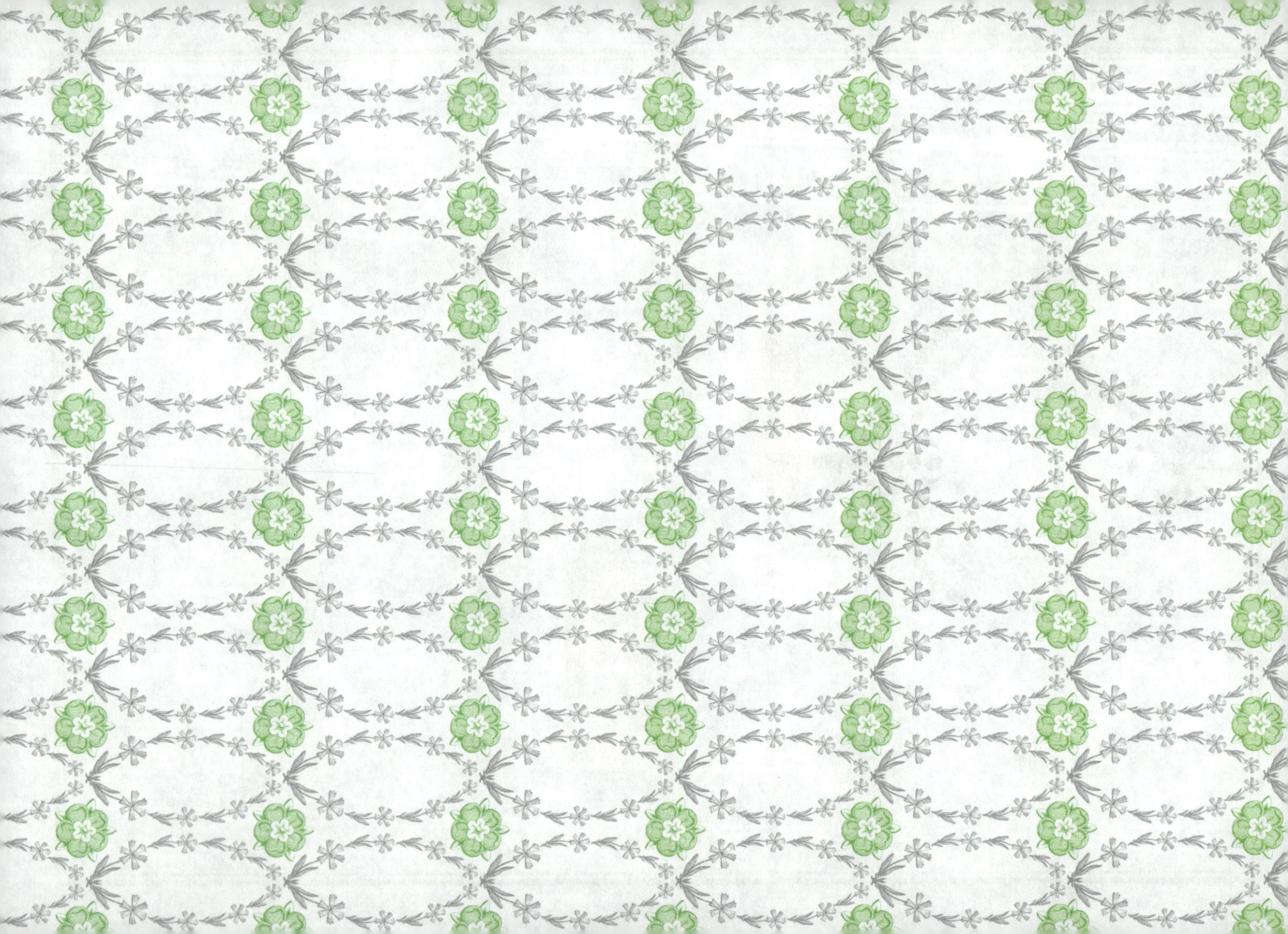

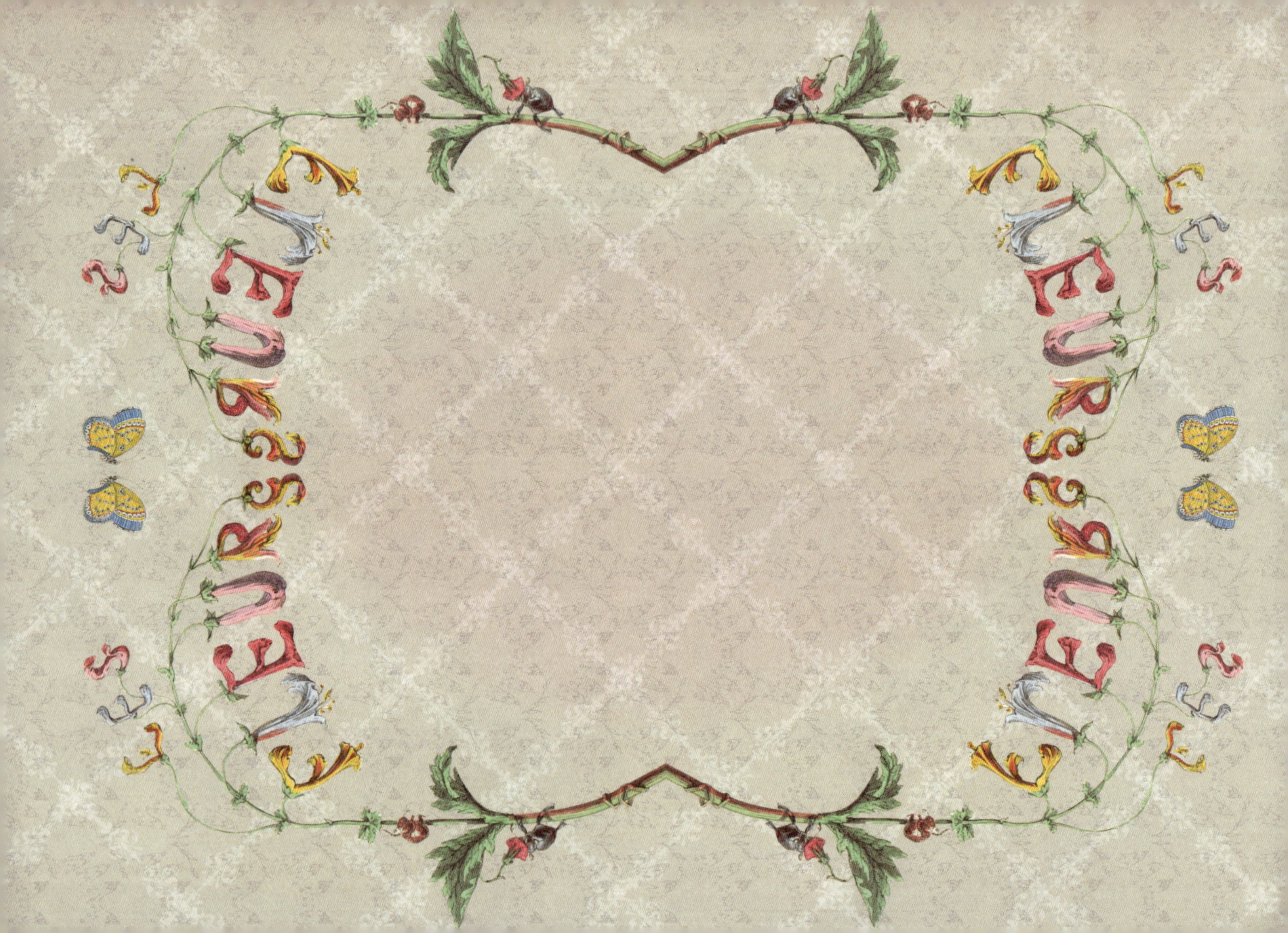

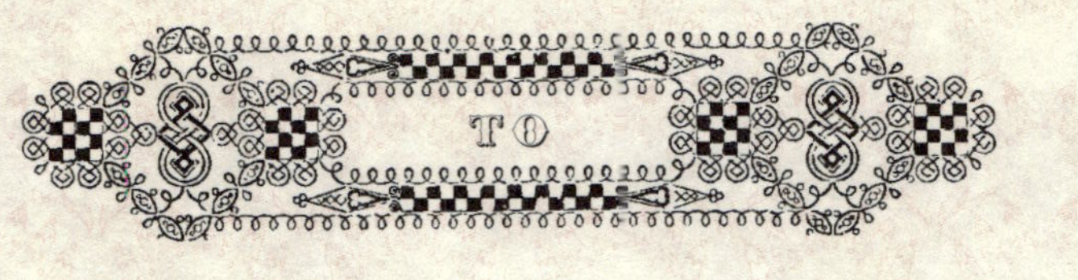

TO
FROM

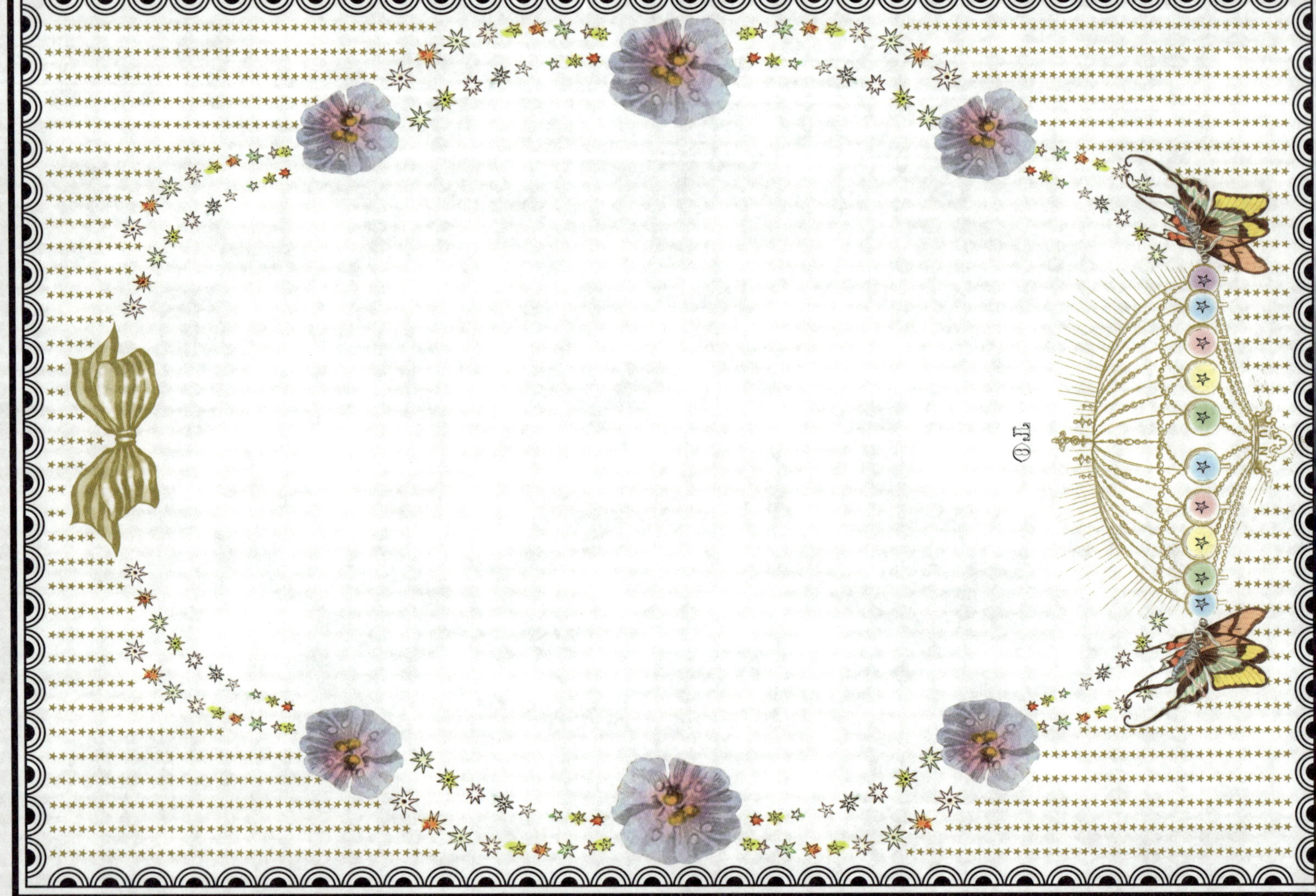

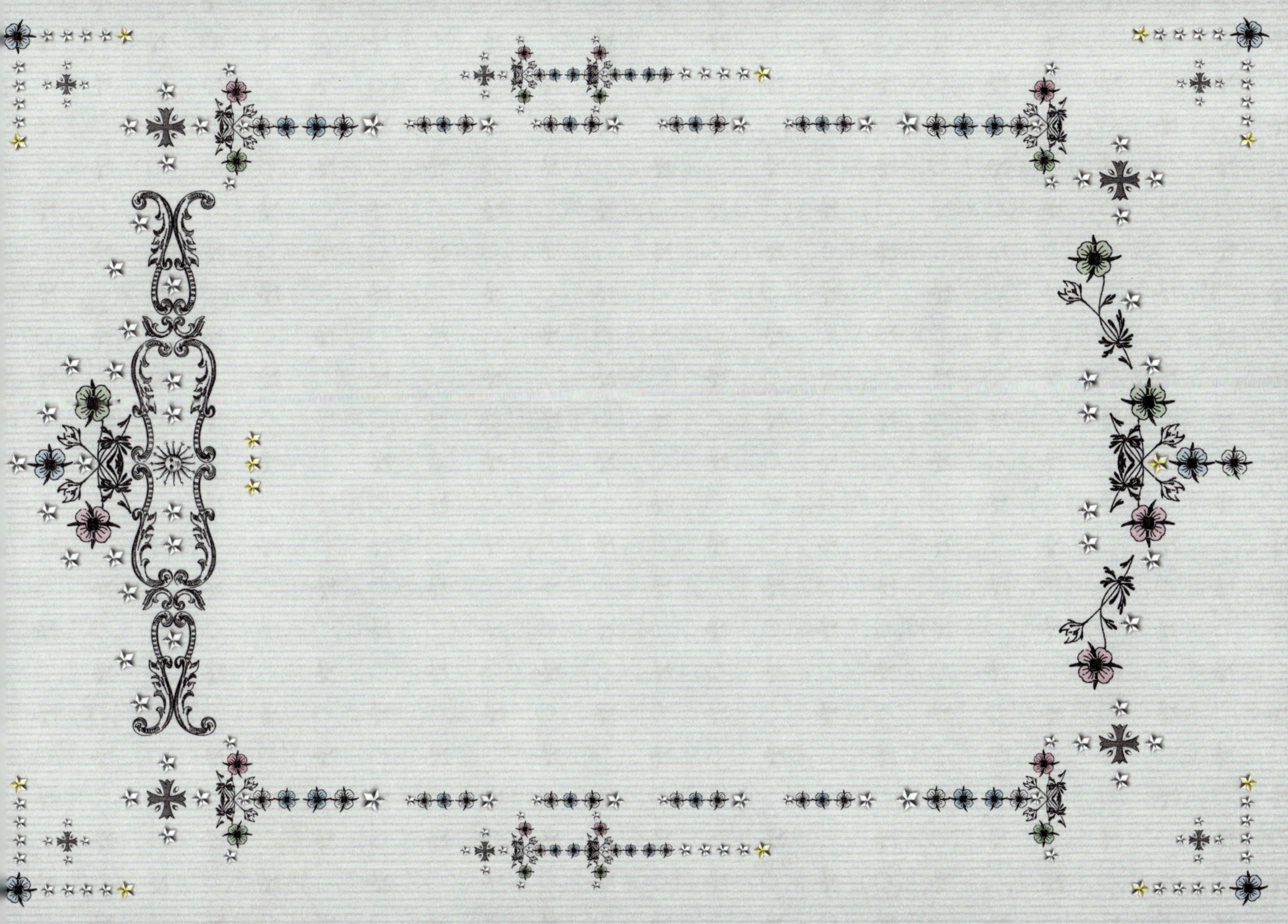

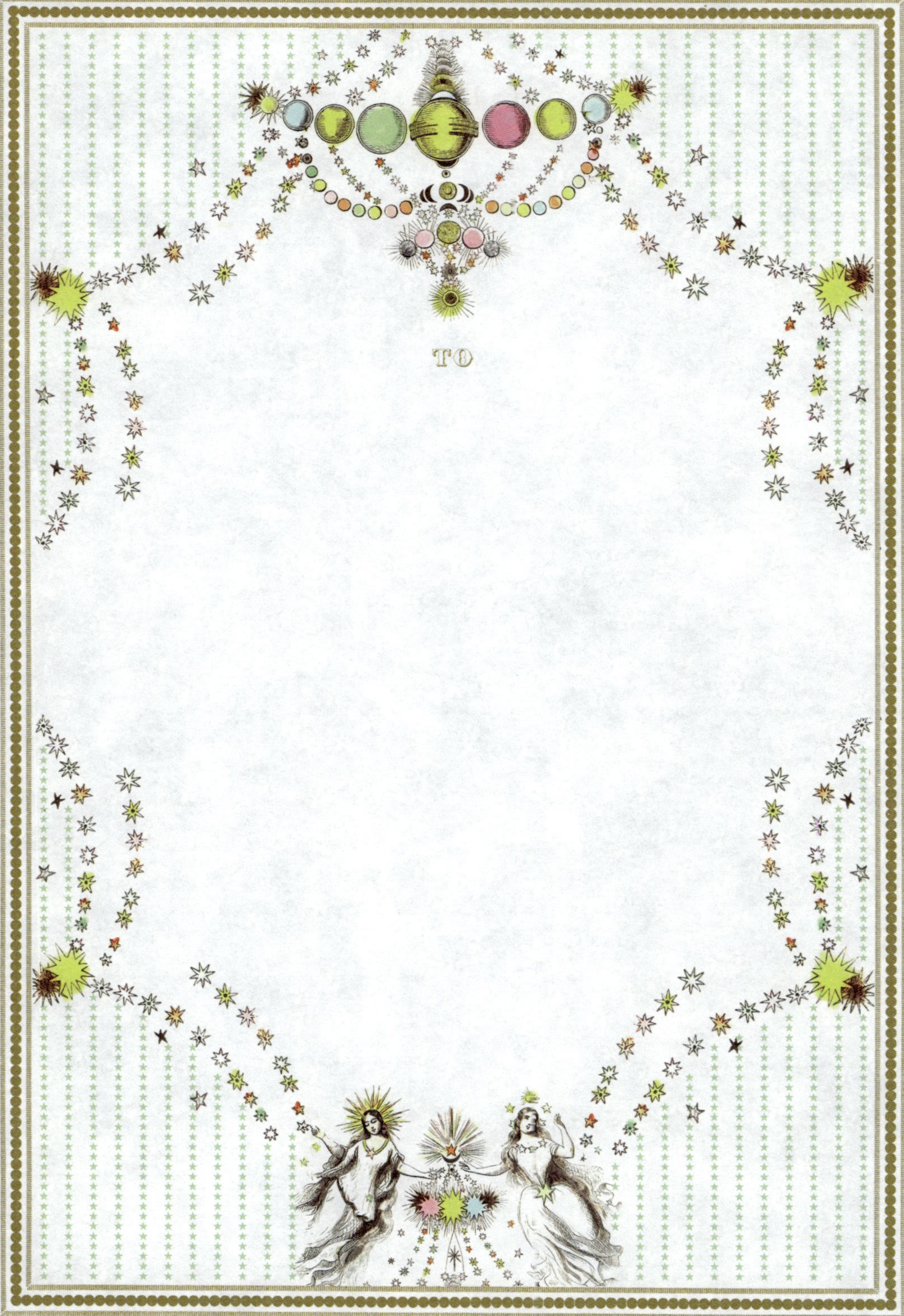

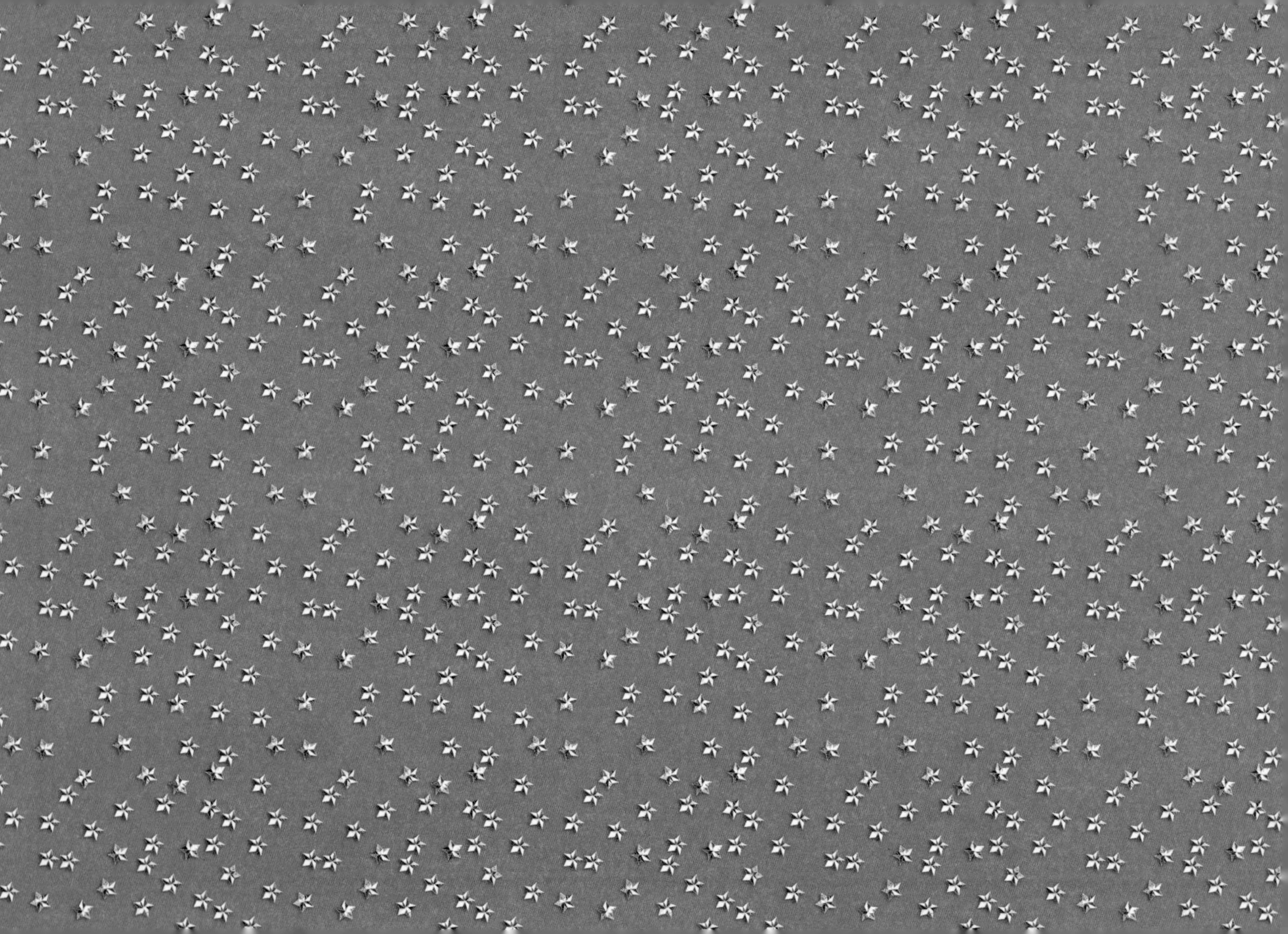

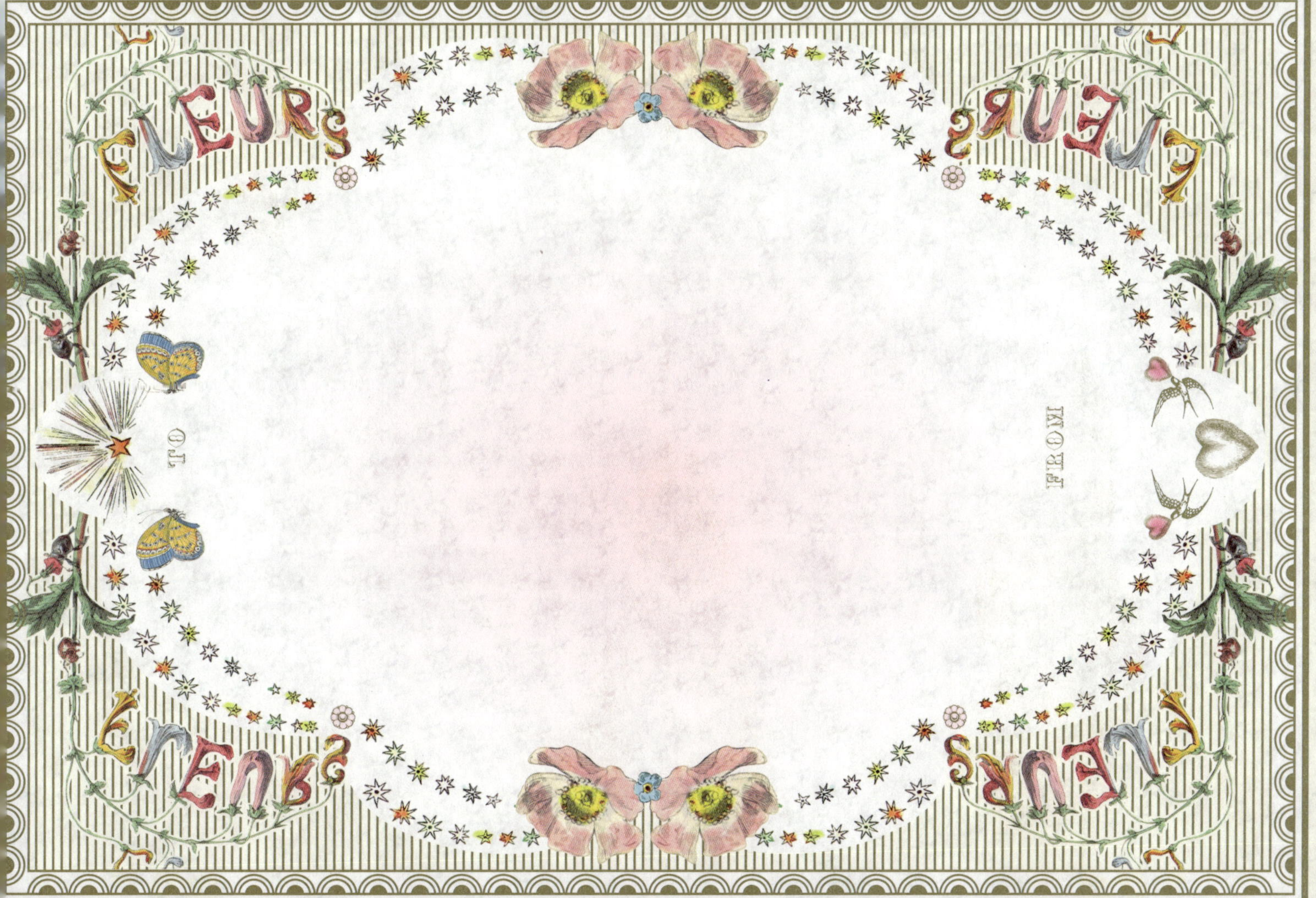

FLEURS
FLEURS
FLEURS
FLEURS
TO
FROM

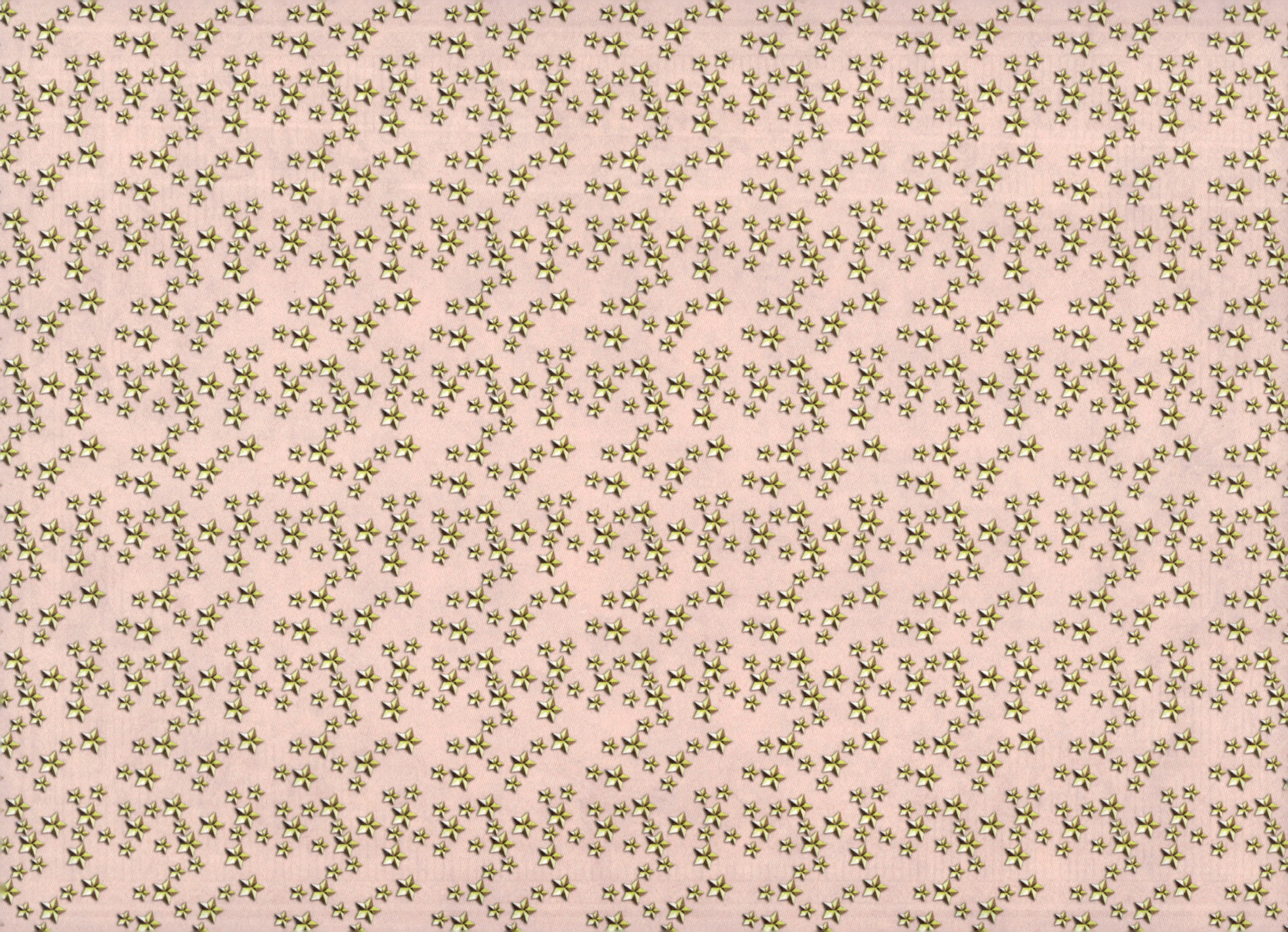

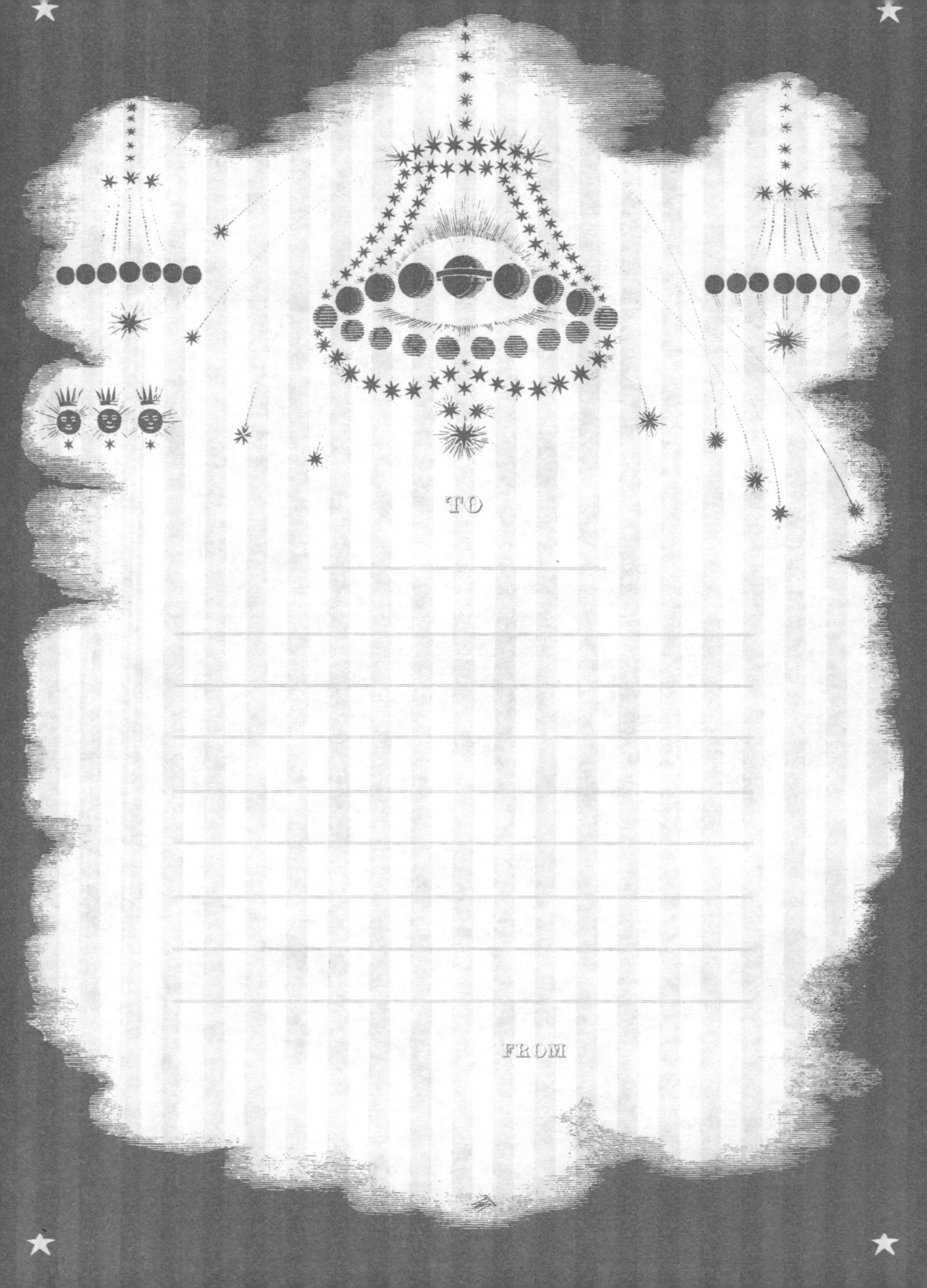

TO
FROM

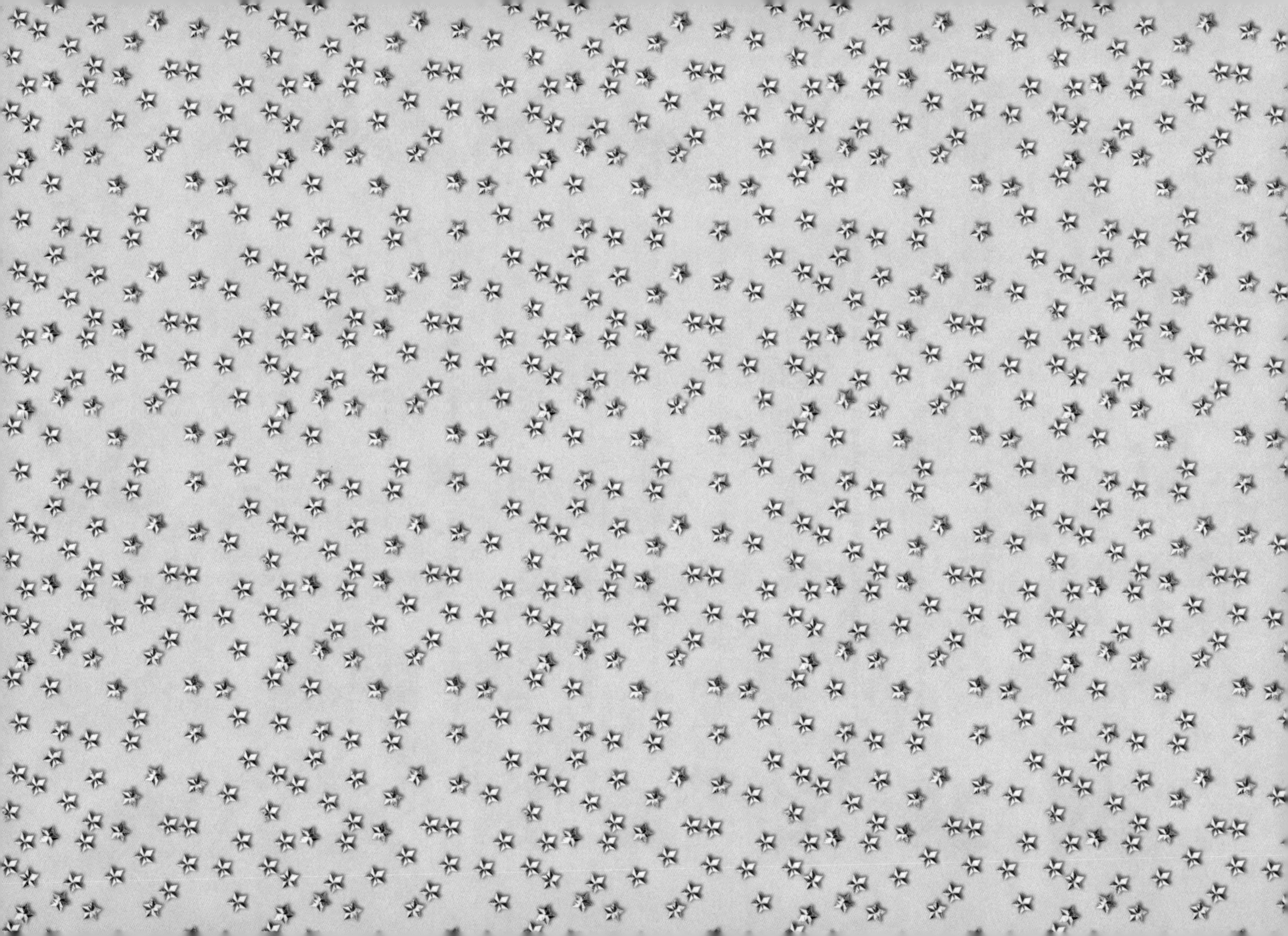

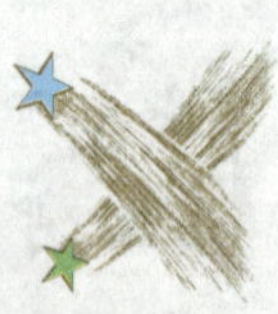
FROM
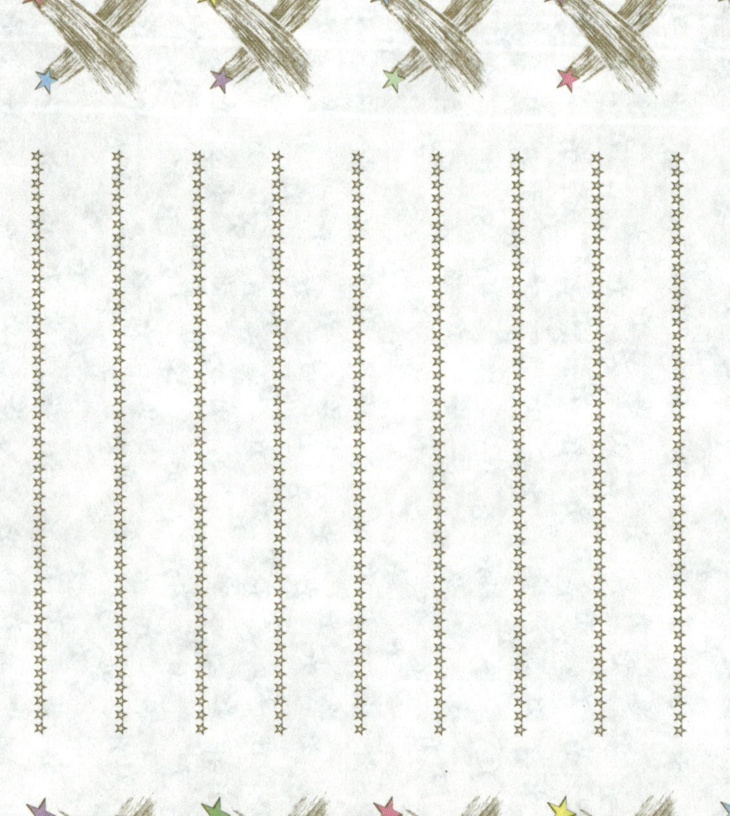
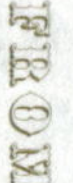

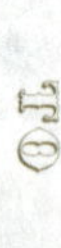
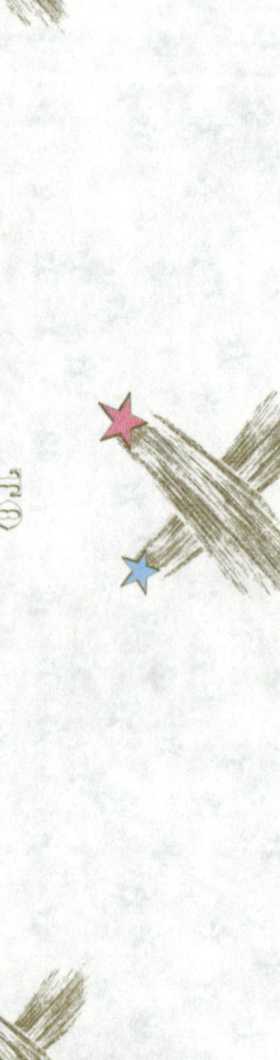
TO

TO
FROM

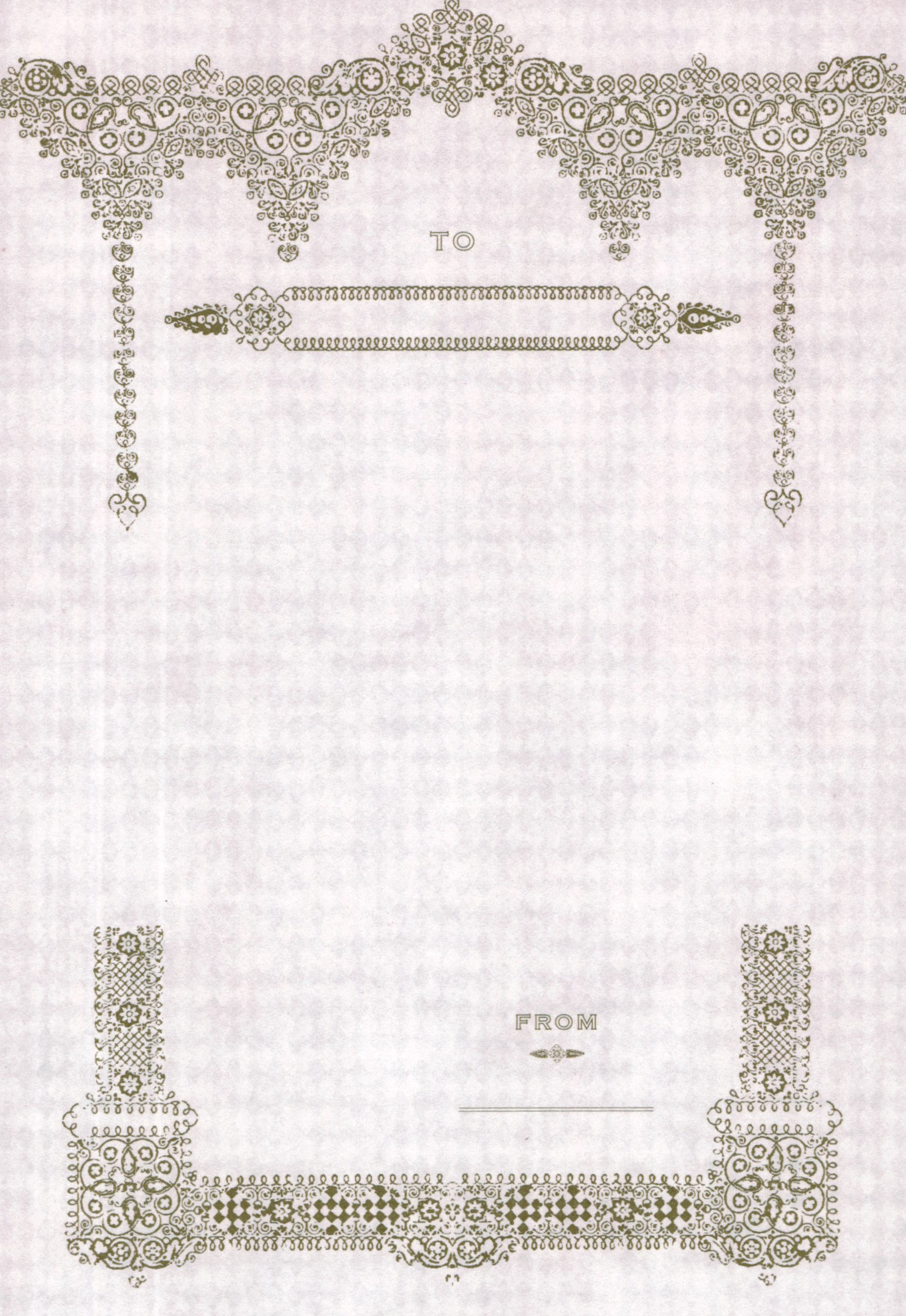

TO
FROM

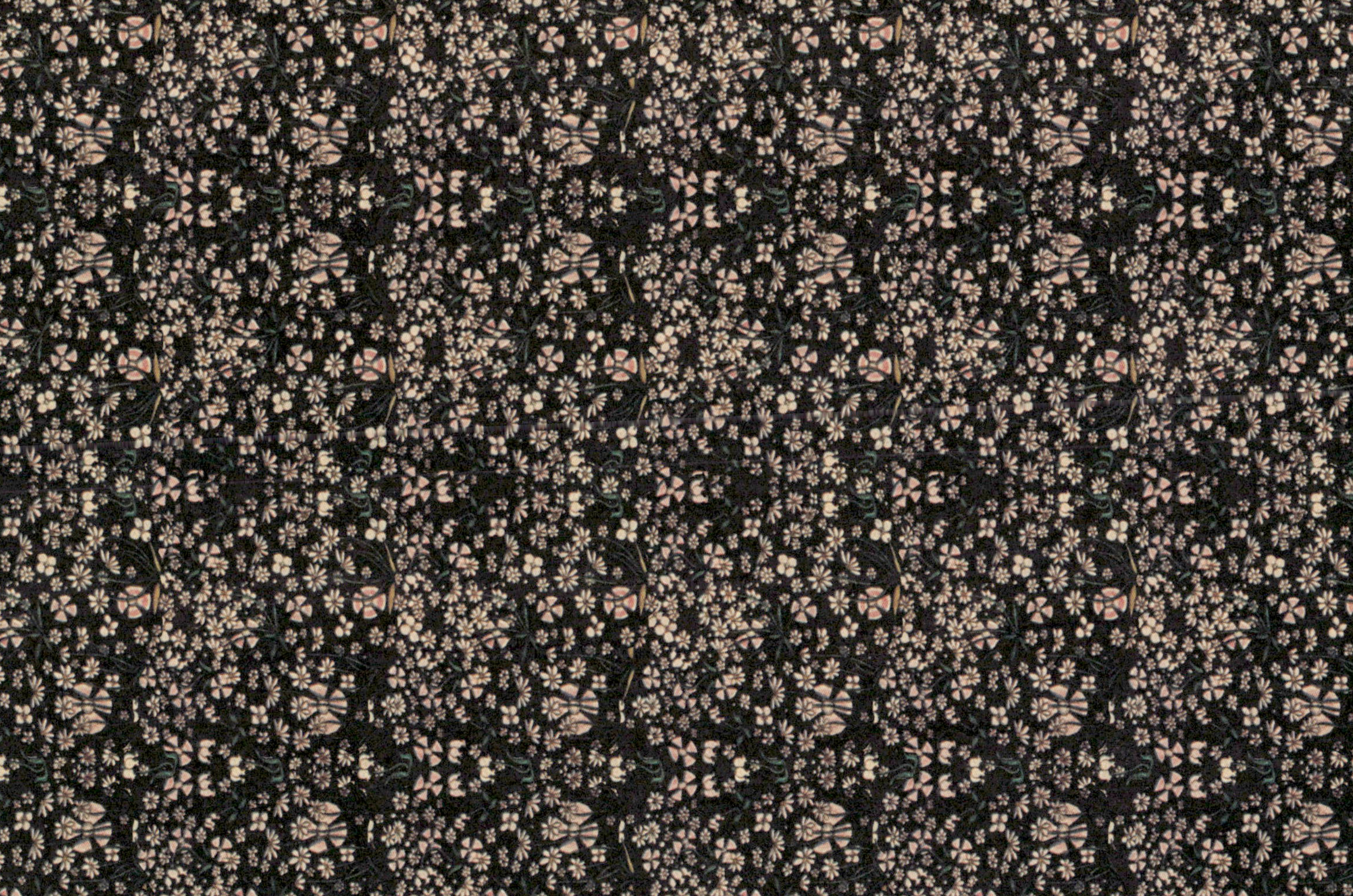

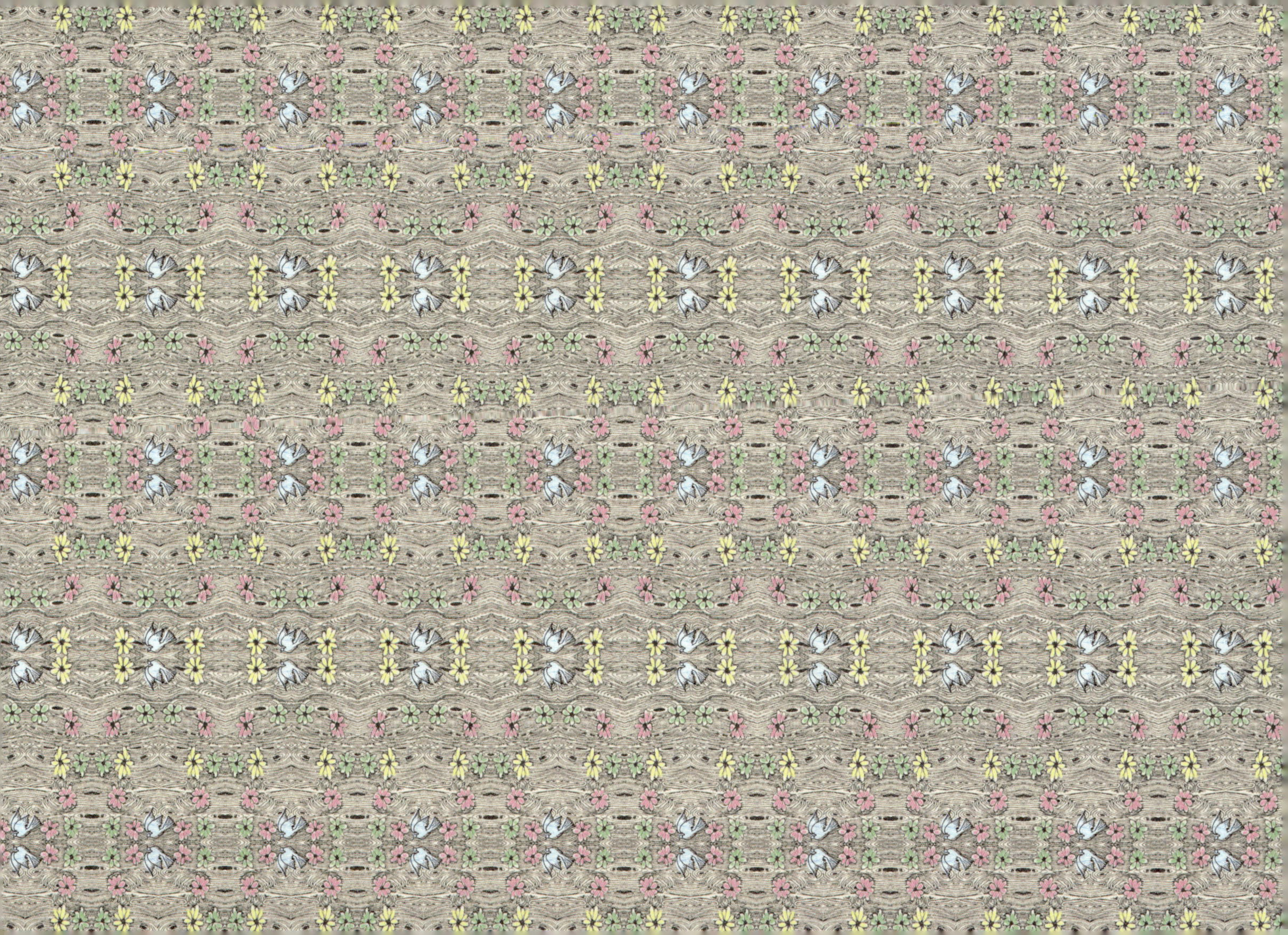

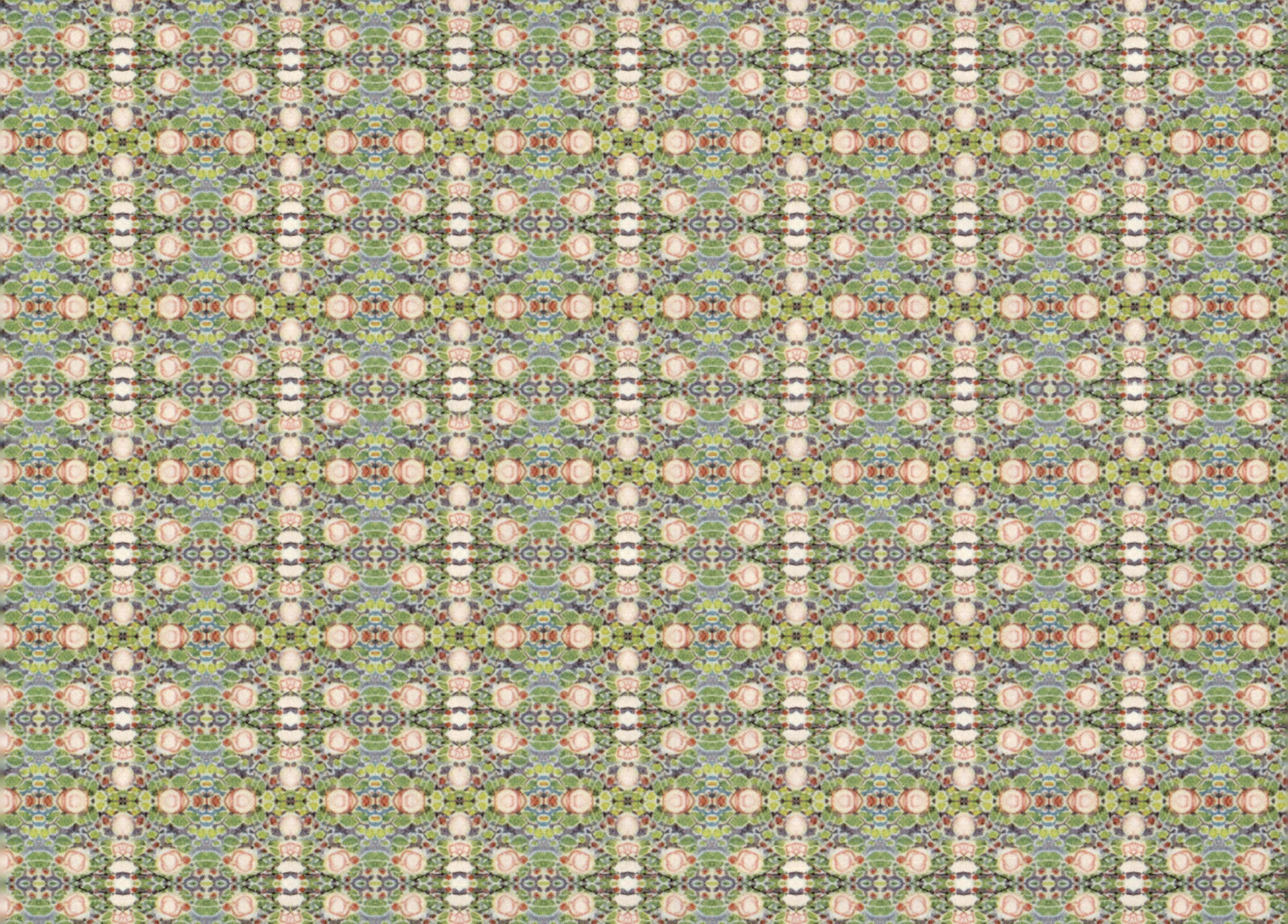

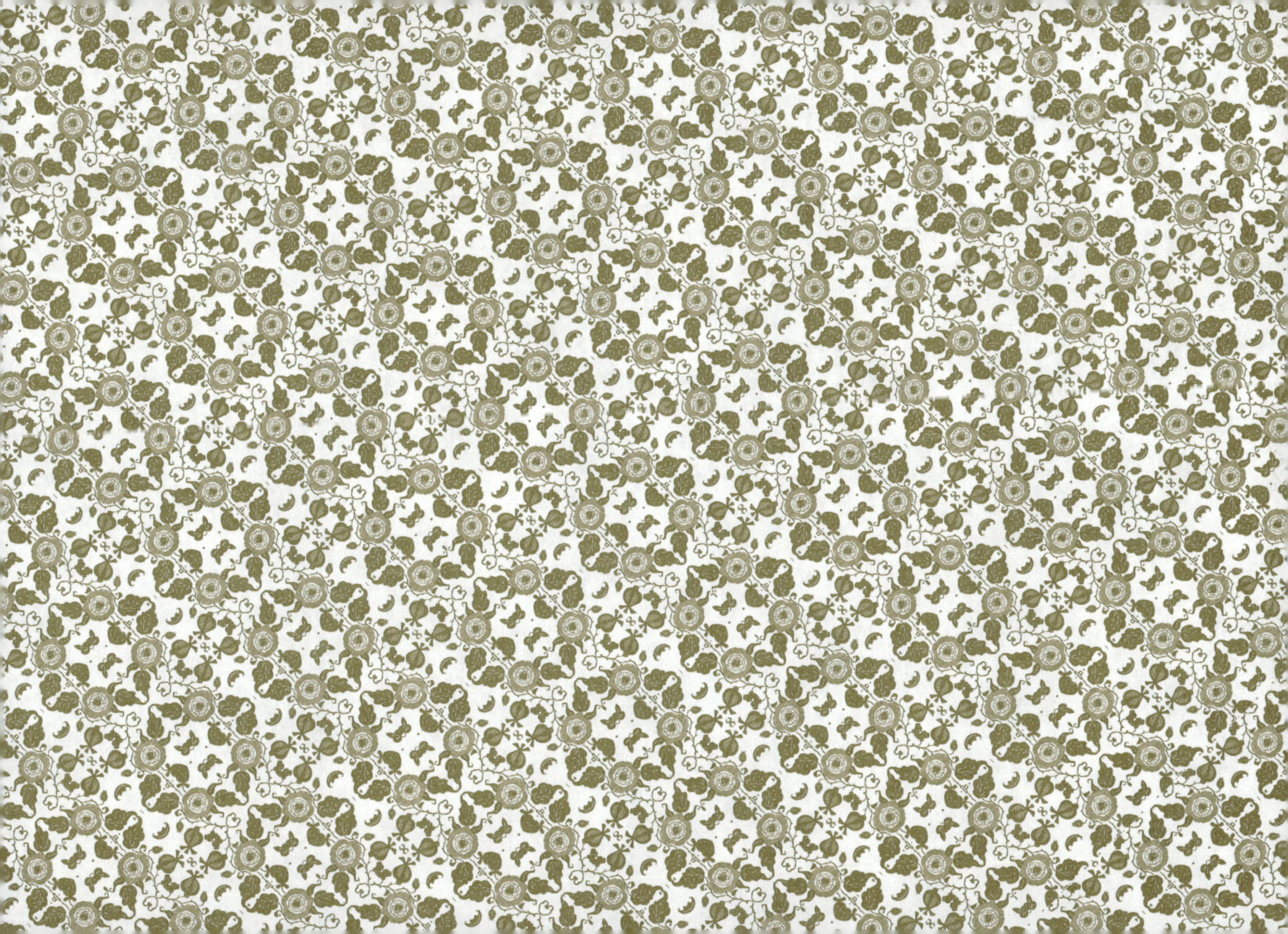

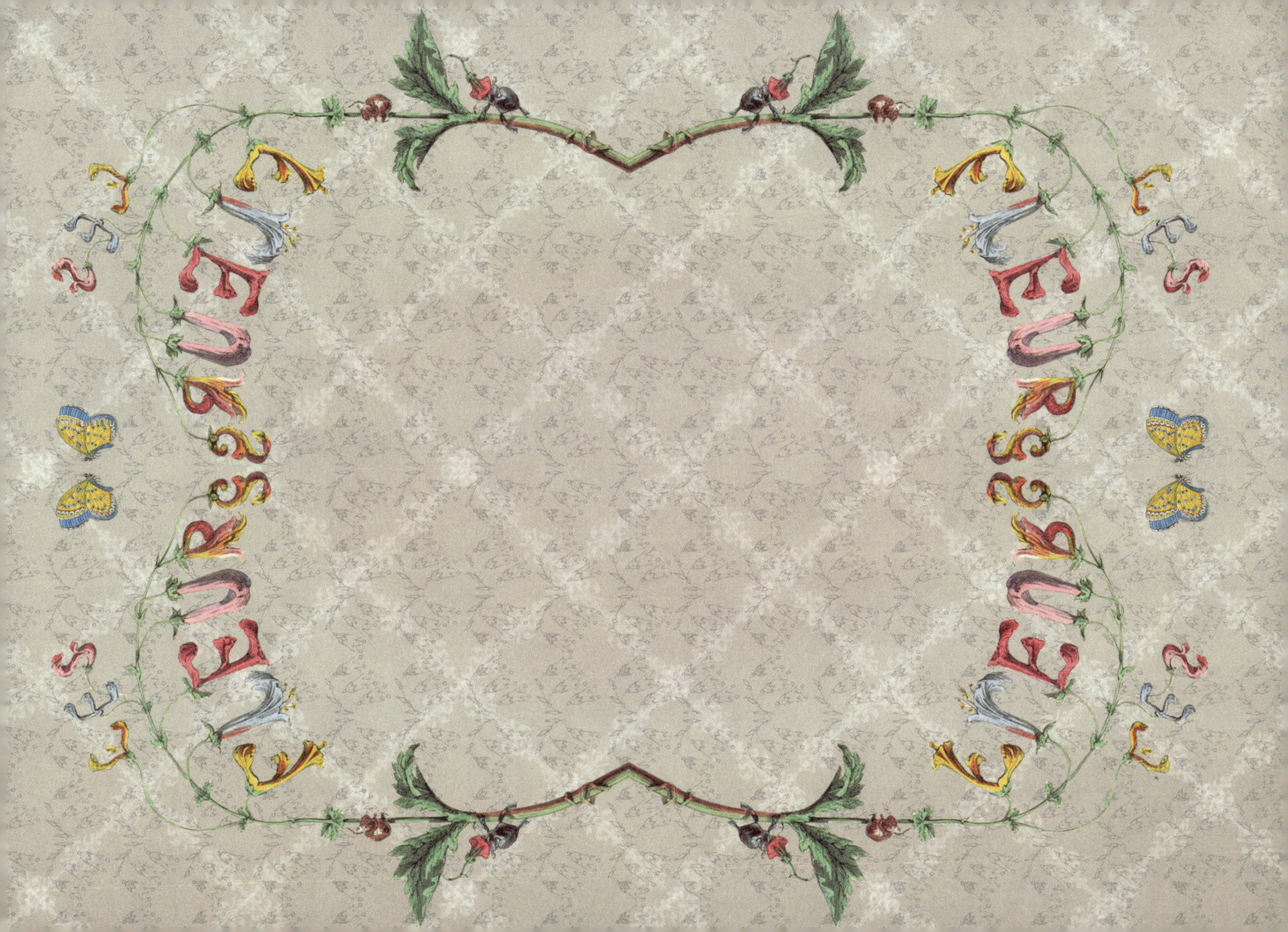

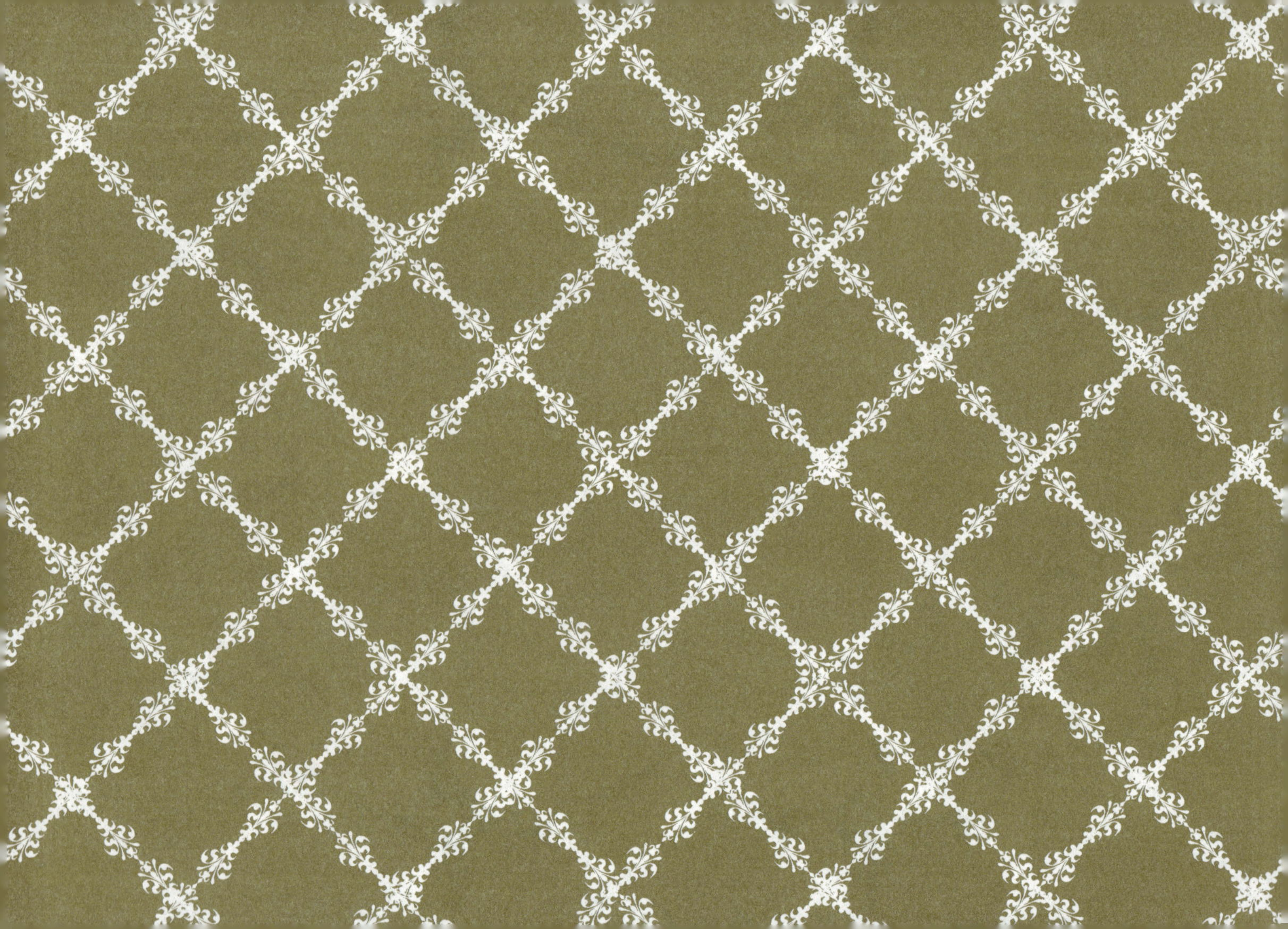

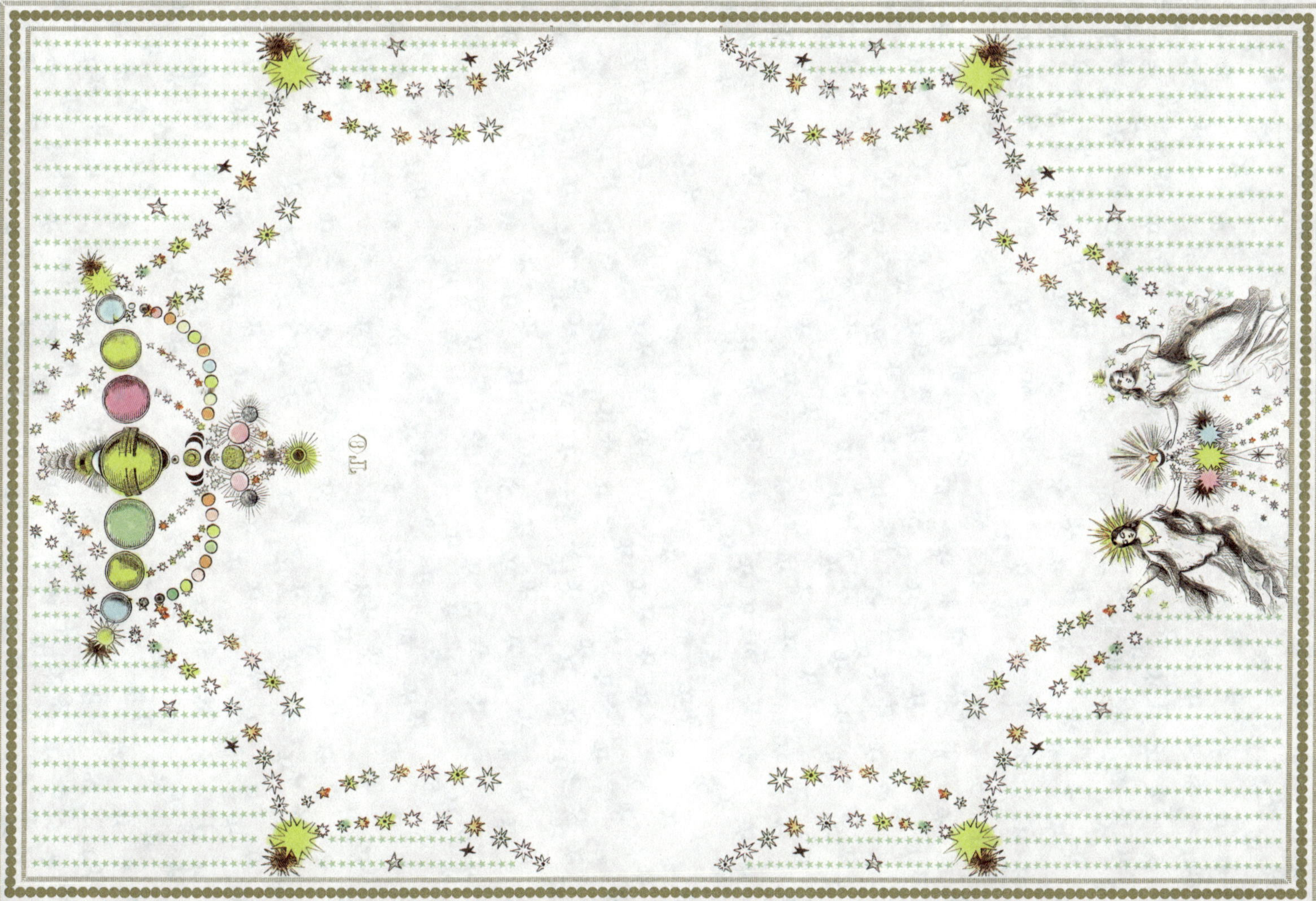

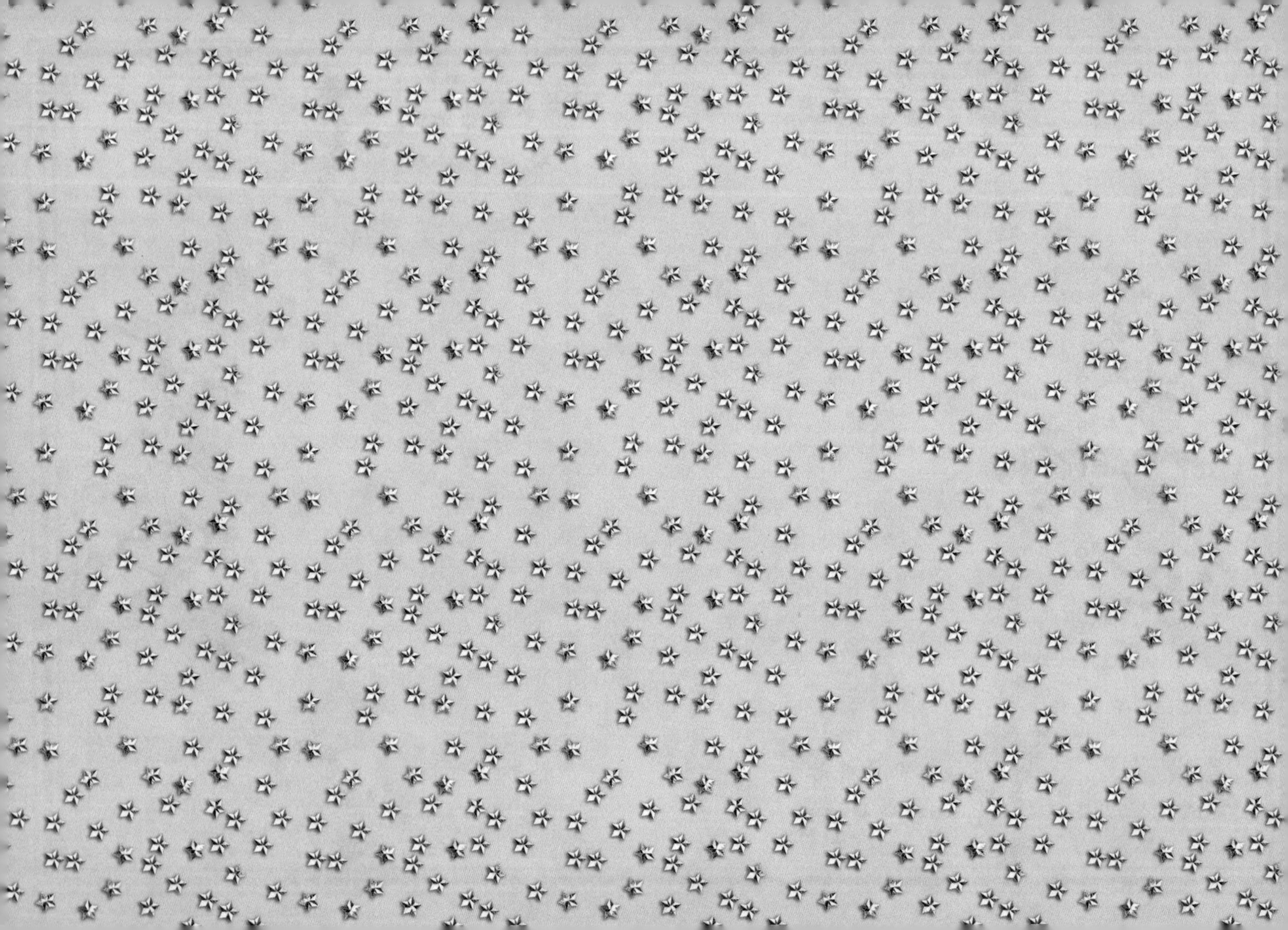

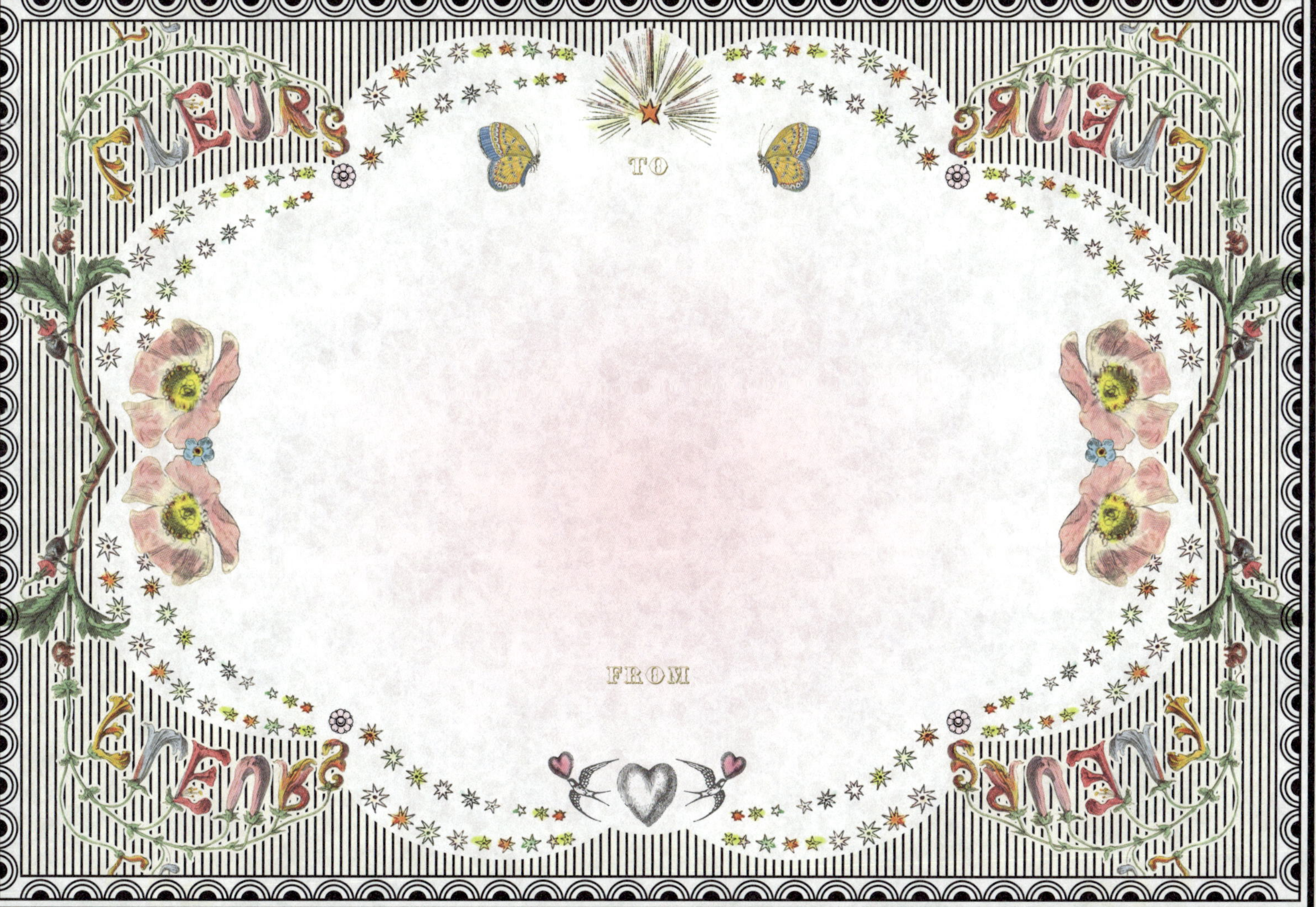
FLEURS
TO
FROM

To
From

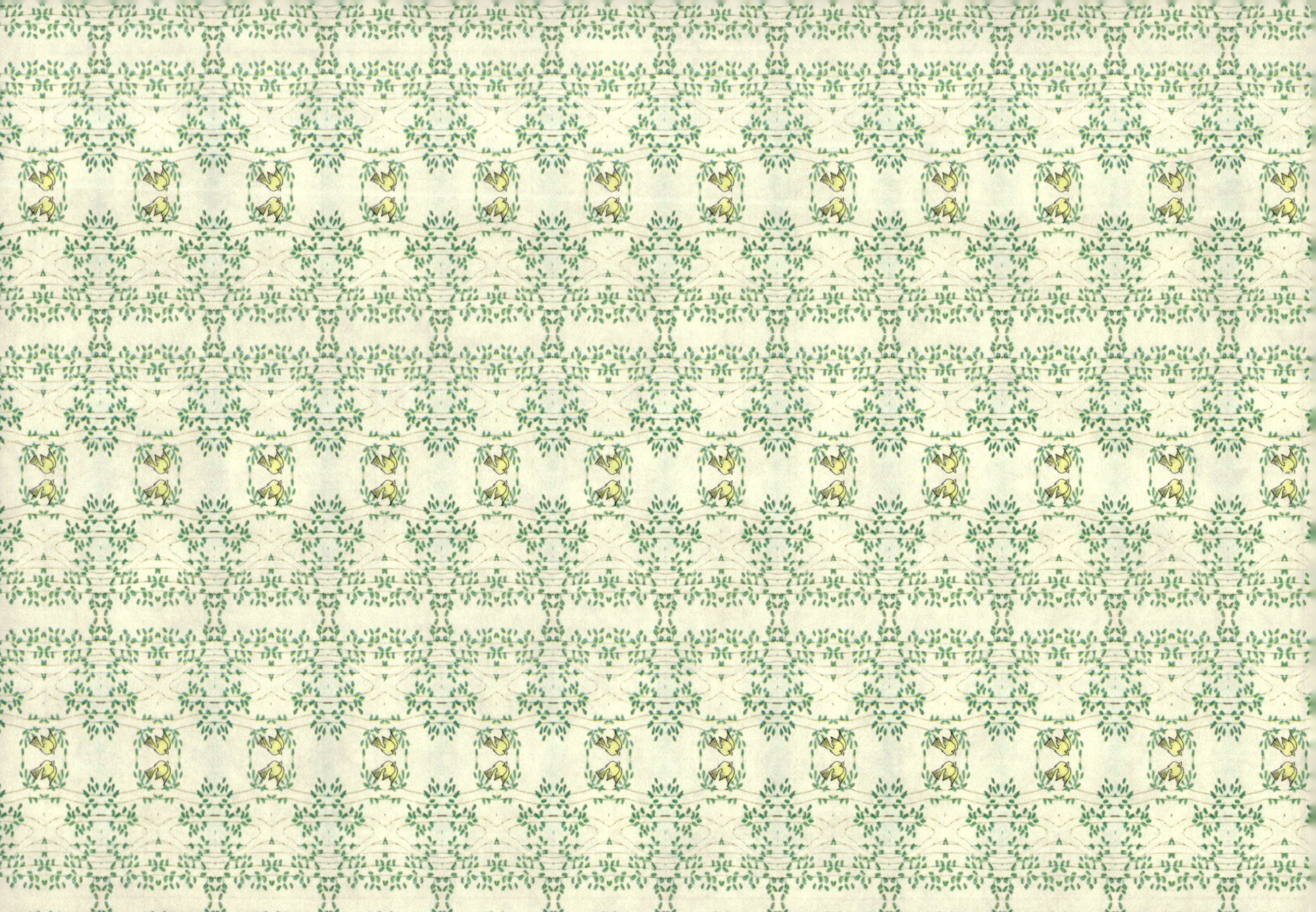

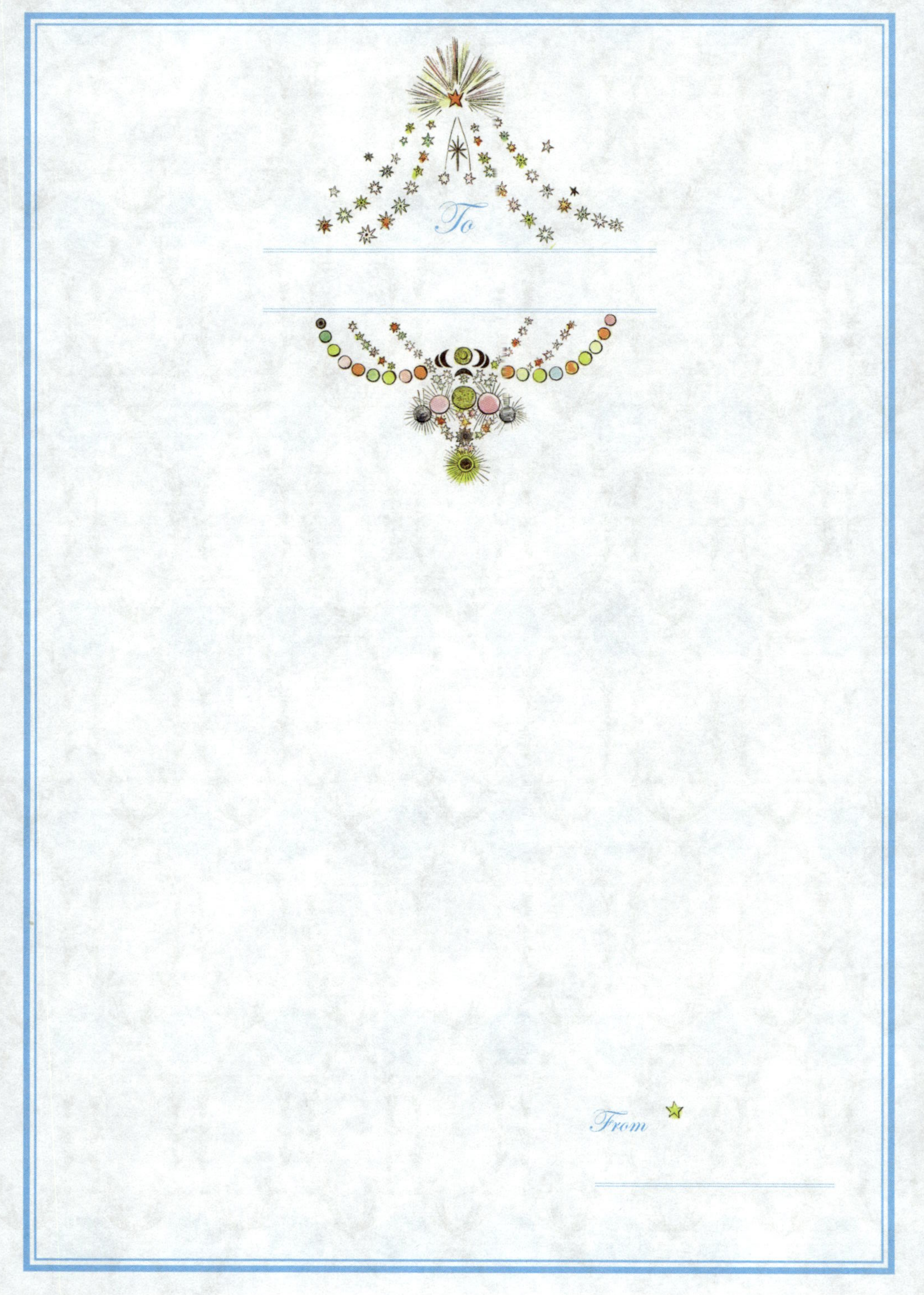
To
From

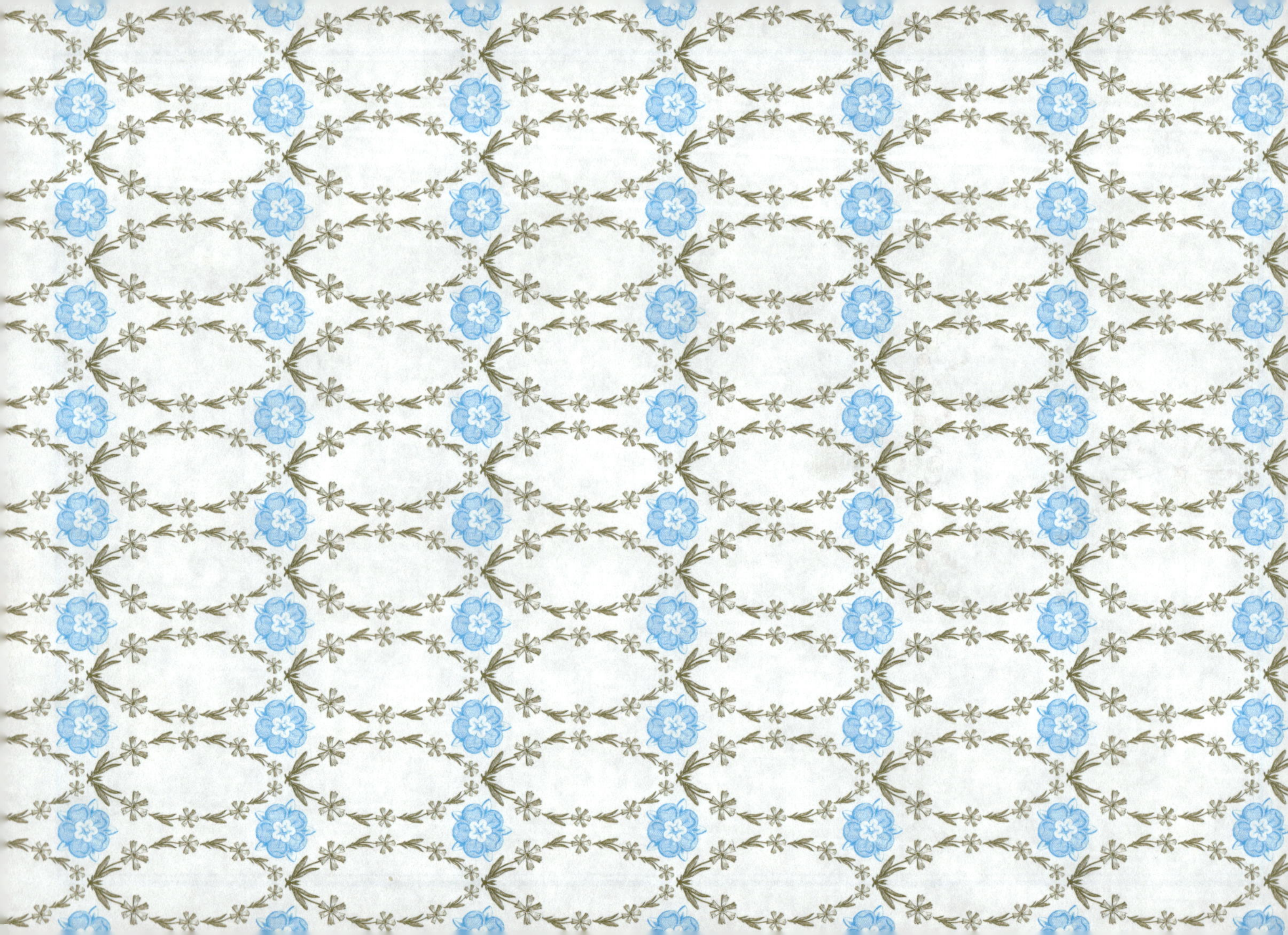

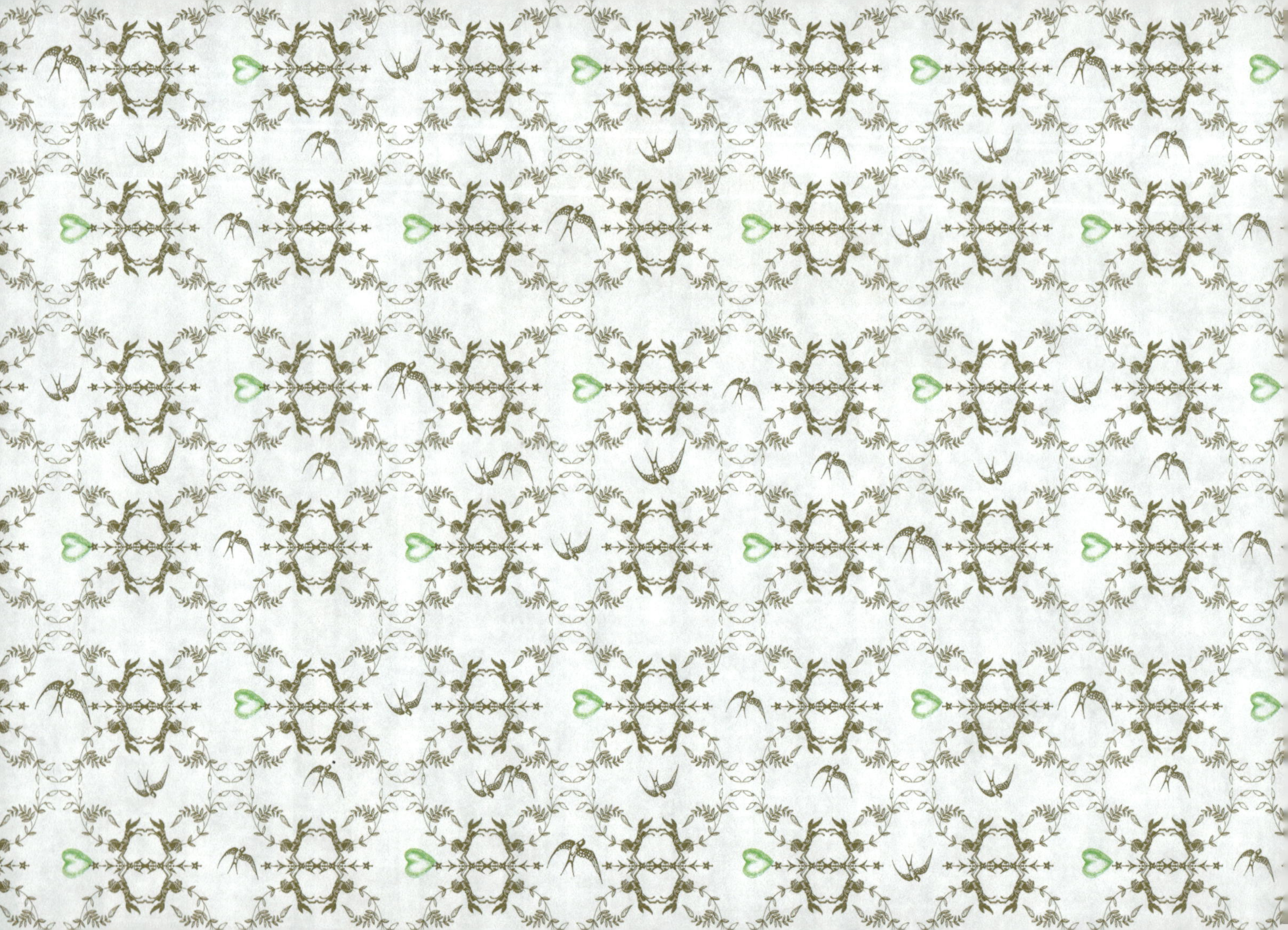

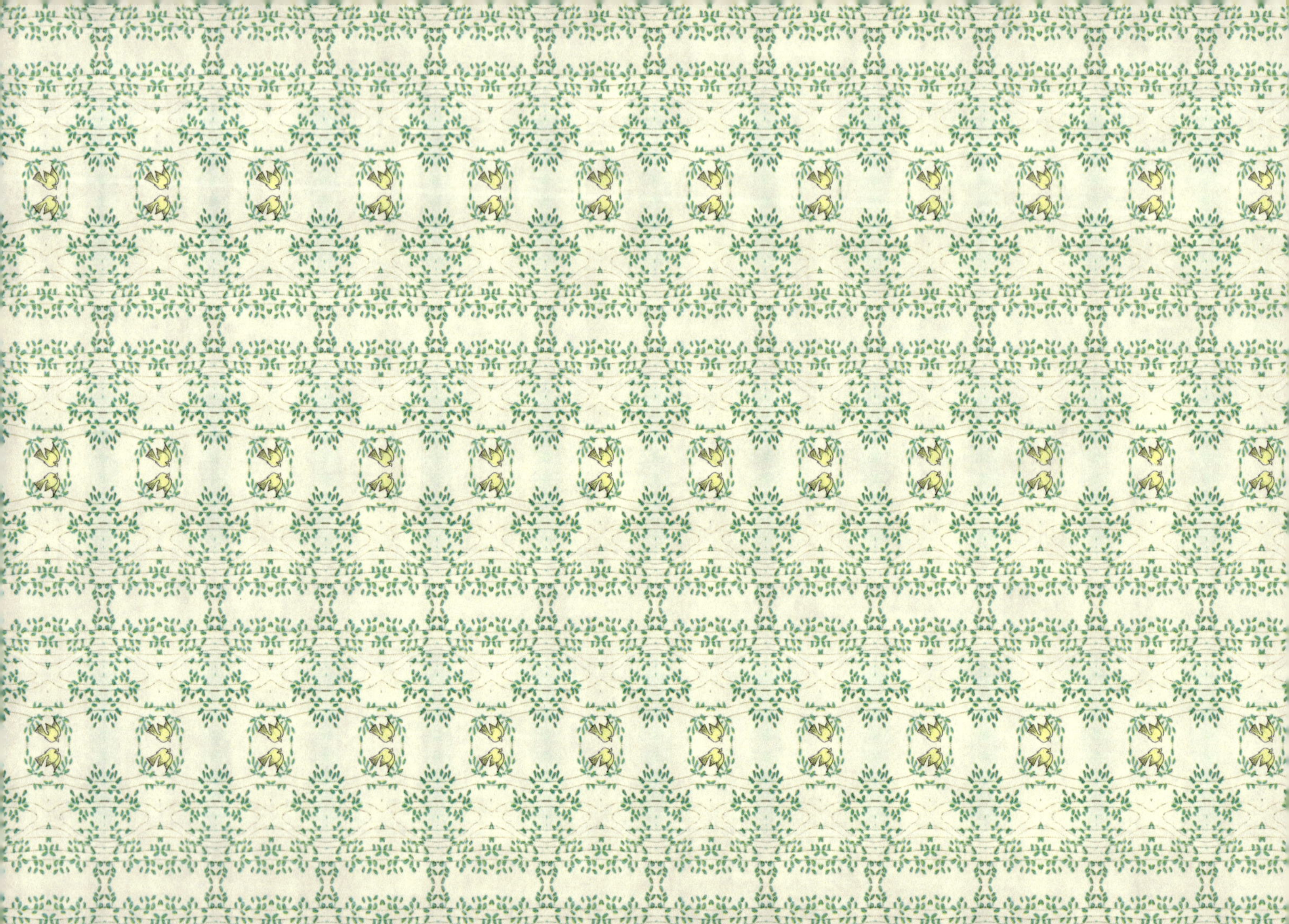

To
From

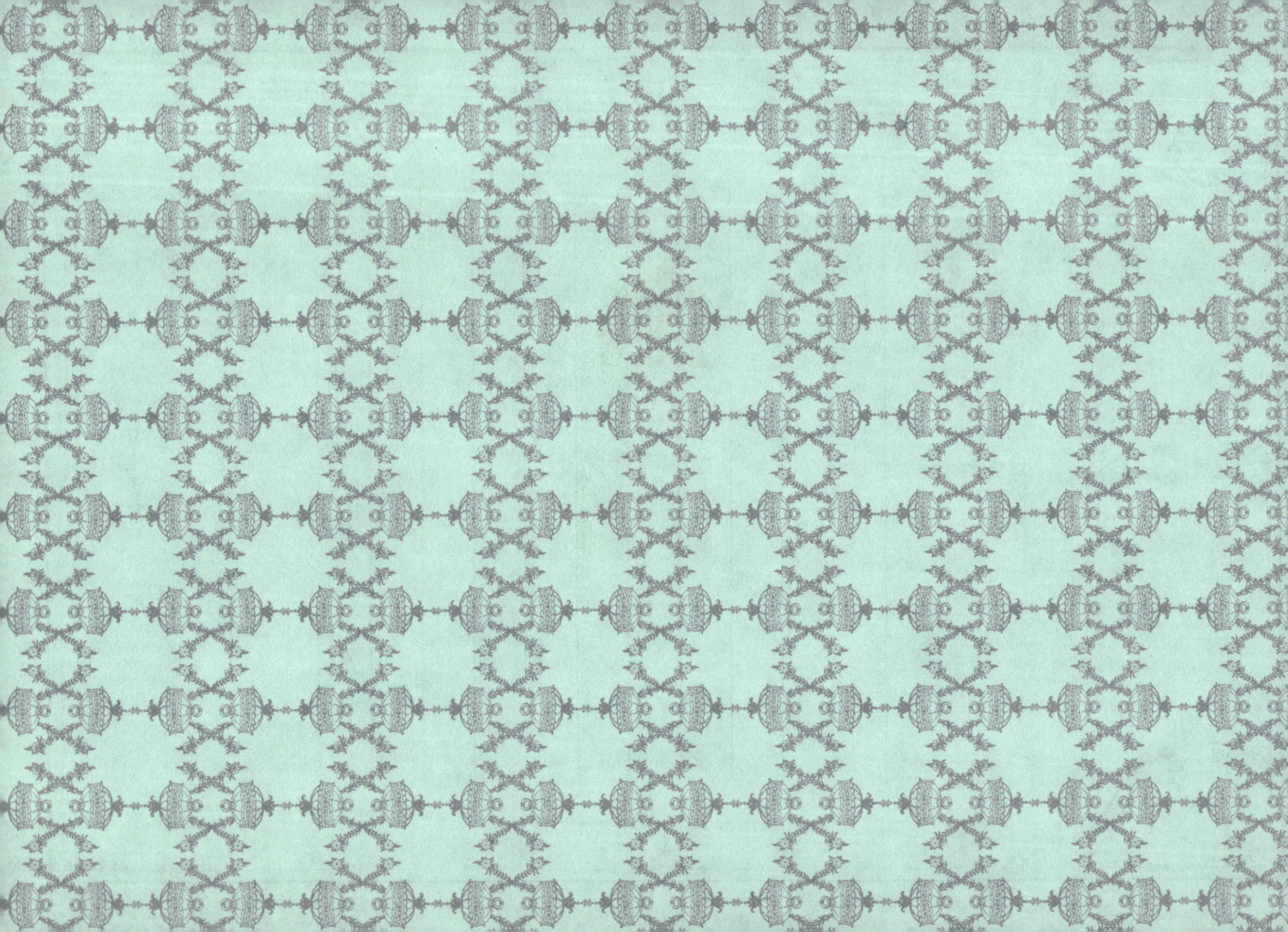

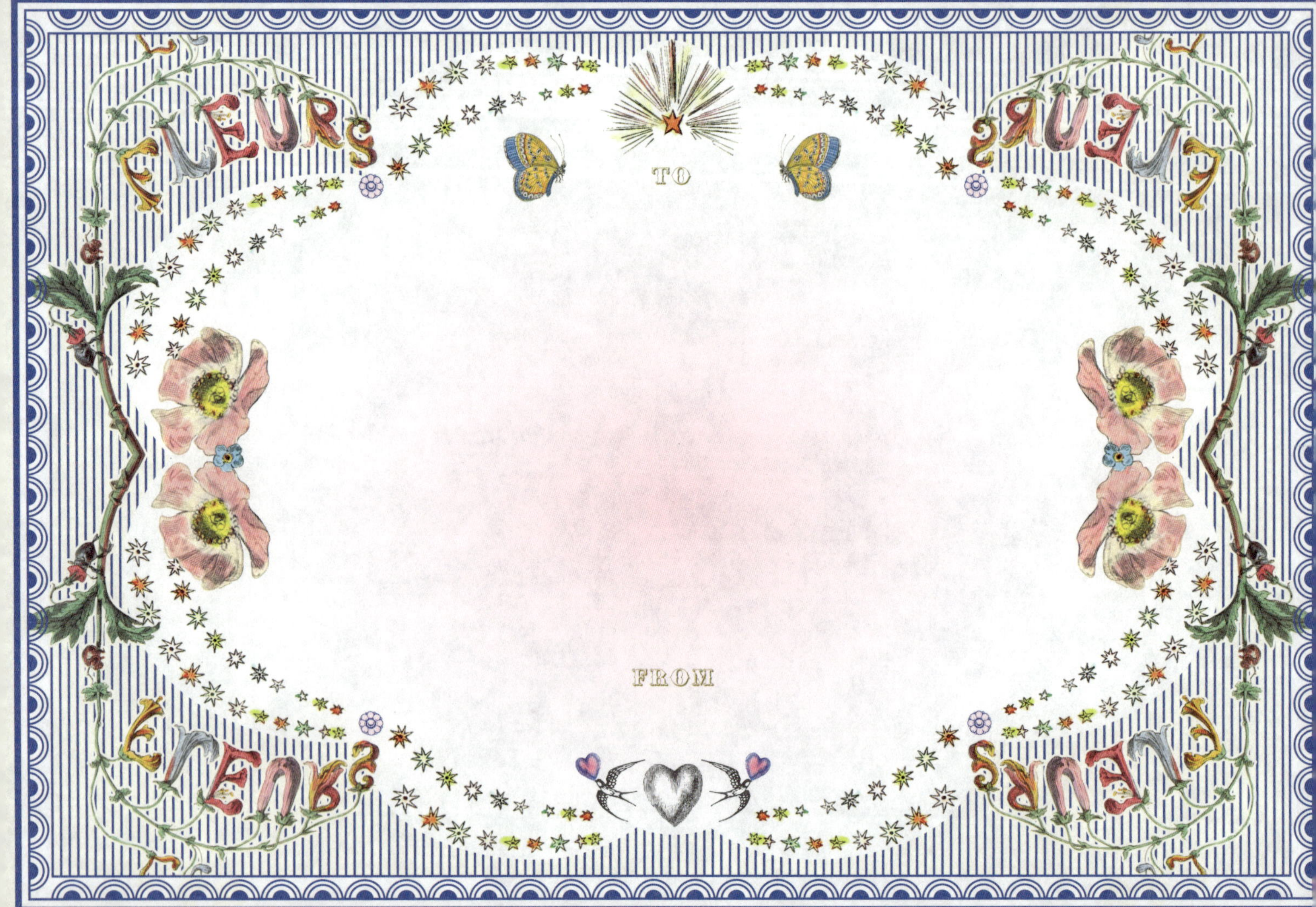

FLEURS
FLEURS
FLEURS
FLEURS
TO
FROM

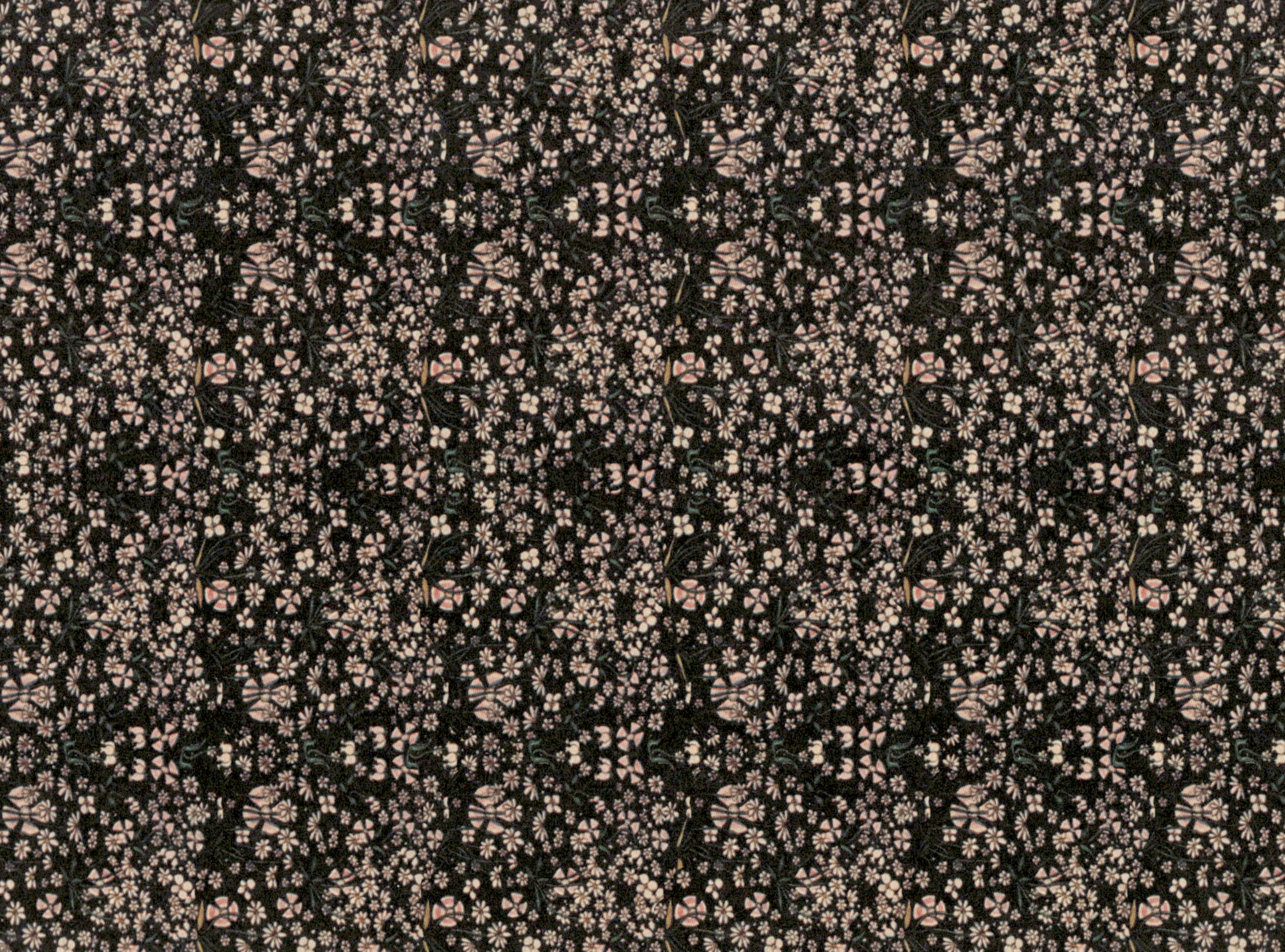

TO
FROM

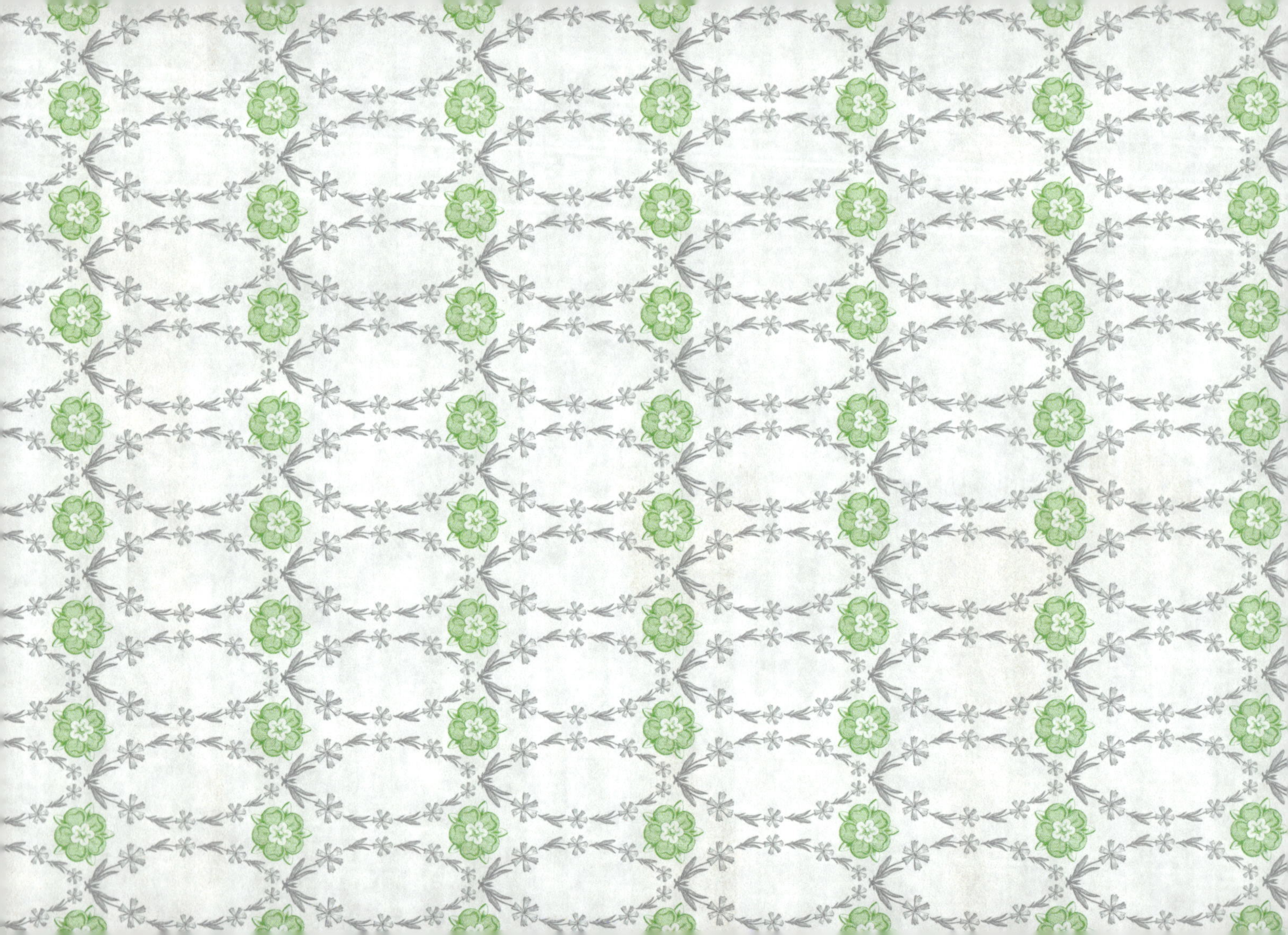

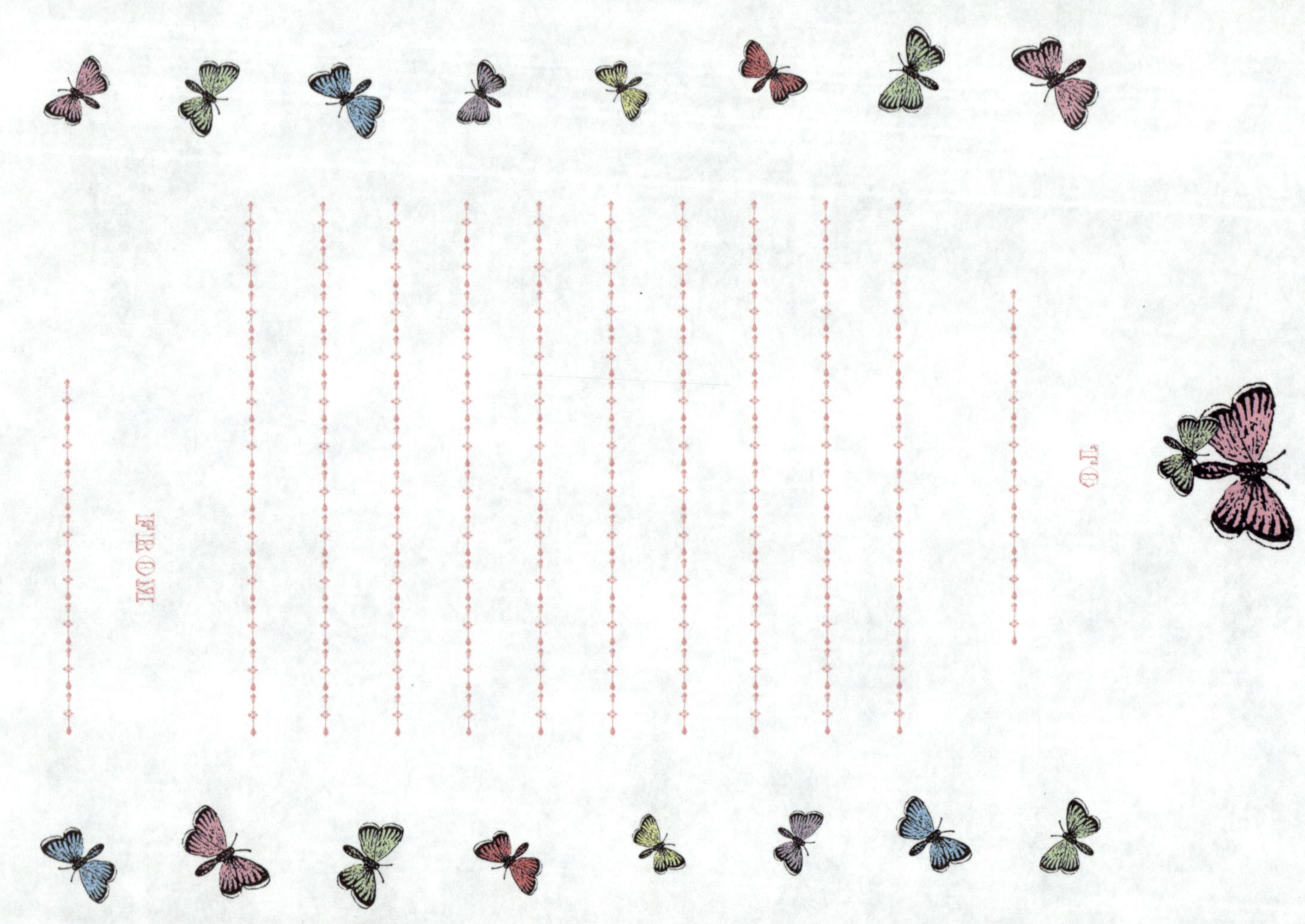

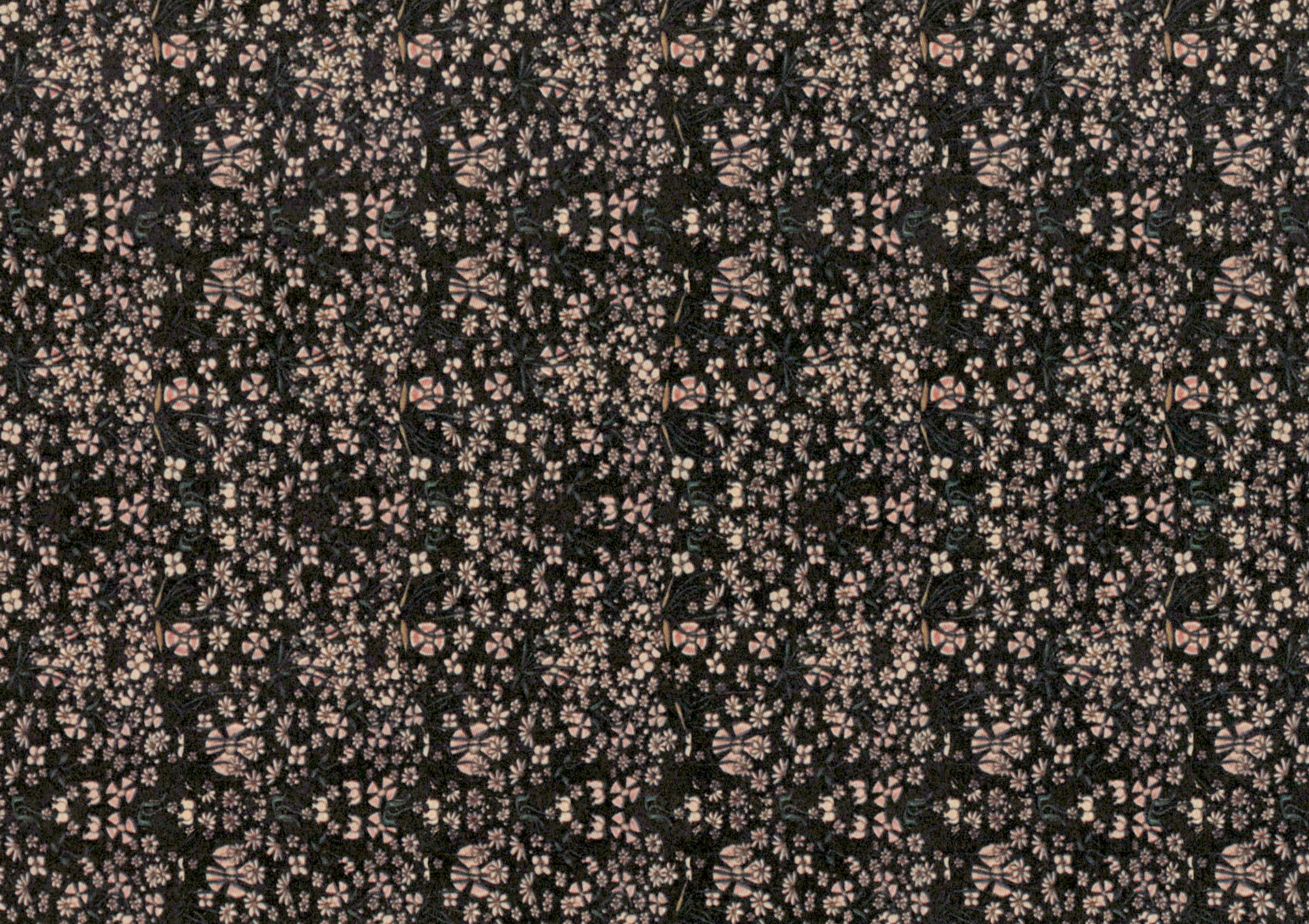

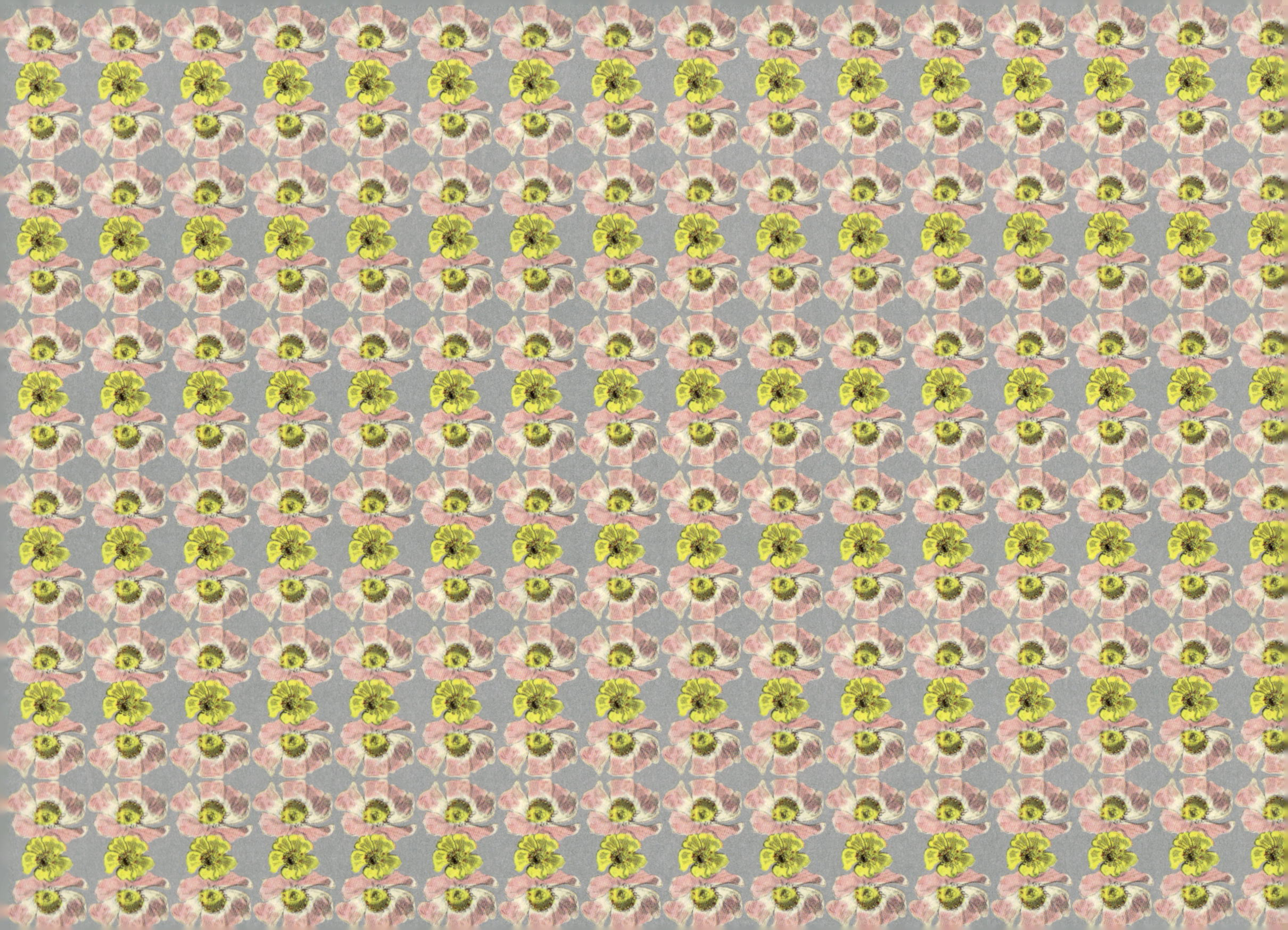

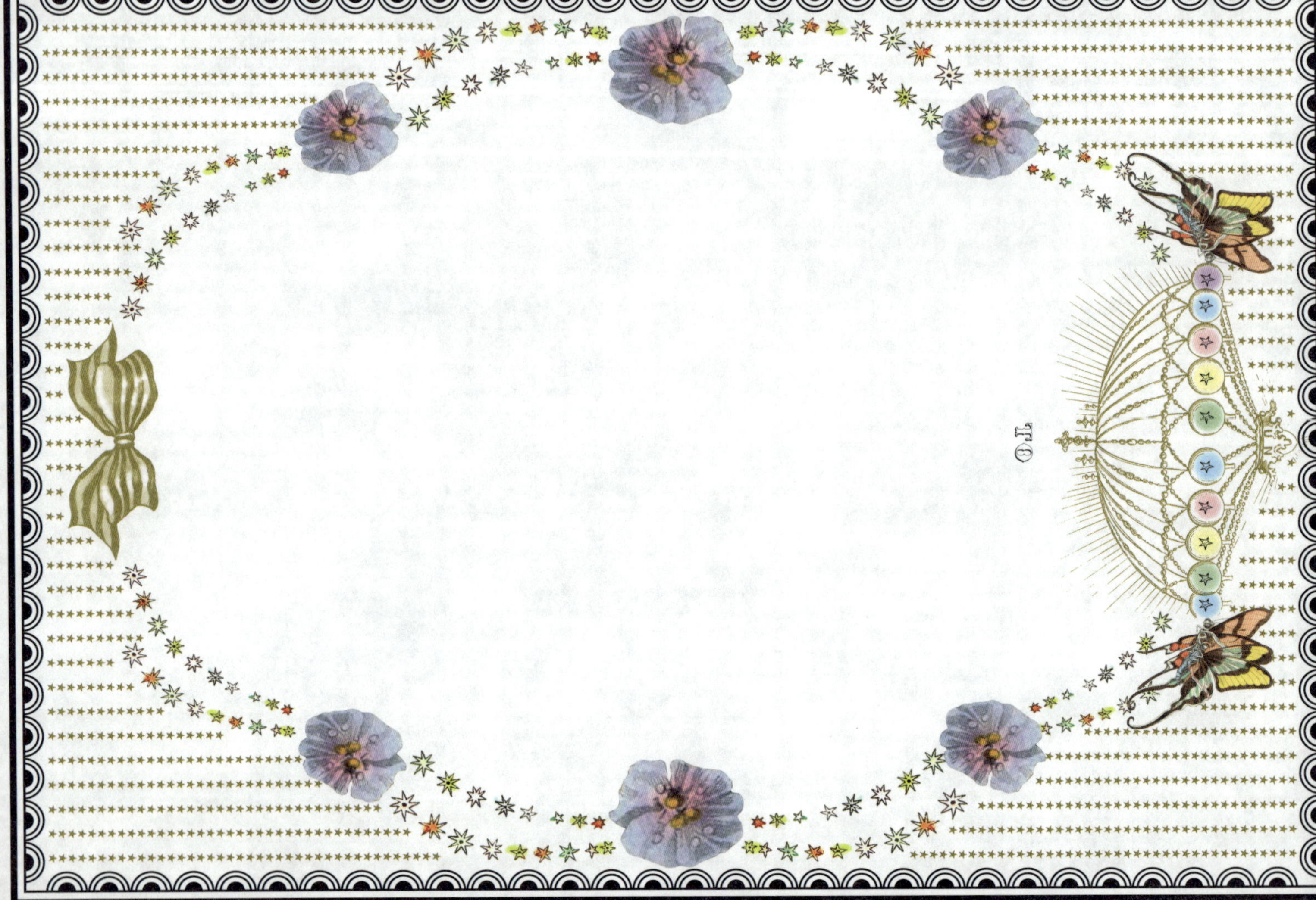

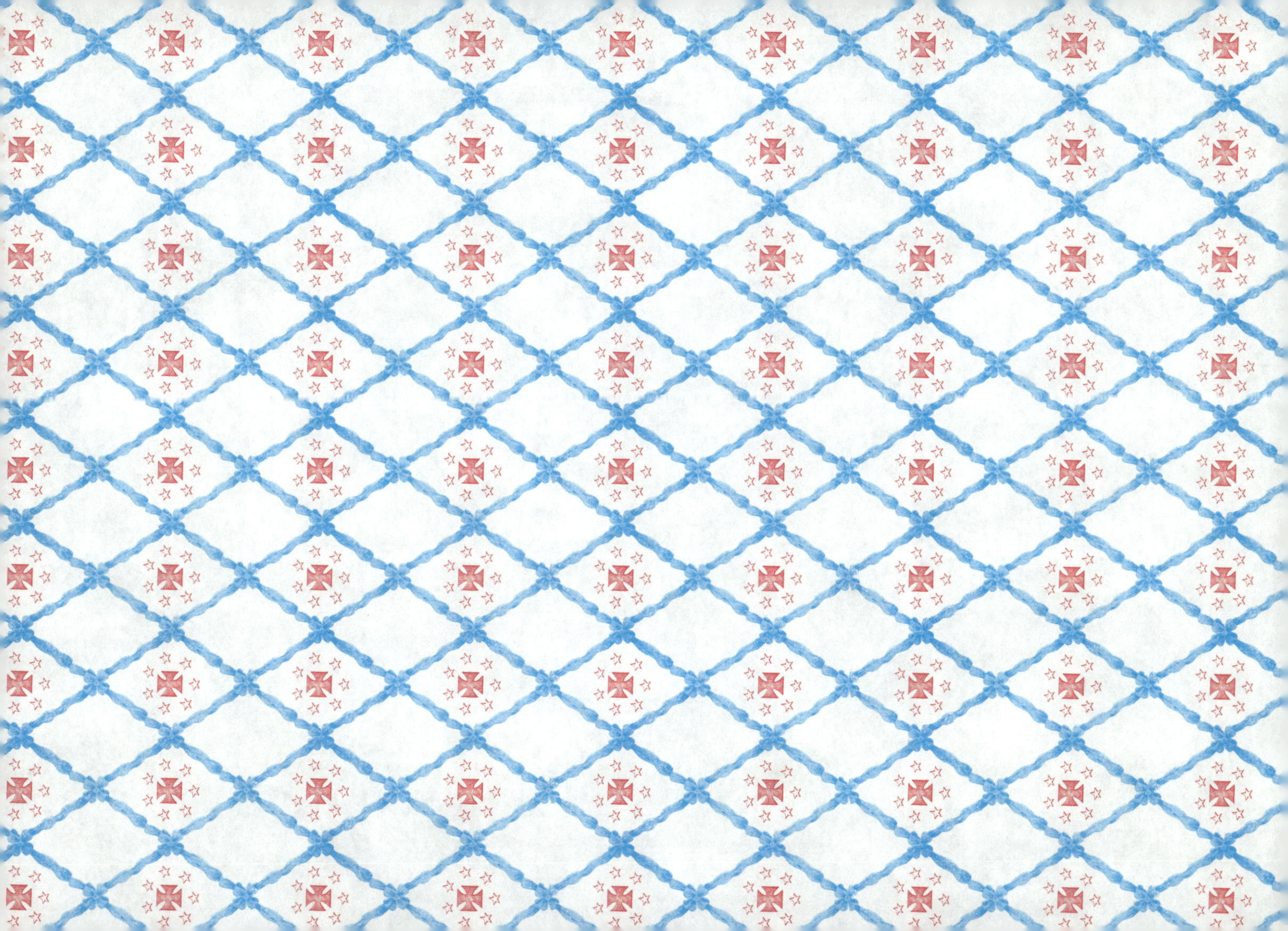

To
From

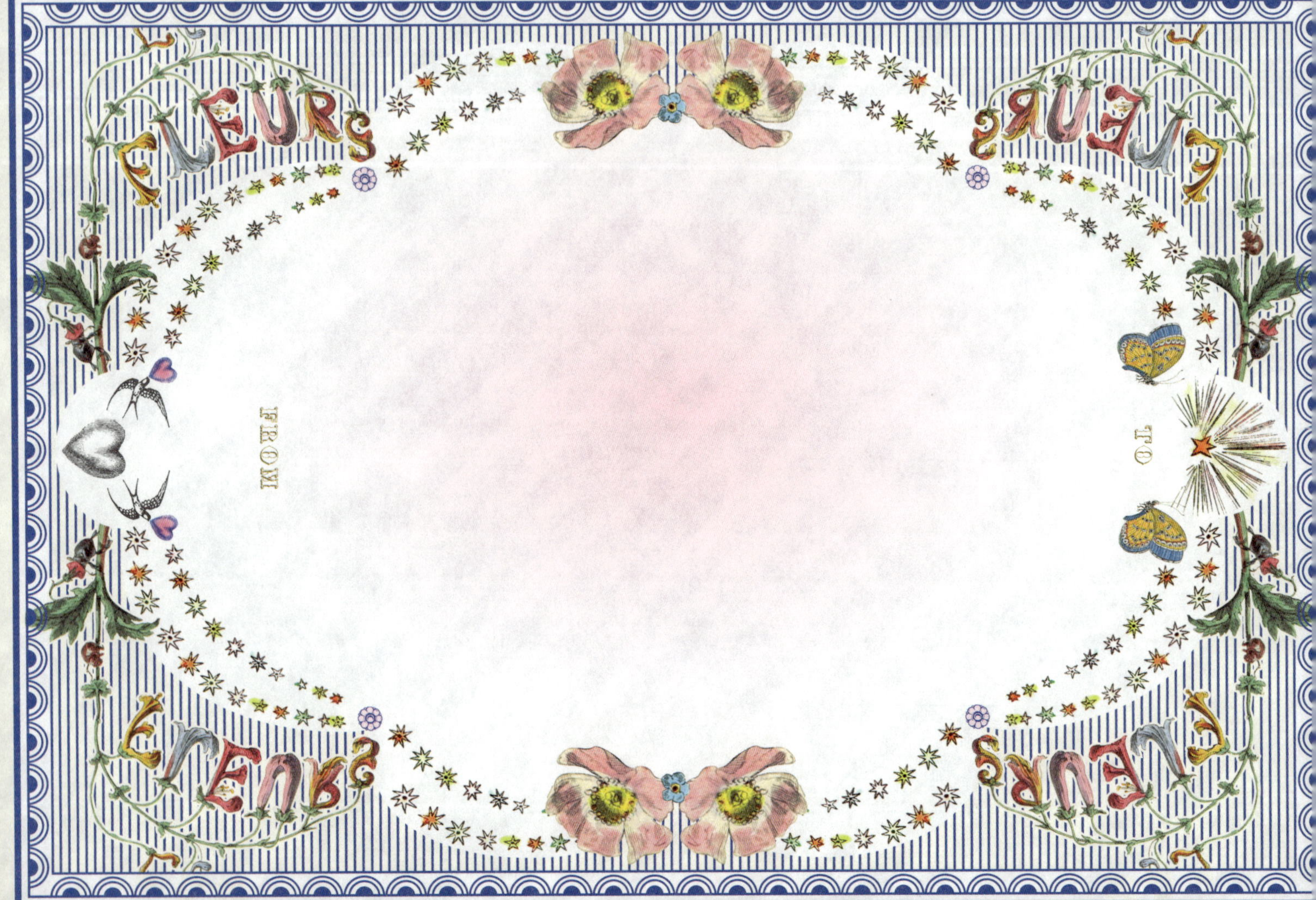

FLEURS
FLEURS
FLEURS
FLEURS
FROM
TO

To
From

TO

FROM

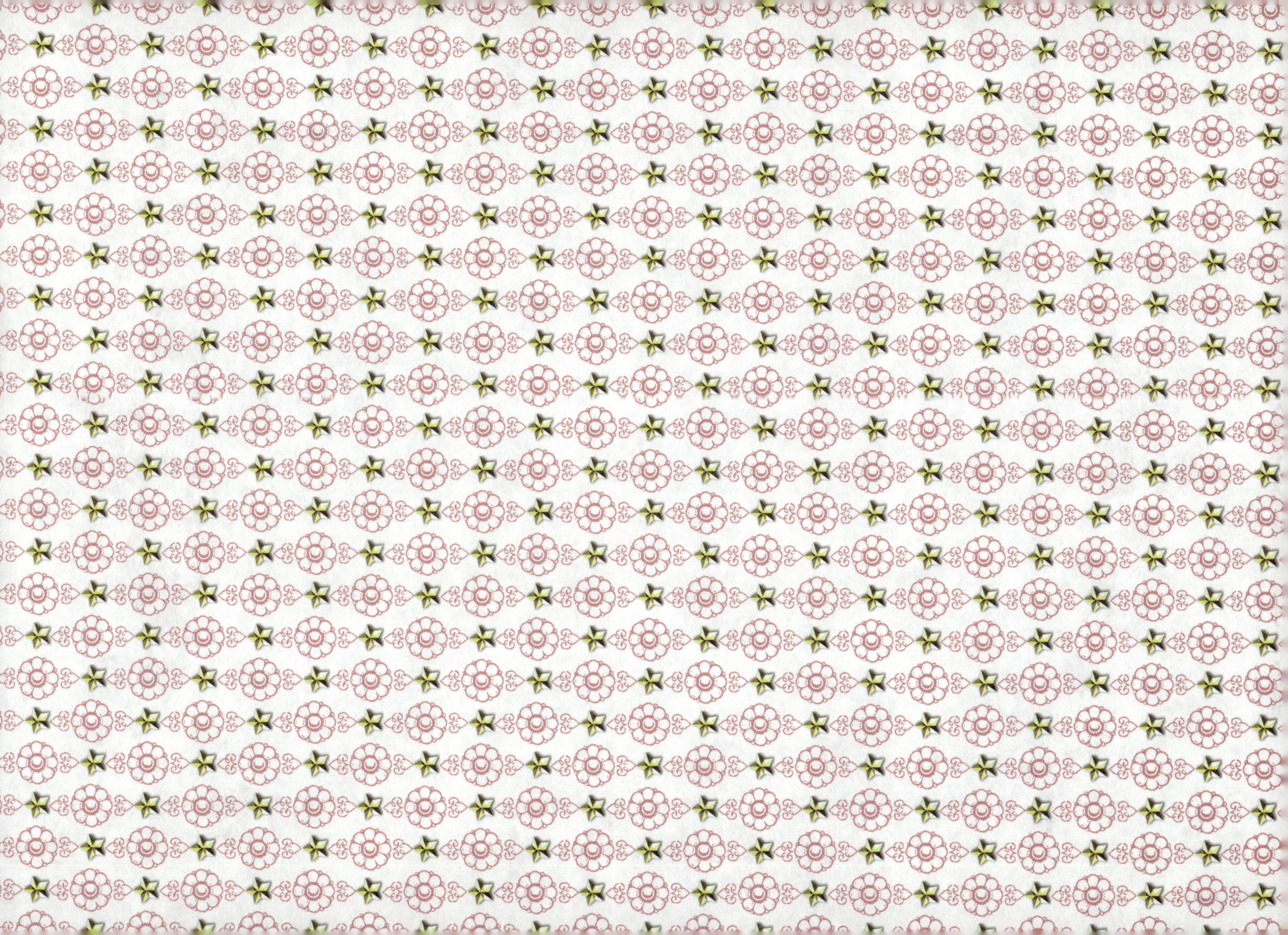

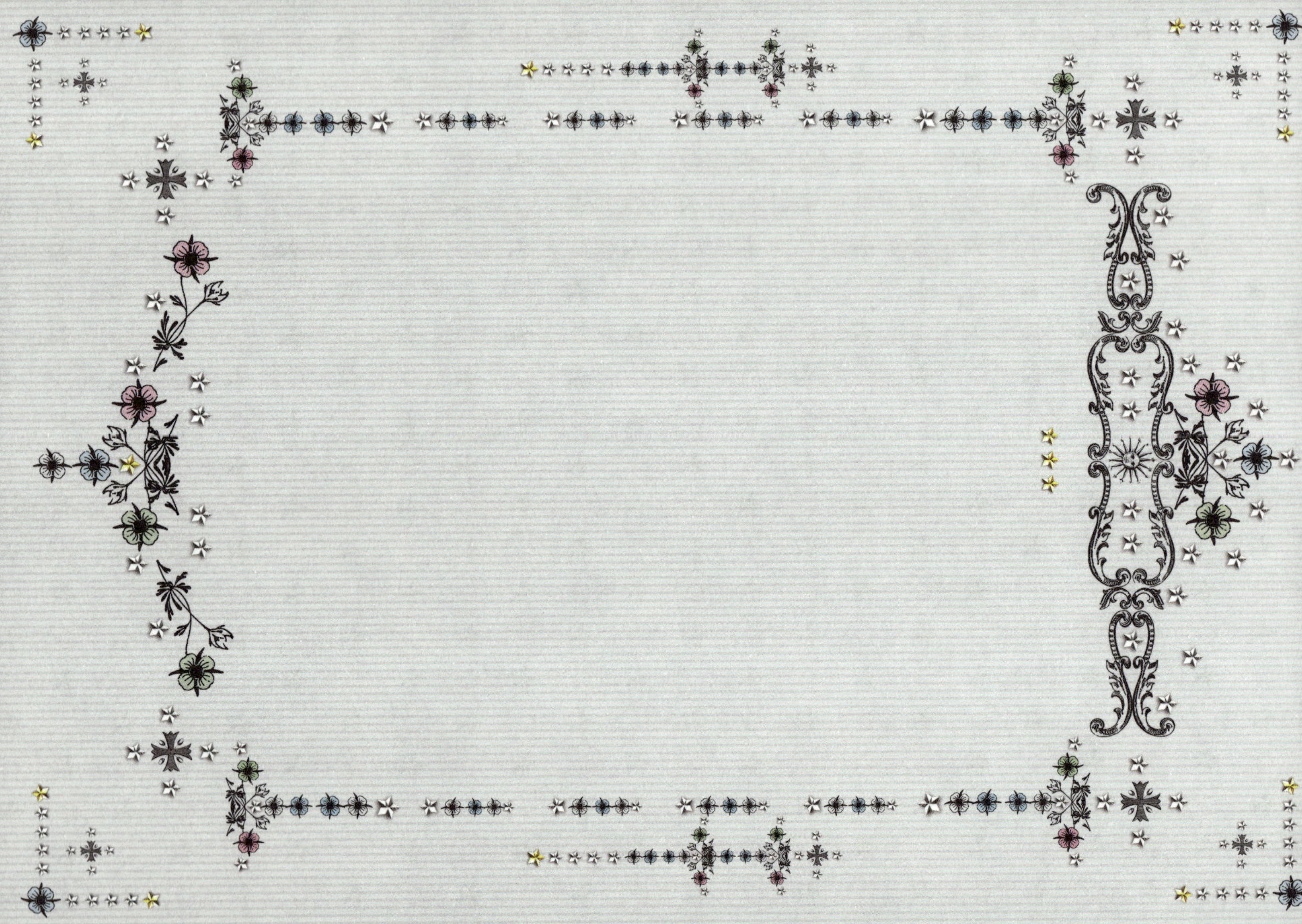

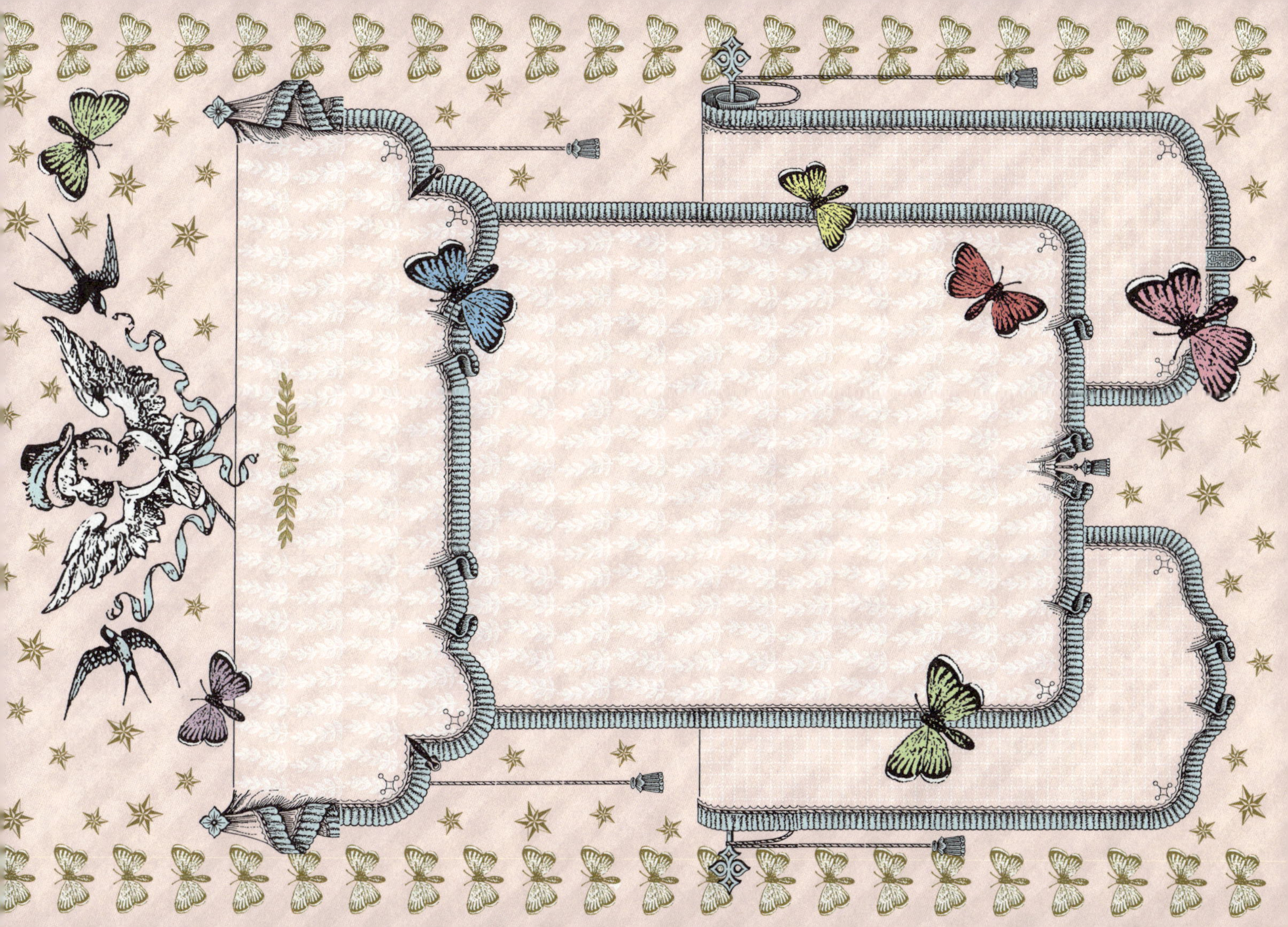

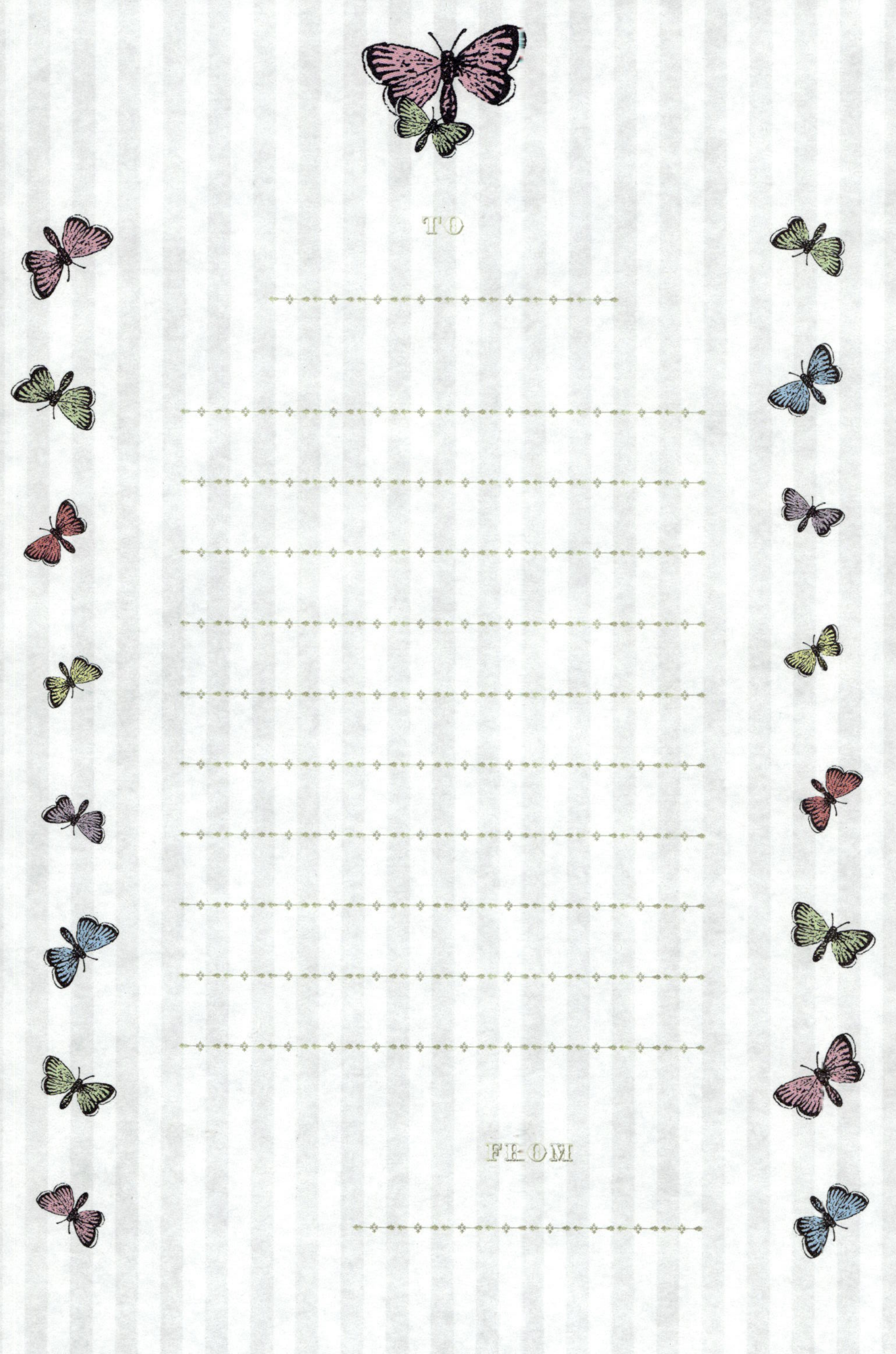

TO
FROM

To
From

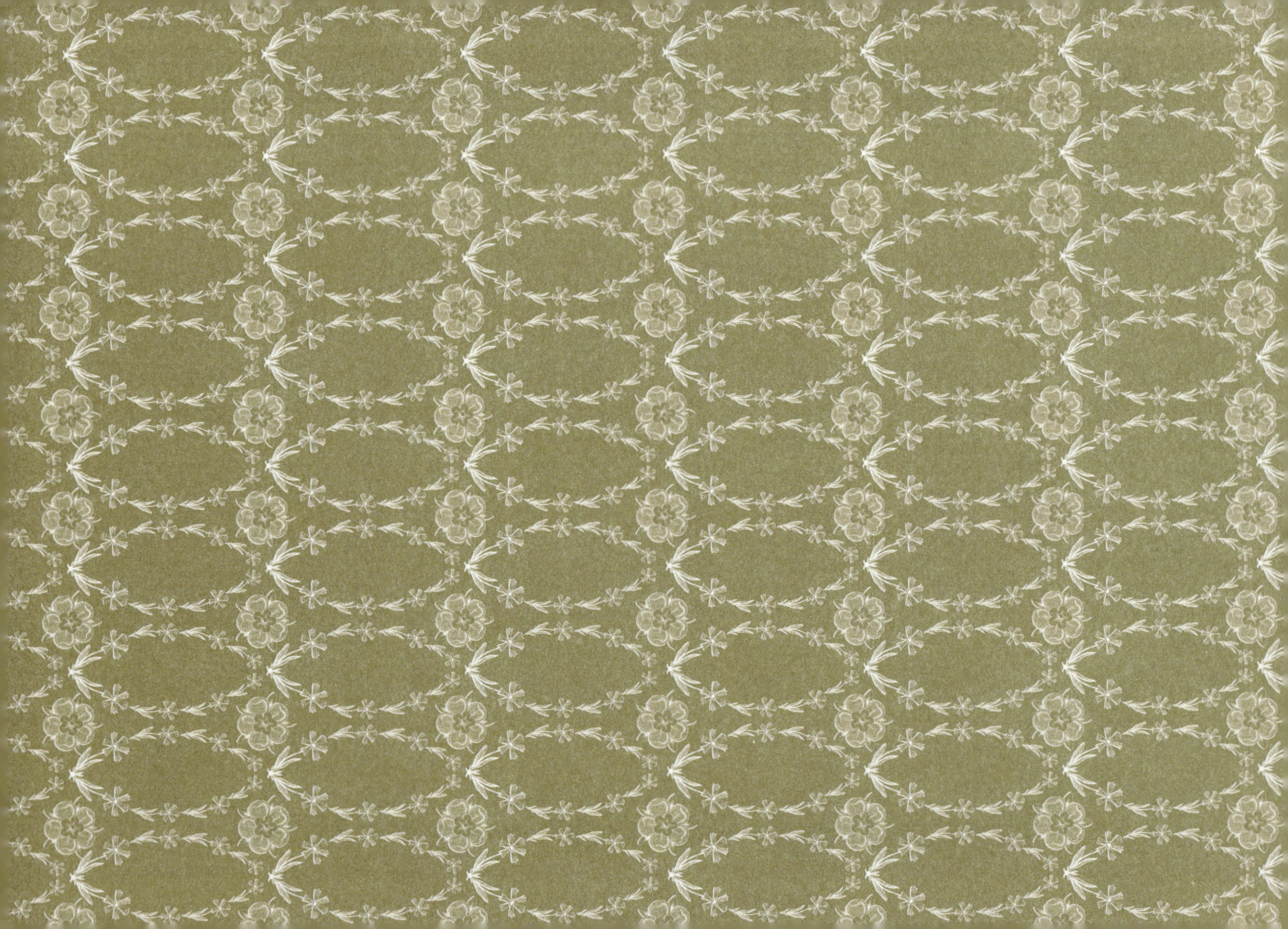

TO

FROM

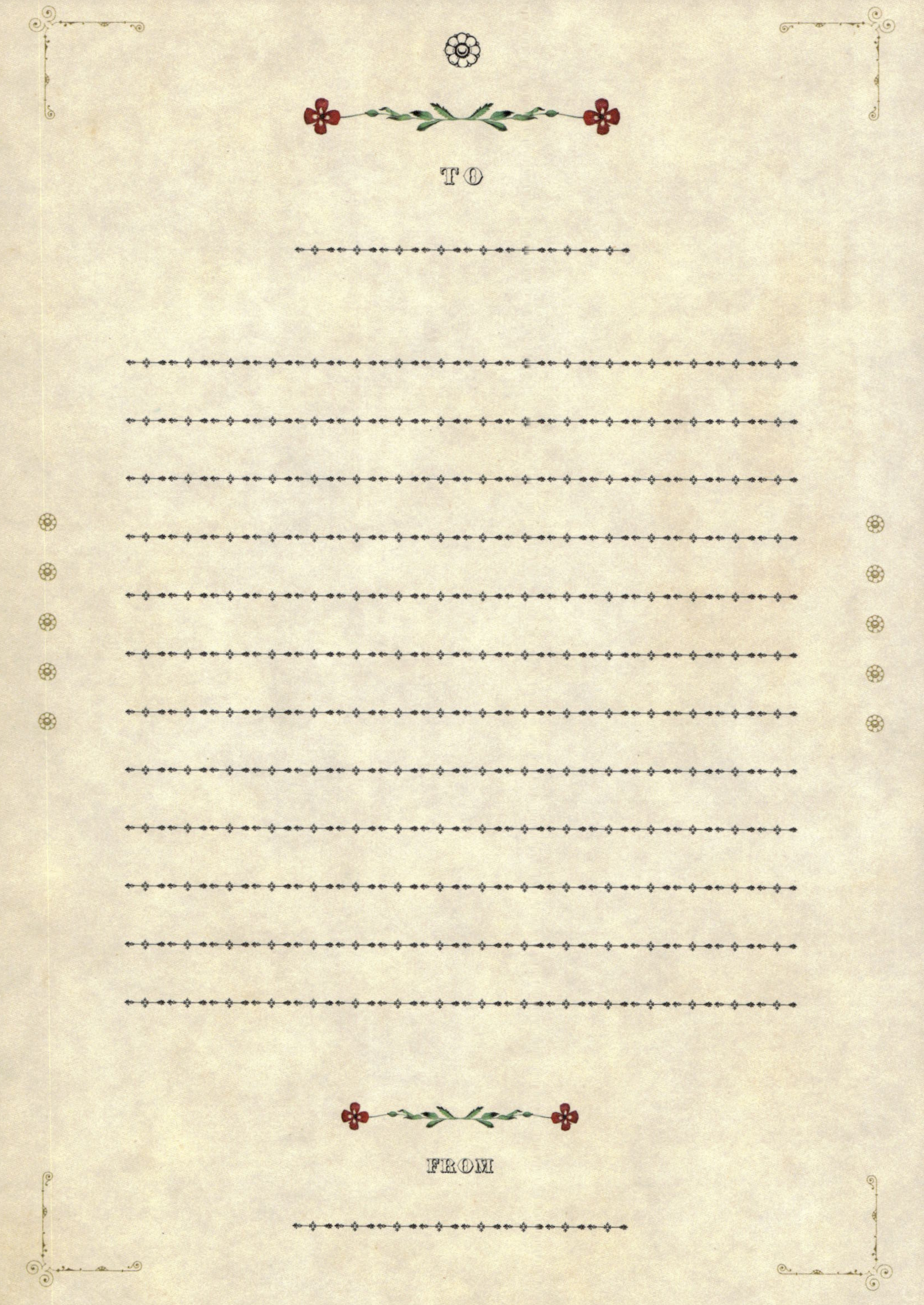

TO
FROM

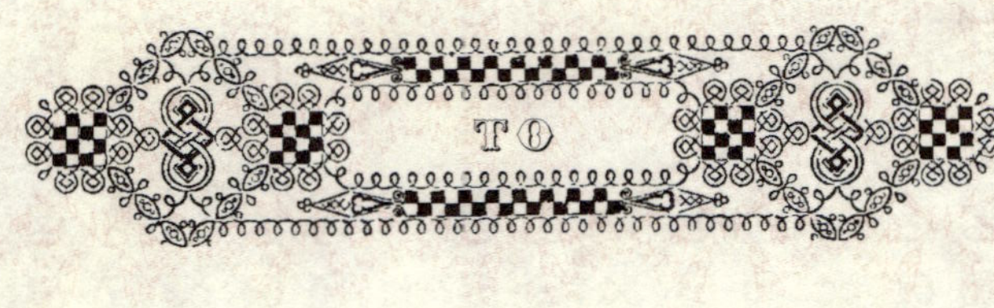

FROM

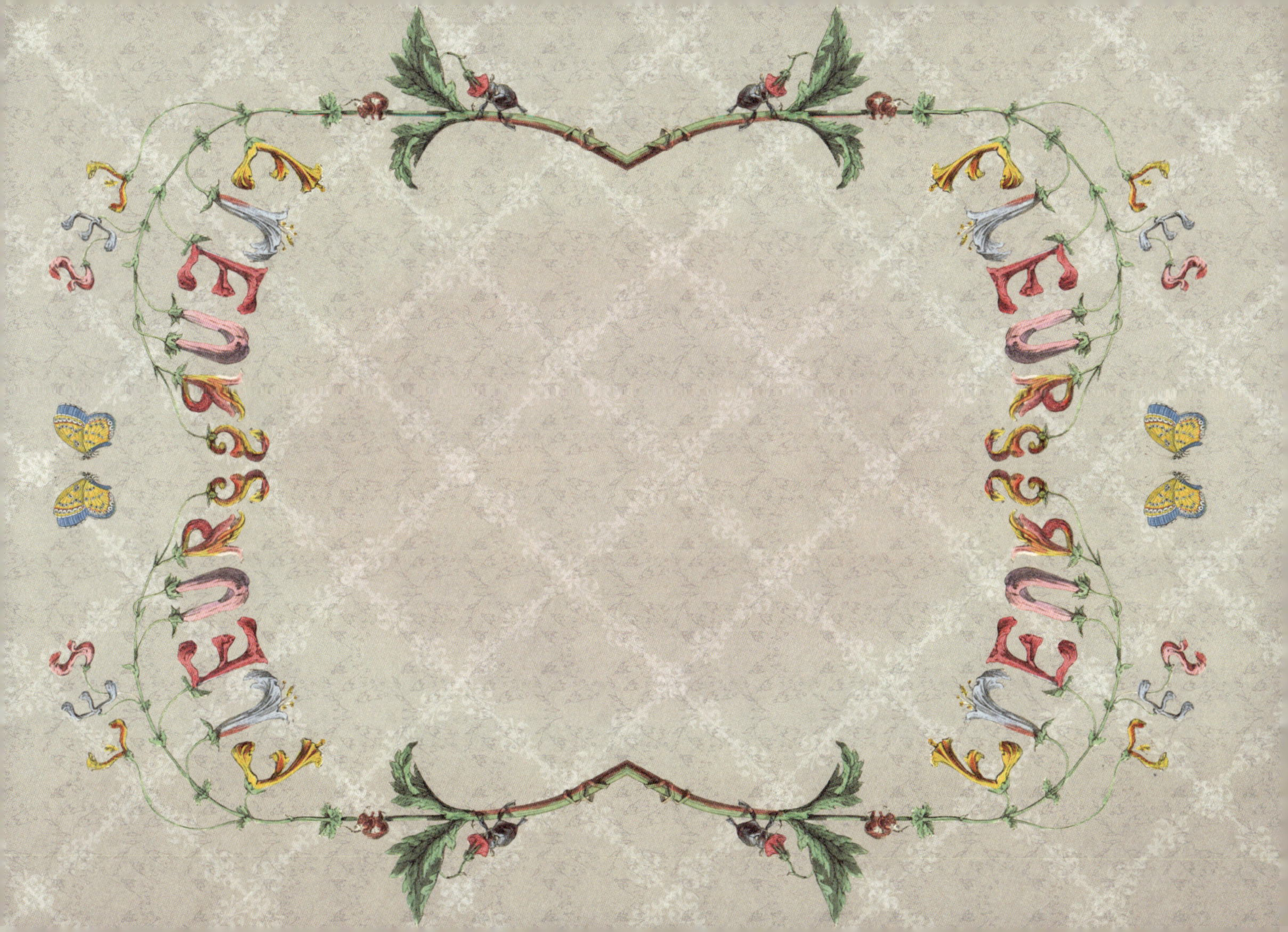

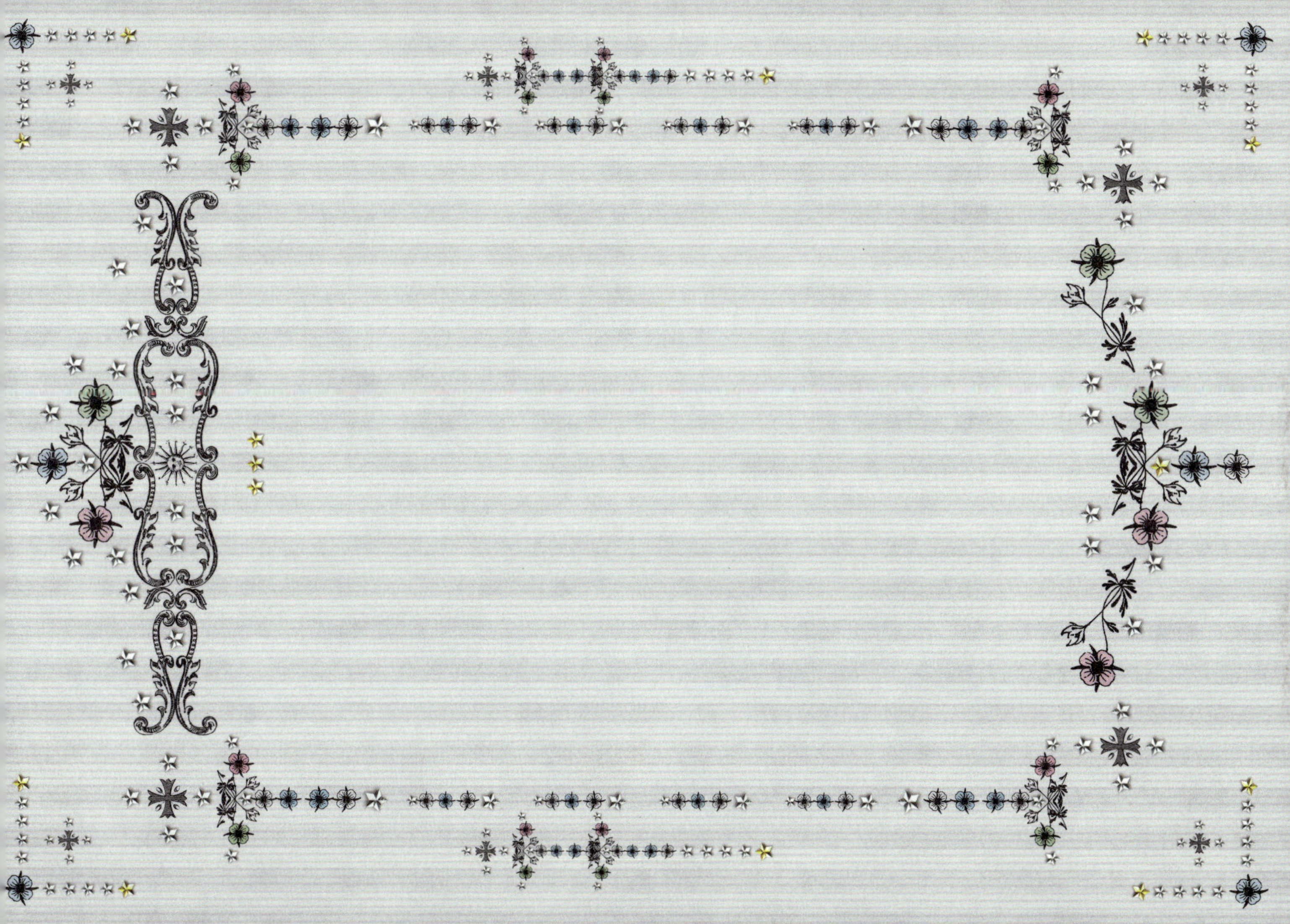

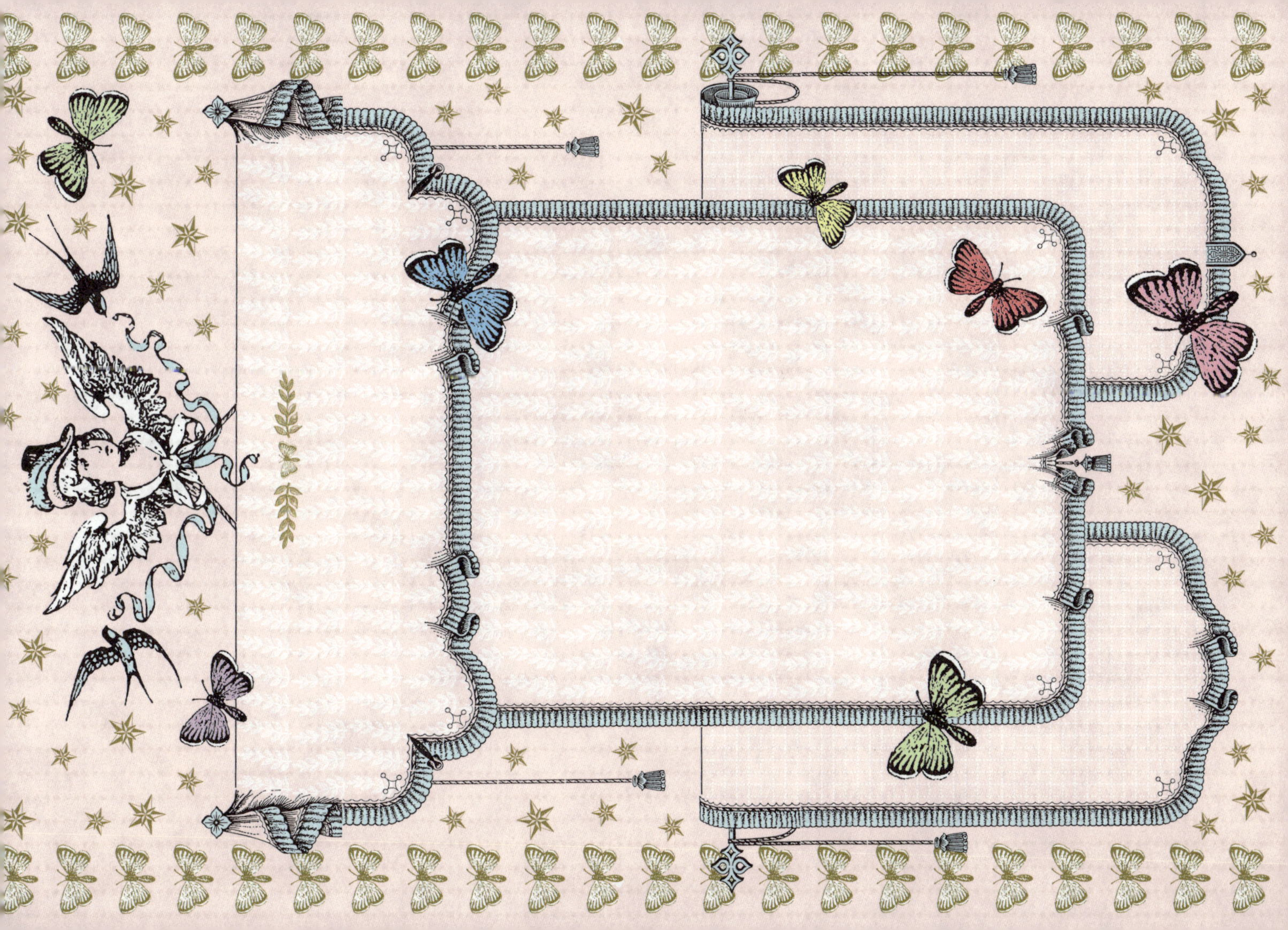

＊＊＊
＊＊＊
＊＊＊
＊＊＊
＊＊＊
＊＊＊
＊＊＊
＊＊＊
＊＊＊
＊＊＊
＊＊＊
＊＊＊
＊＊＊
＊＊＊
＊＊＊
＊＊＊
＊＊＊
＊＊＊
＊＊＊
＊＊＊
＊＊＊
＊＊＊
＊＊＊
＊＊＊
＊＊＊
＊＊＊
＊＊＊
＊＊＊
＊＊＊
＊＊＊
＊＊＊
＊＊＊
＊＊＊
＊＊＊
＊＊＊
＊＊＊

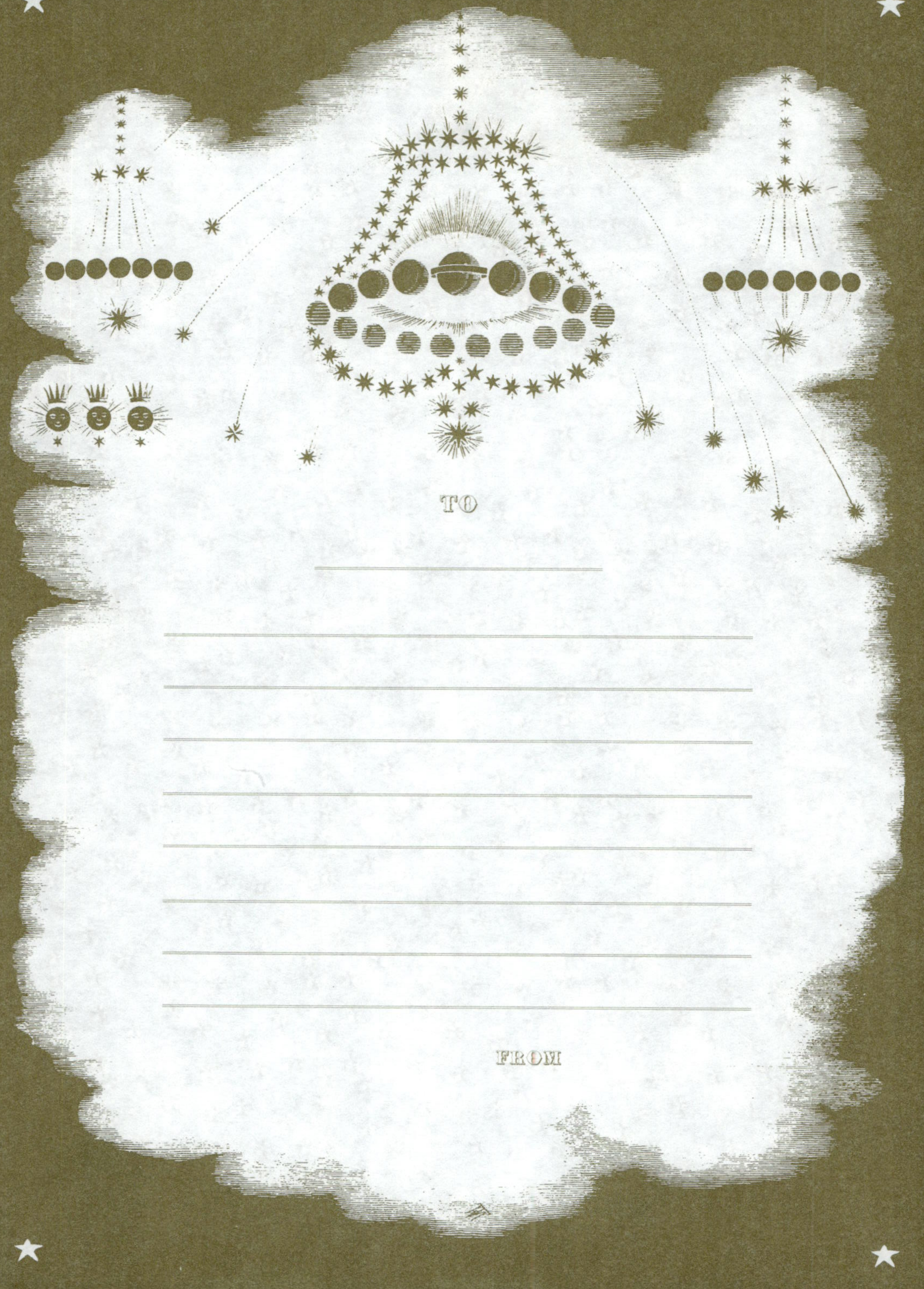
TO
FROM

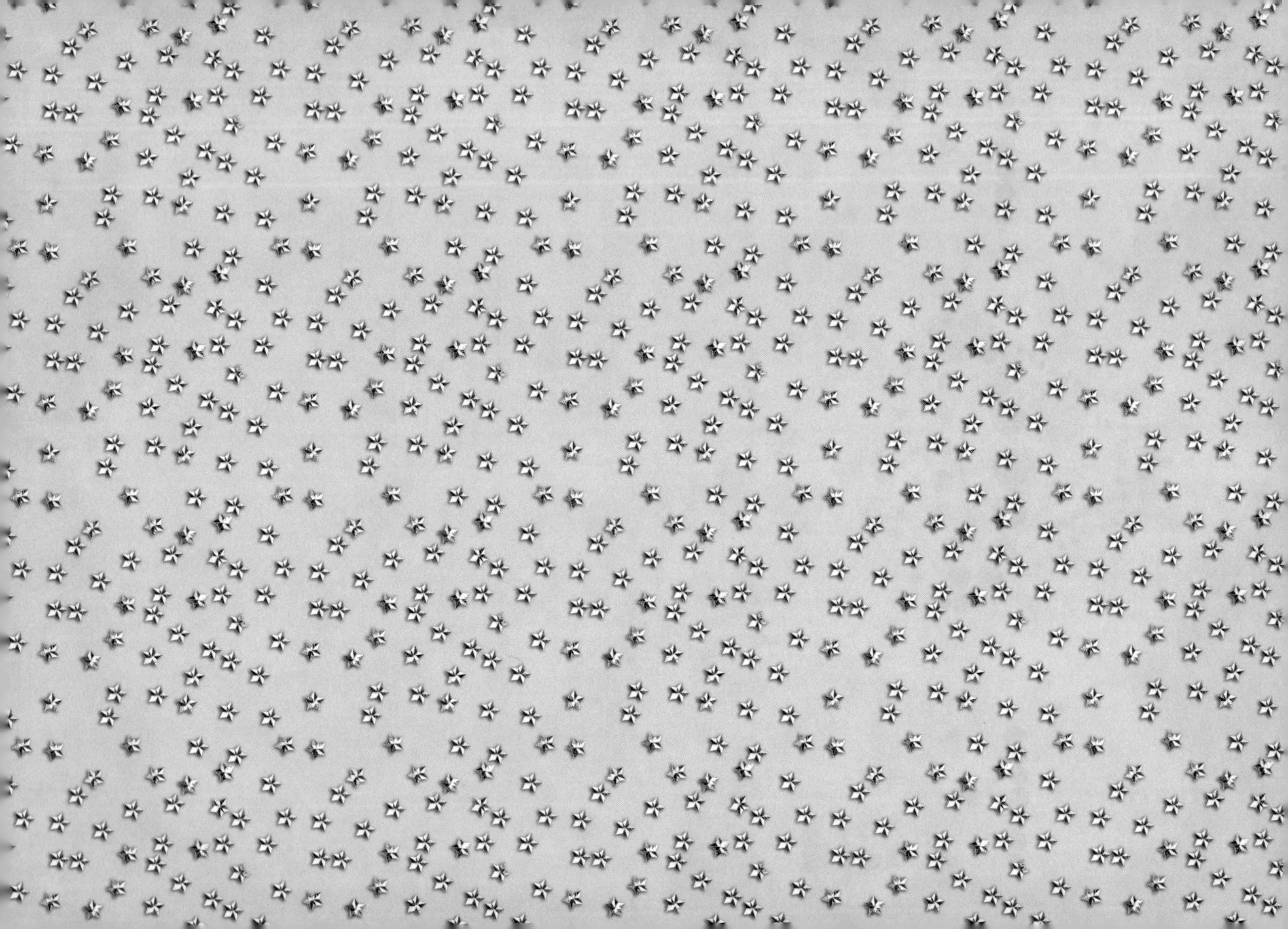

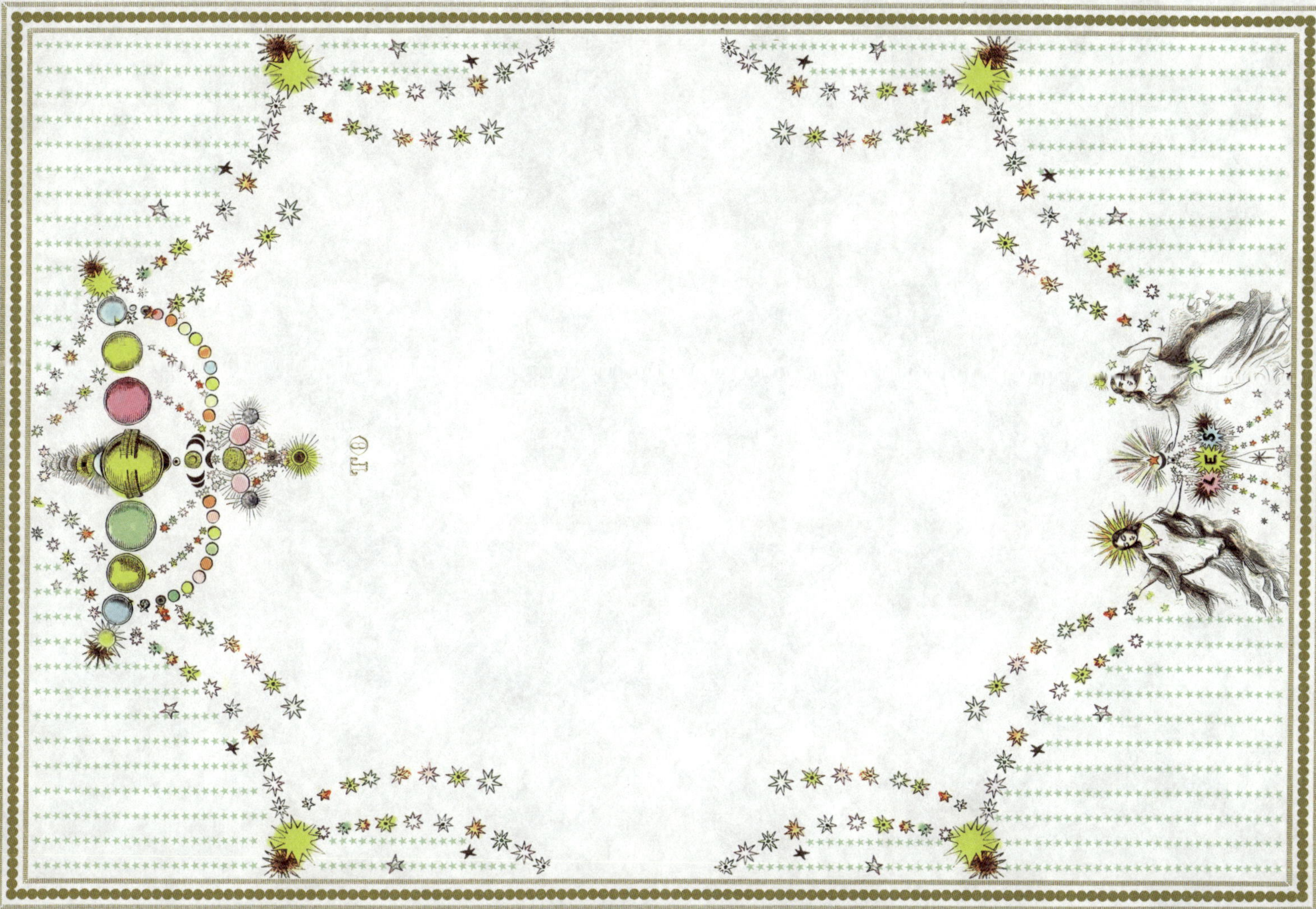

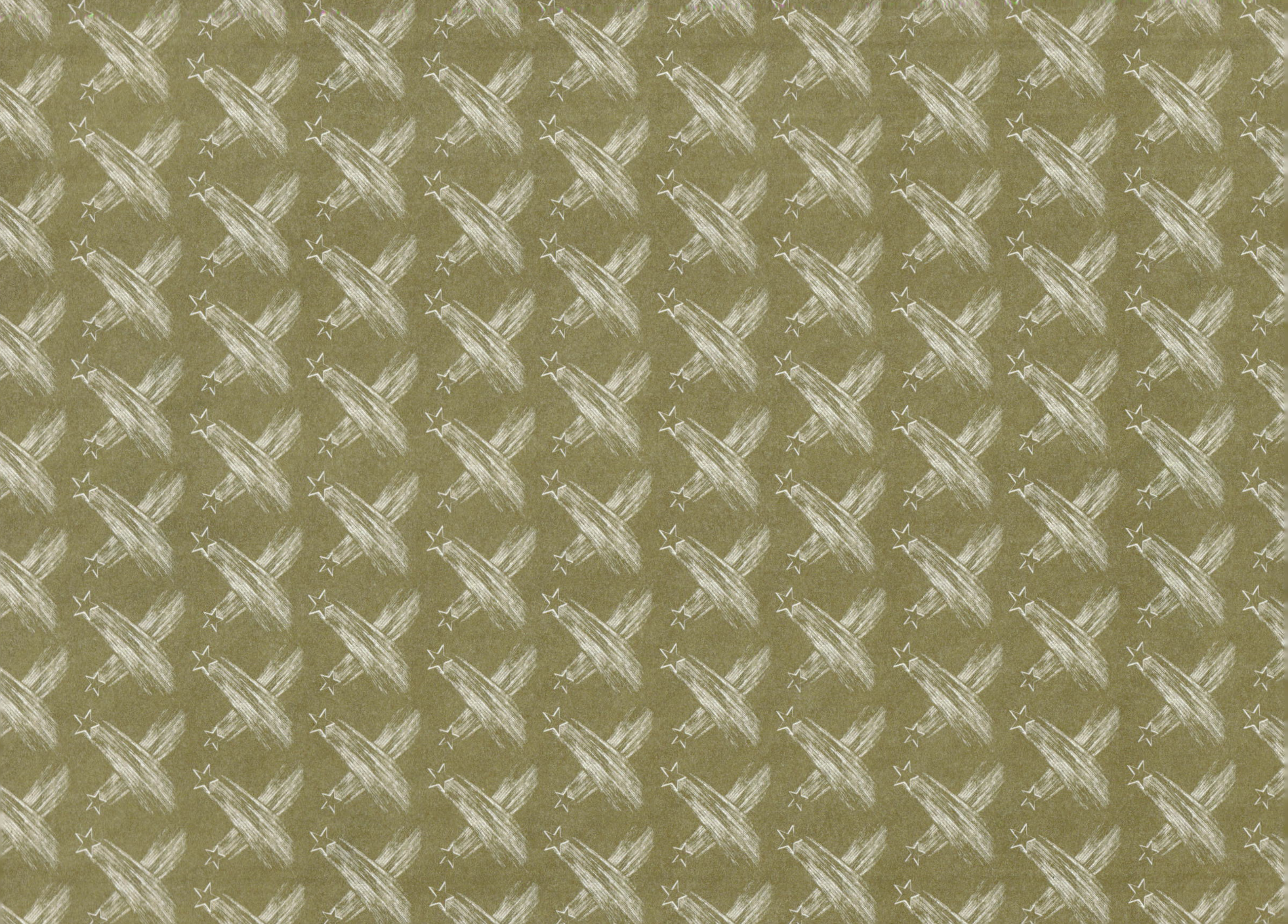

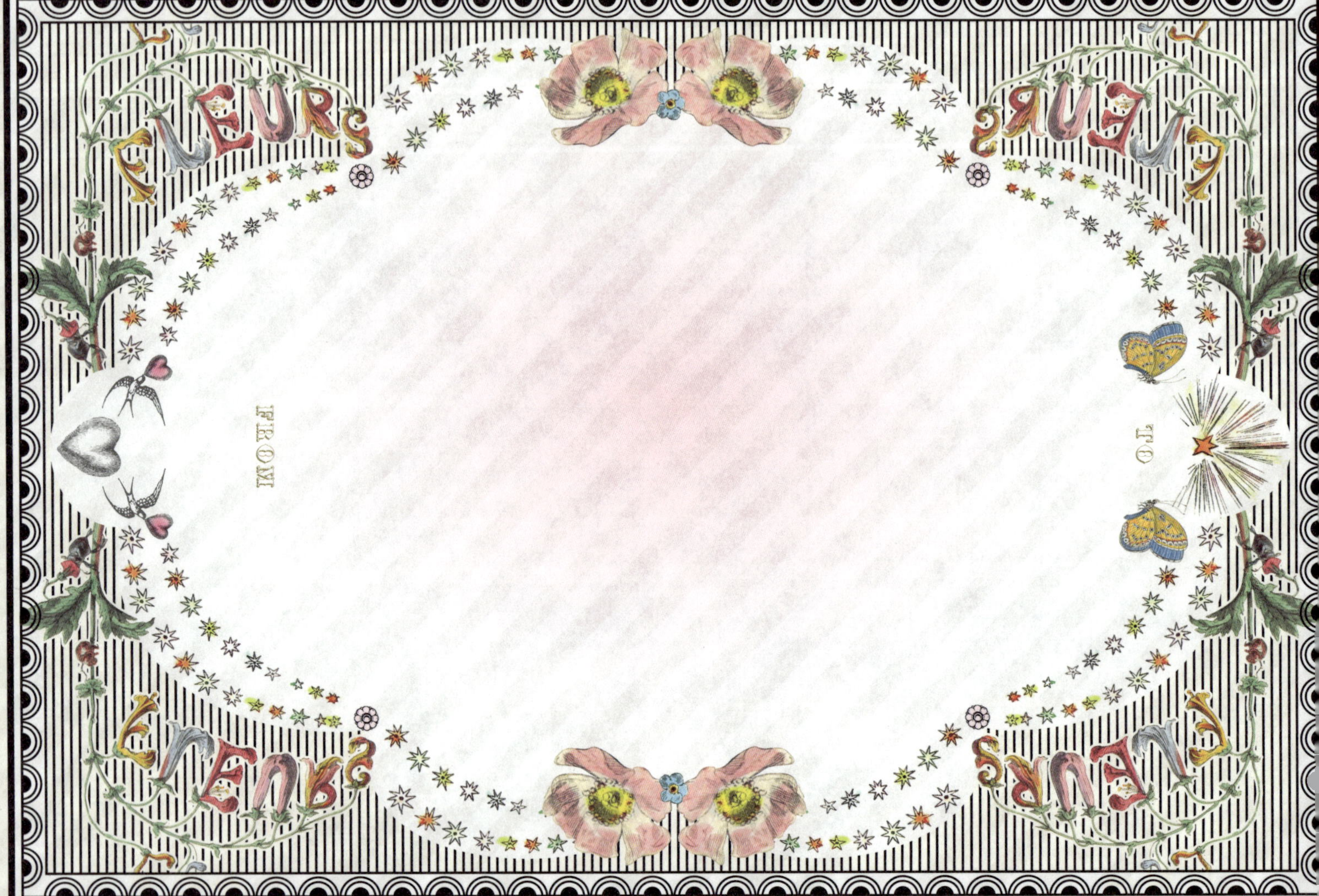

FLEURS
FROM
TO

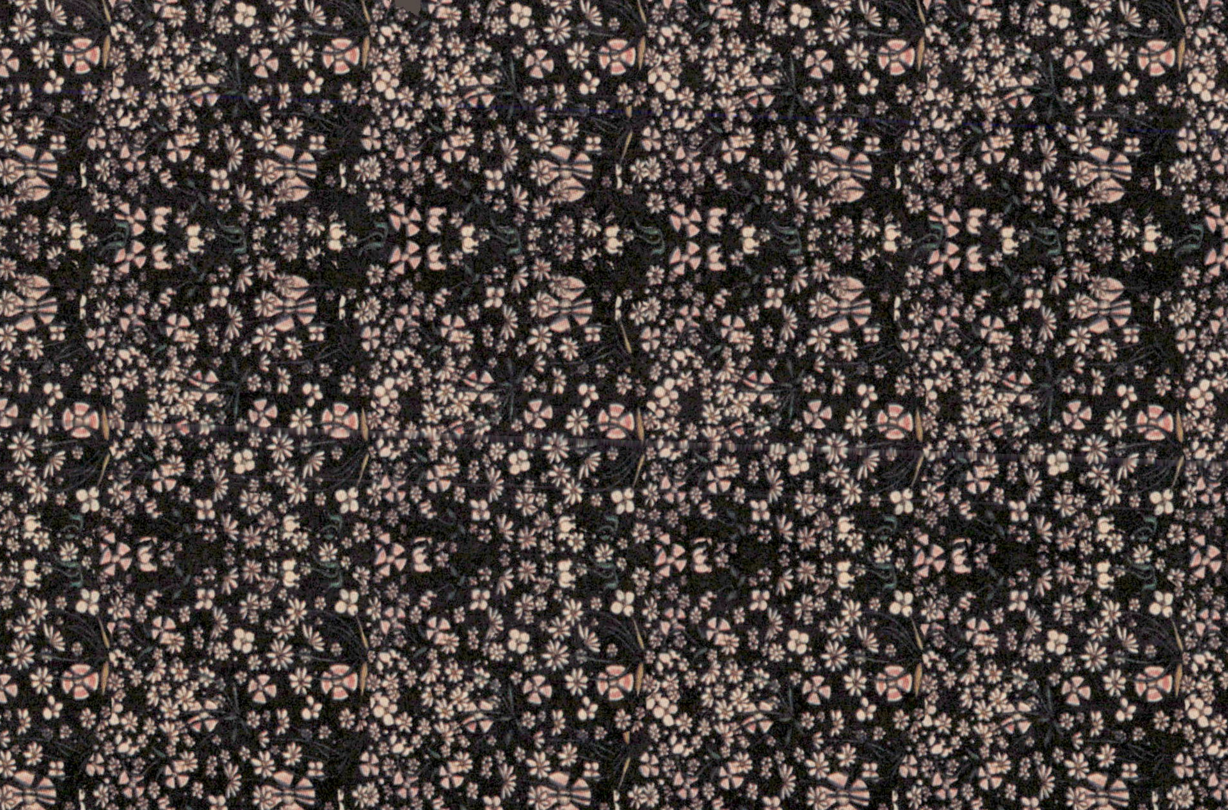

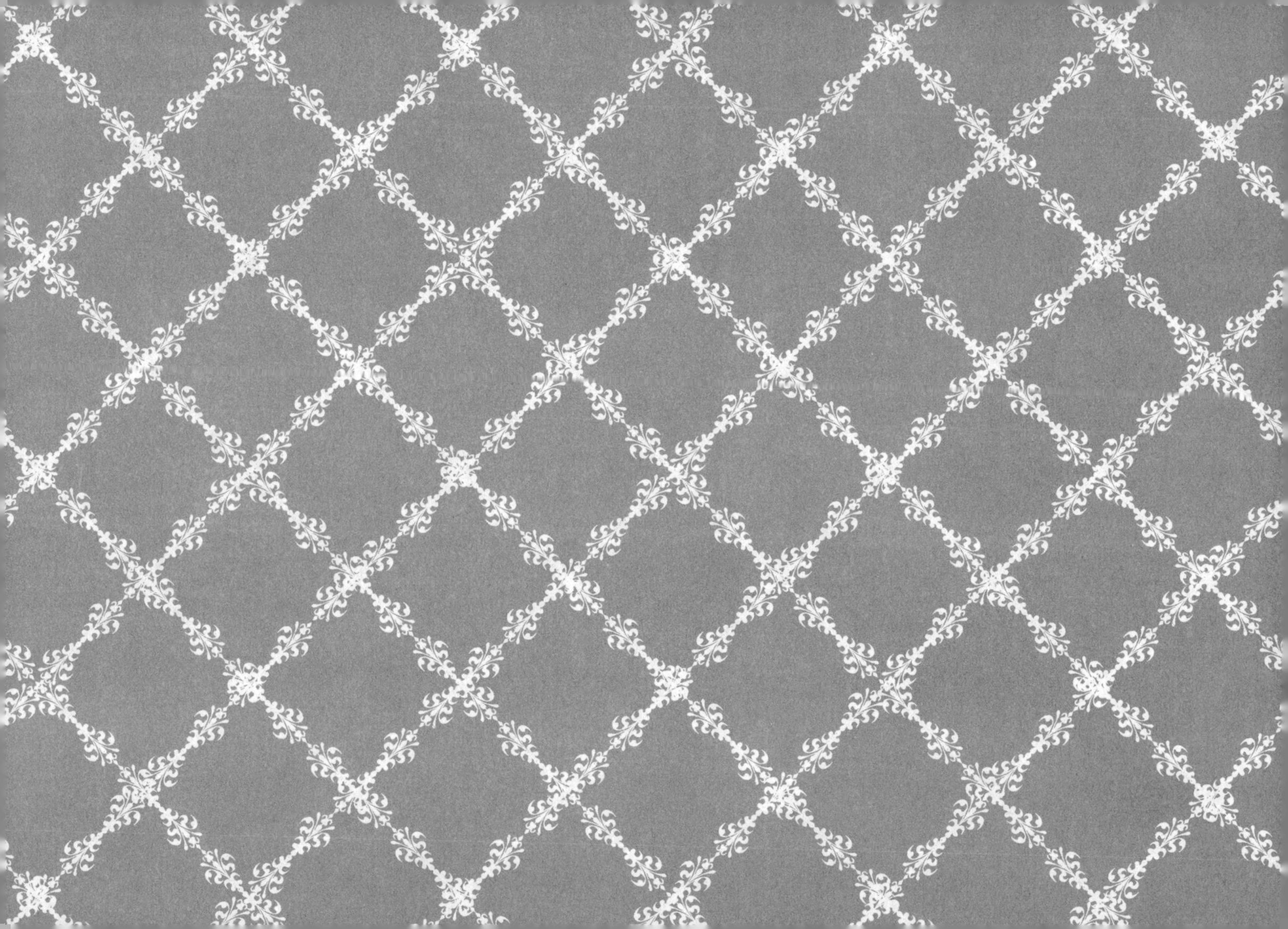

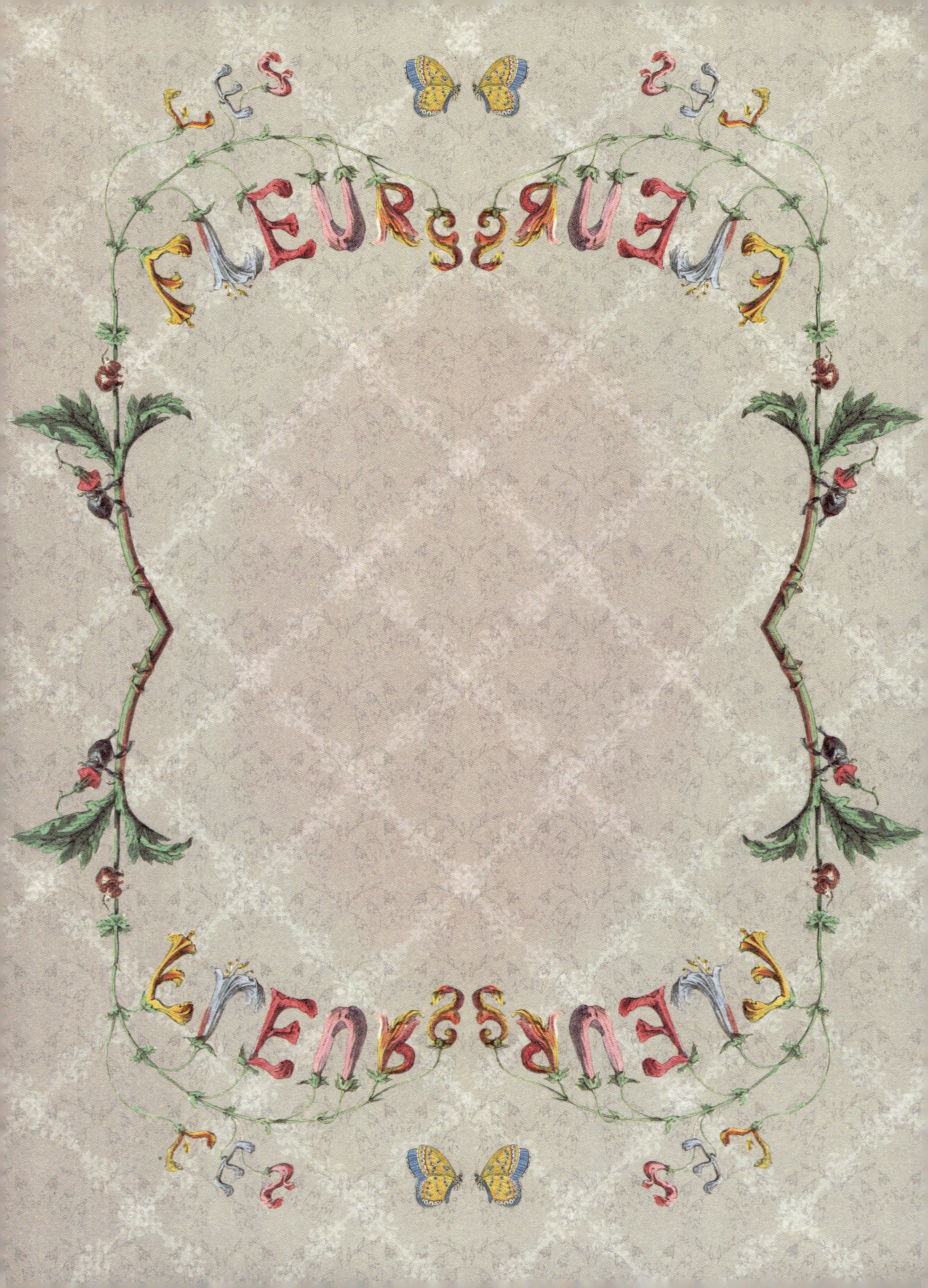

LES FLEURS

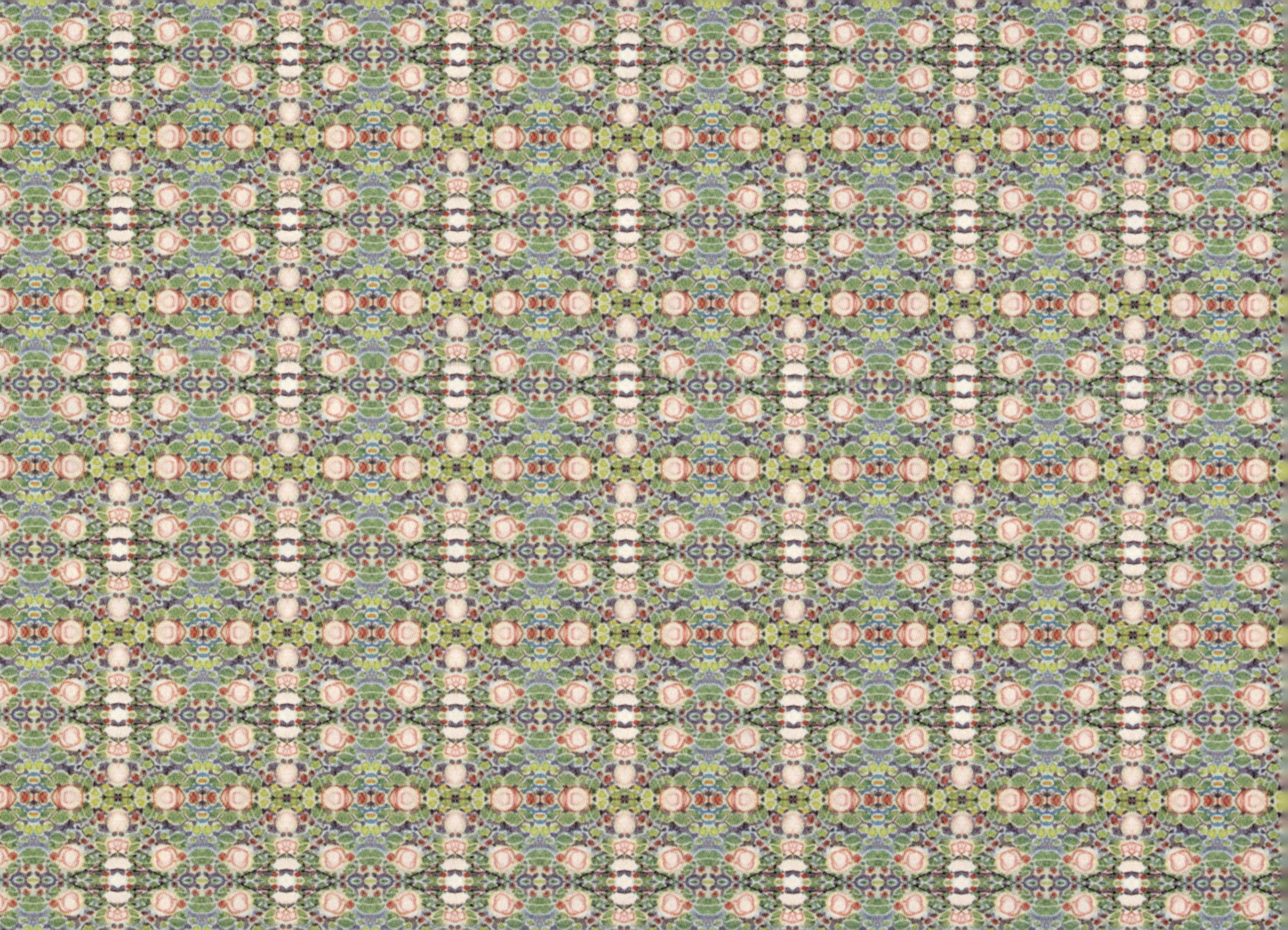

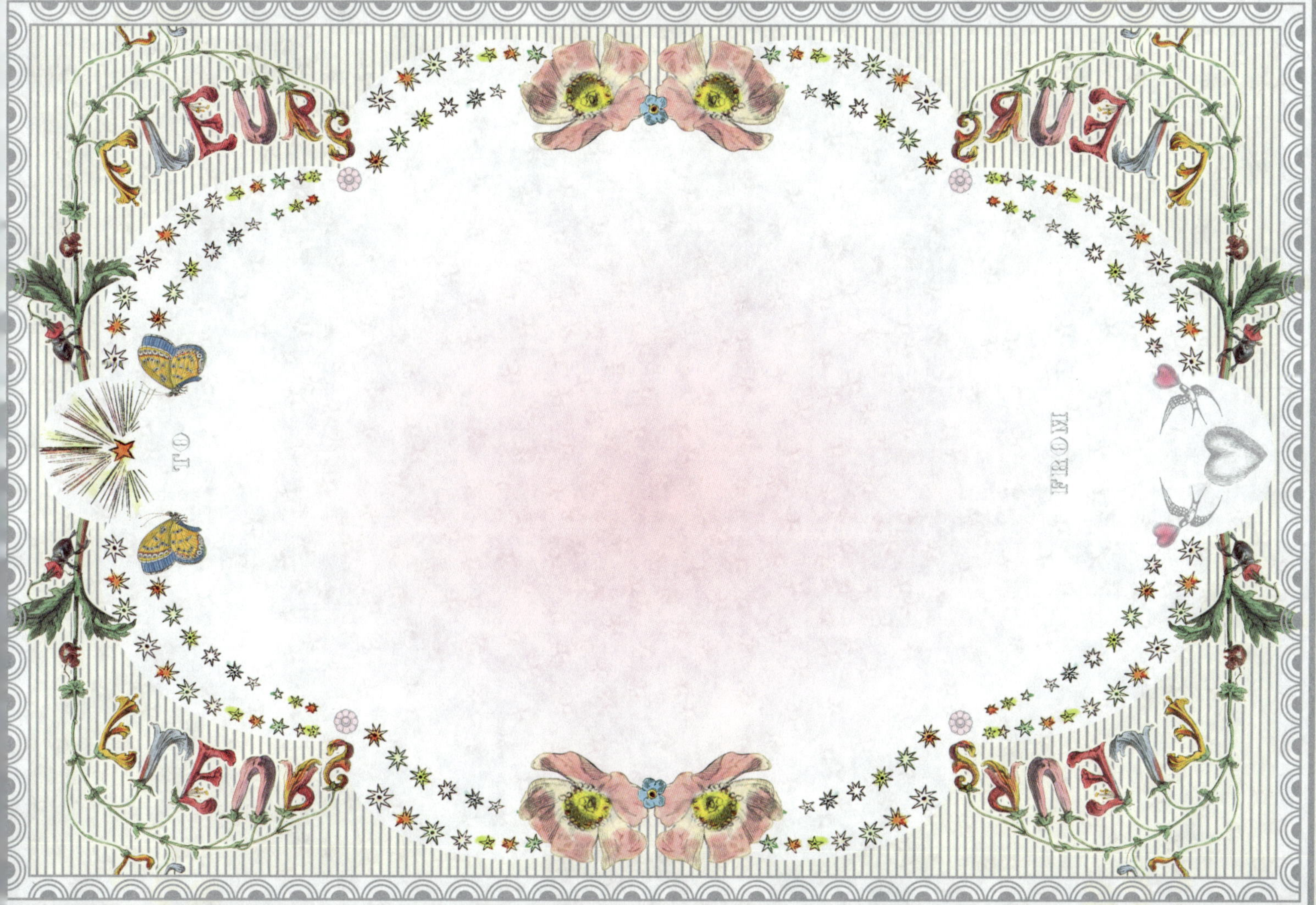

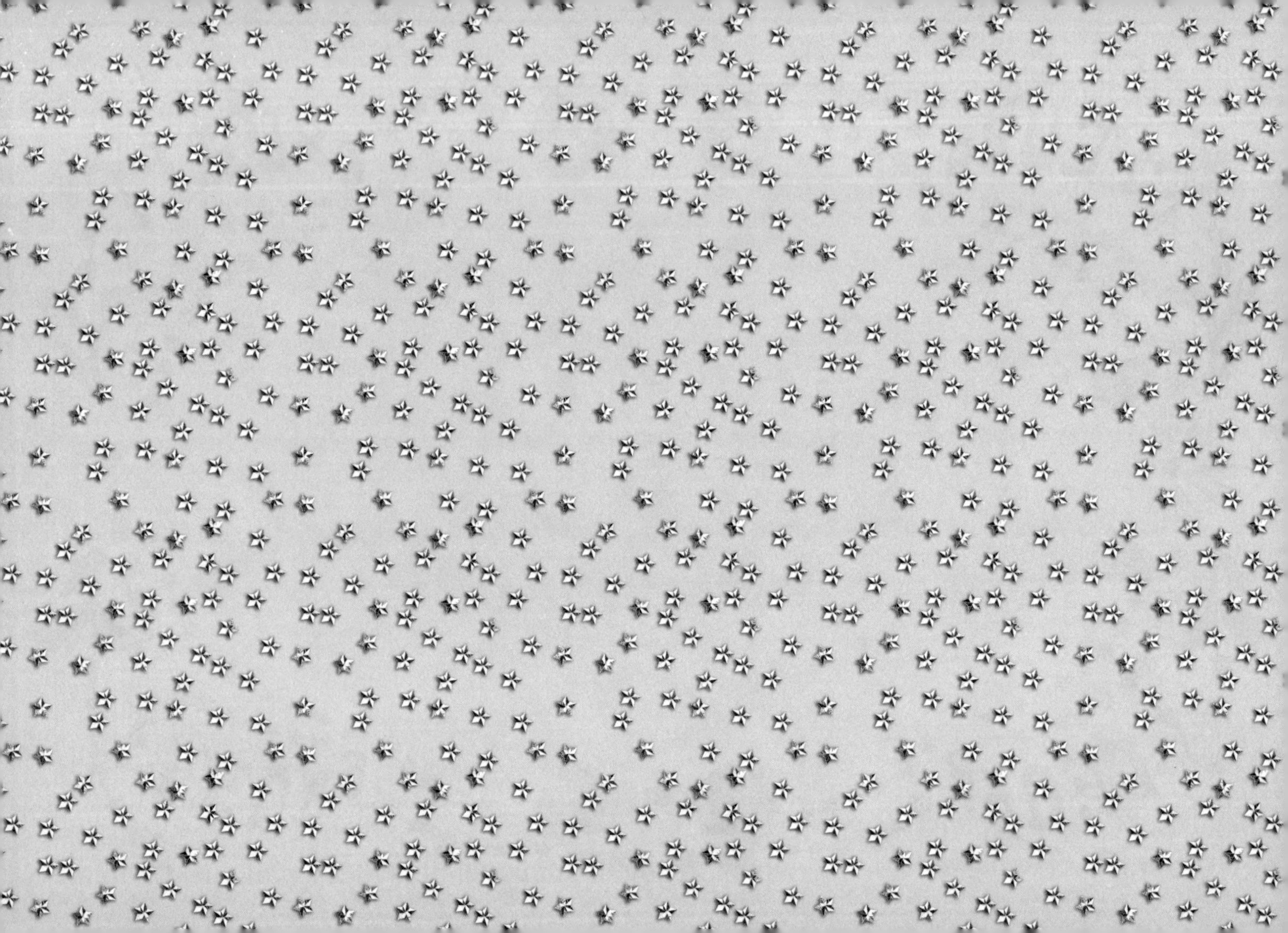

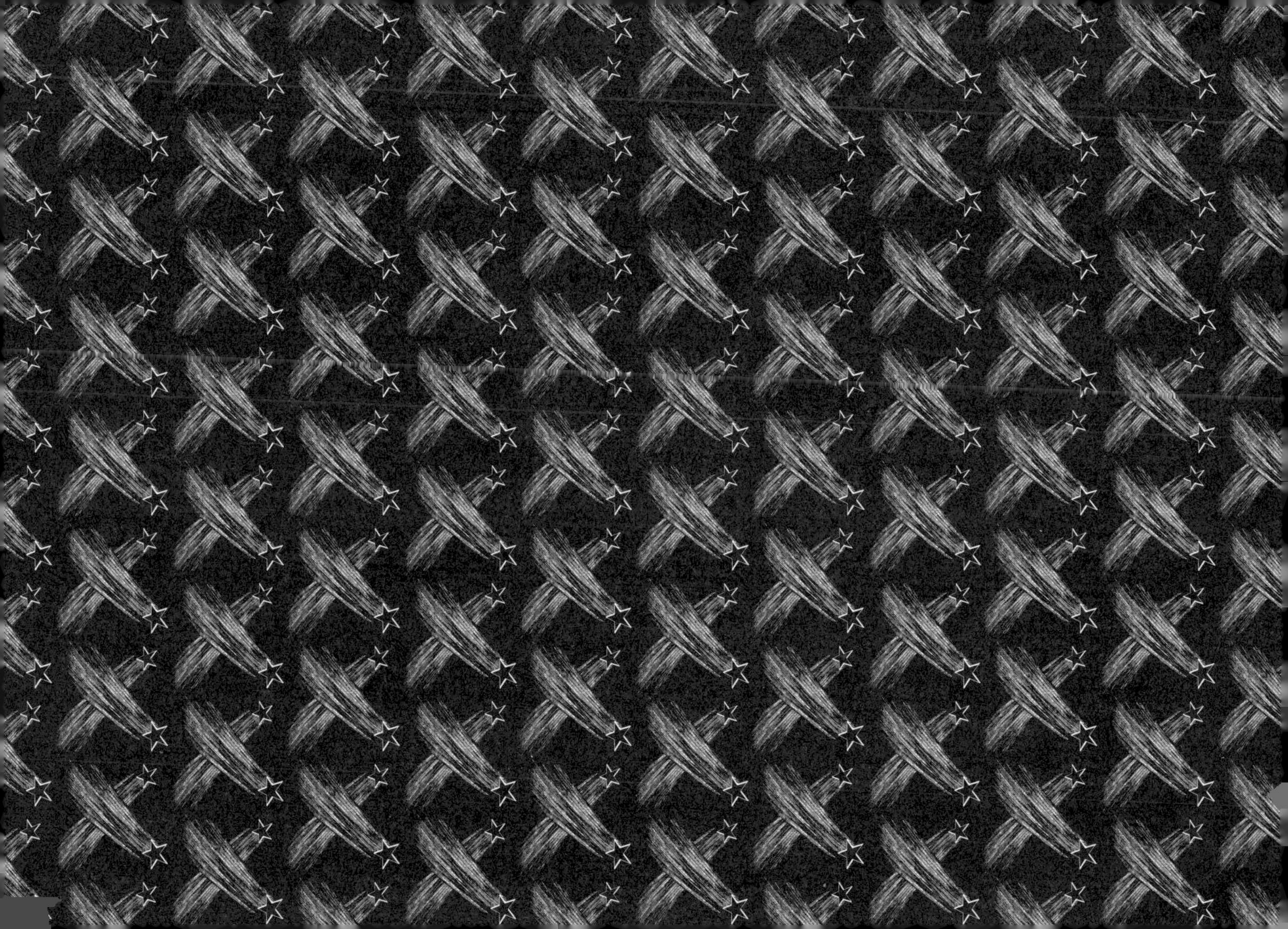

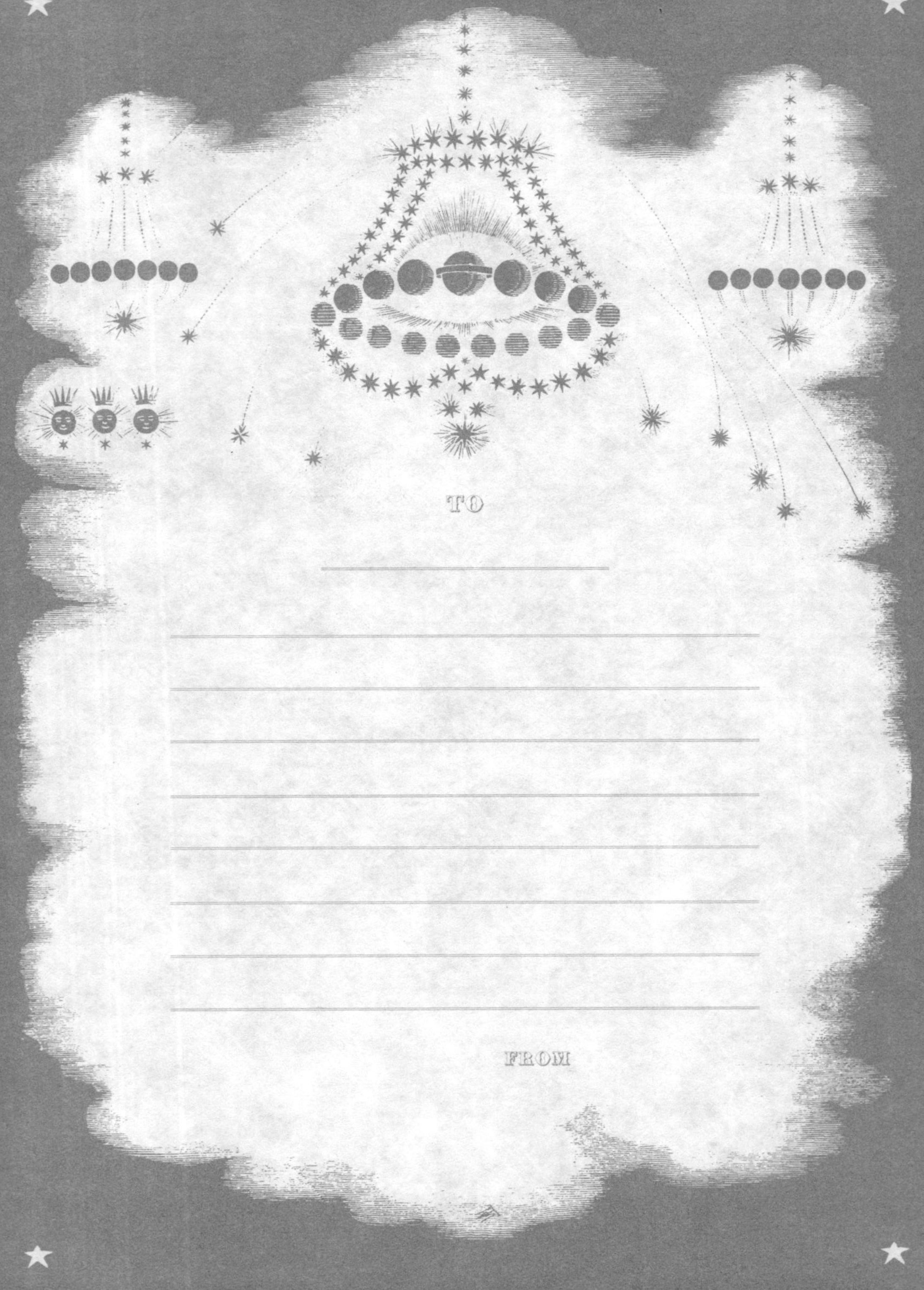

TO
FROM

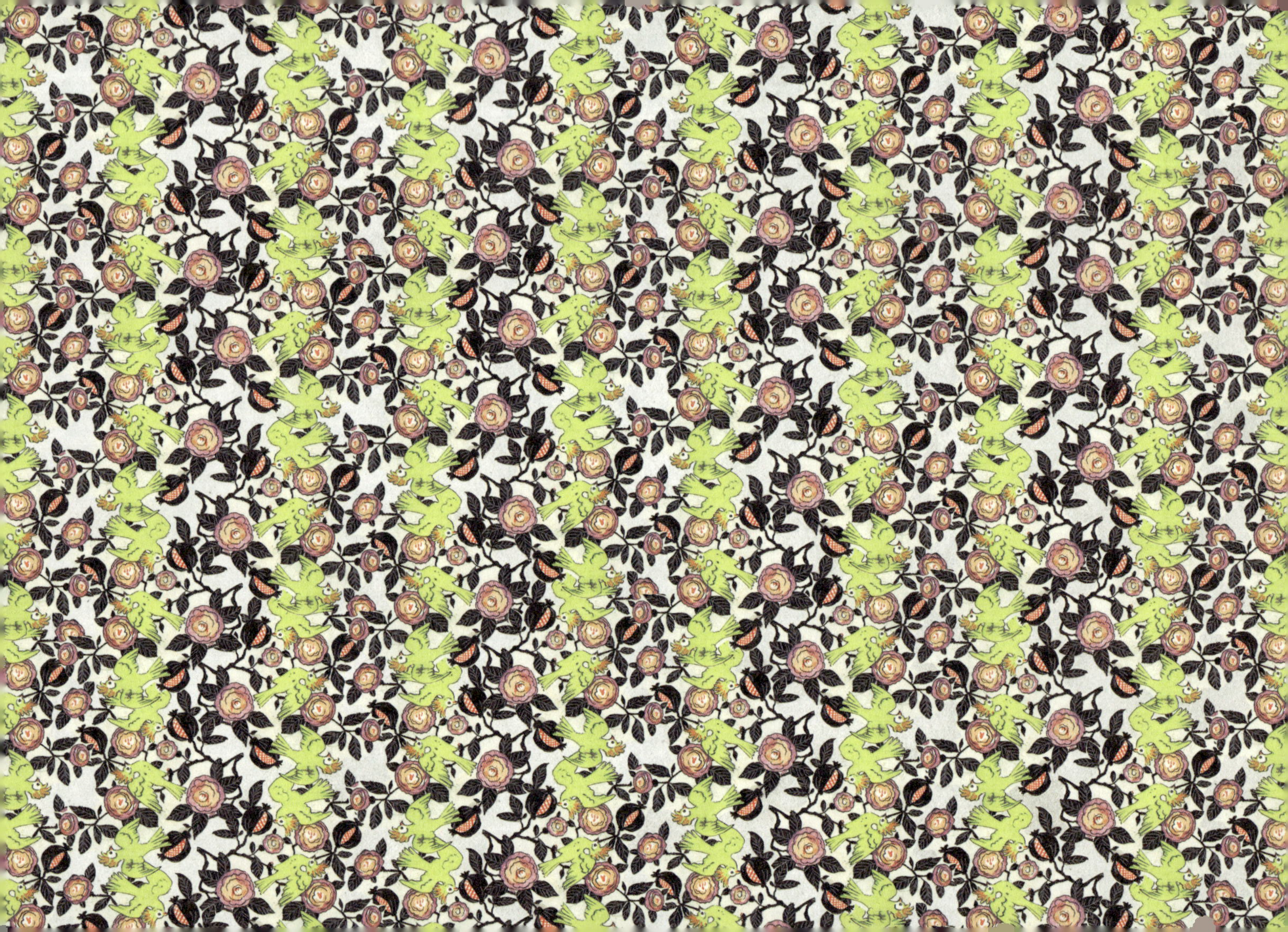

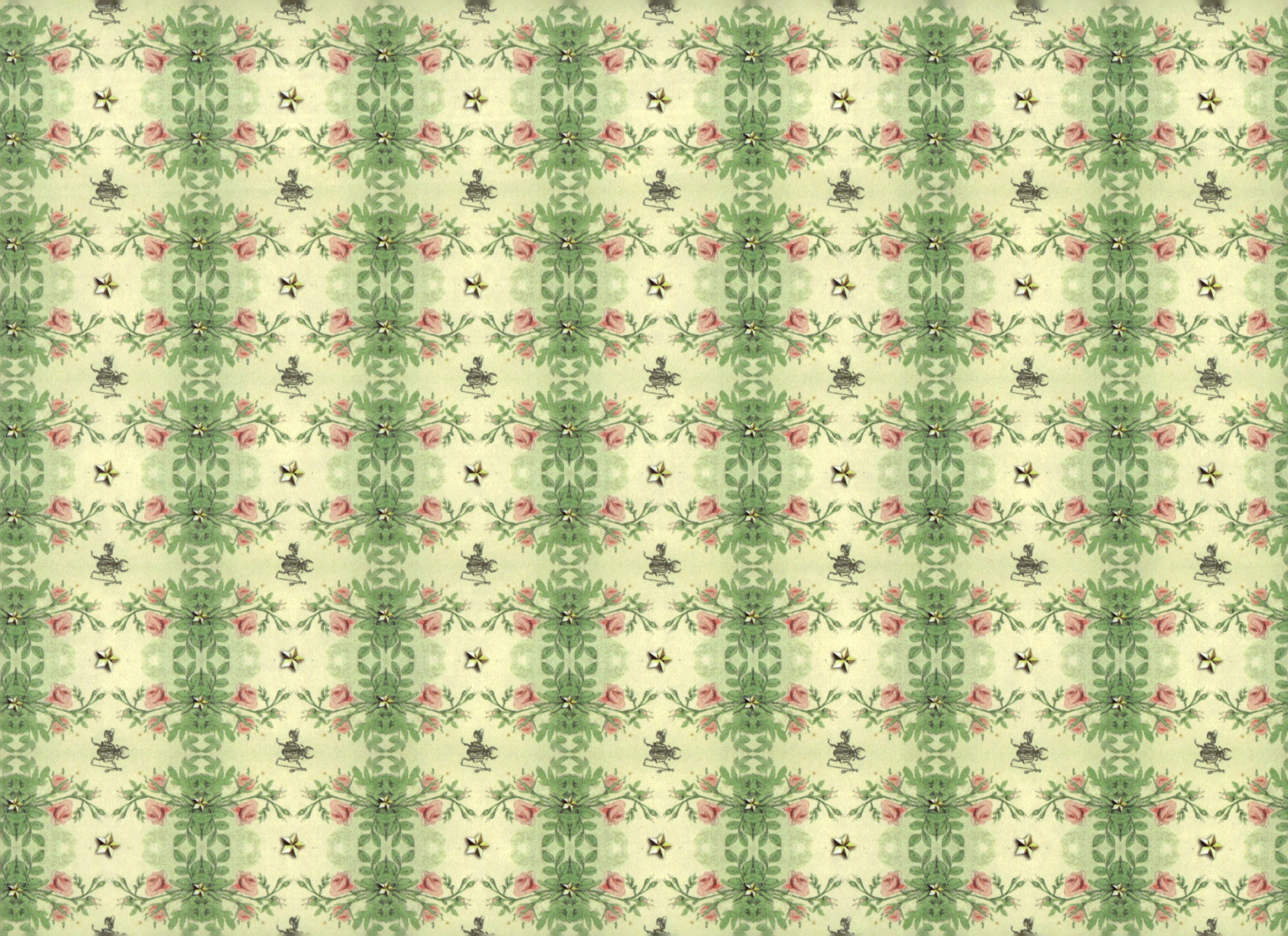

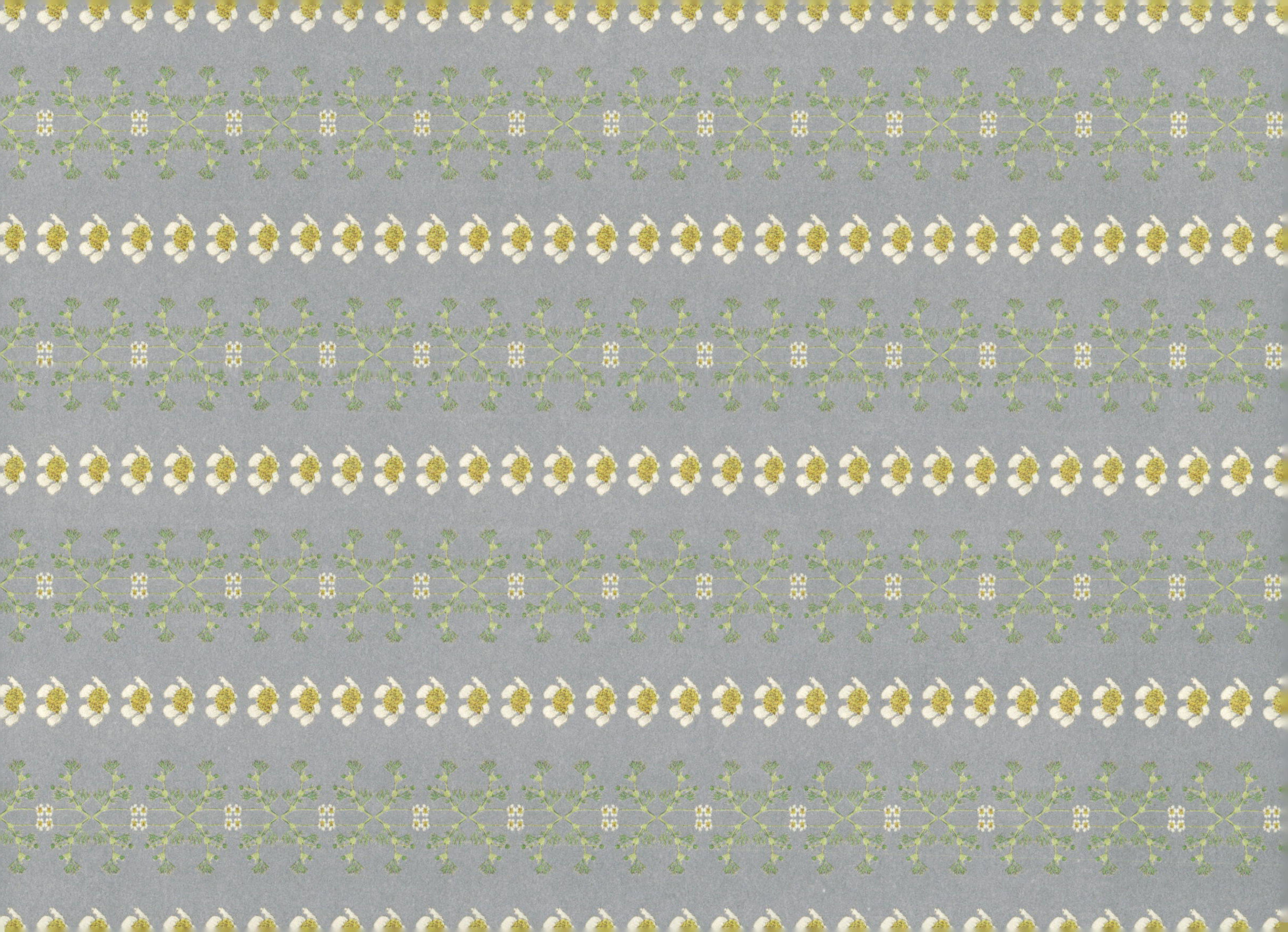

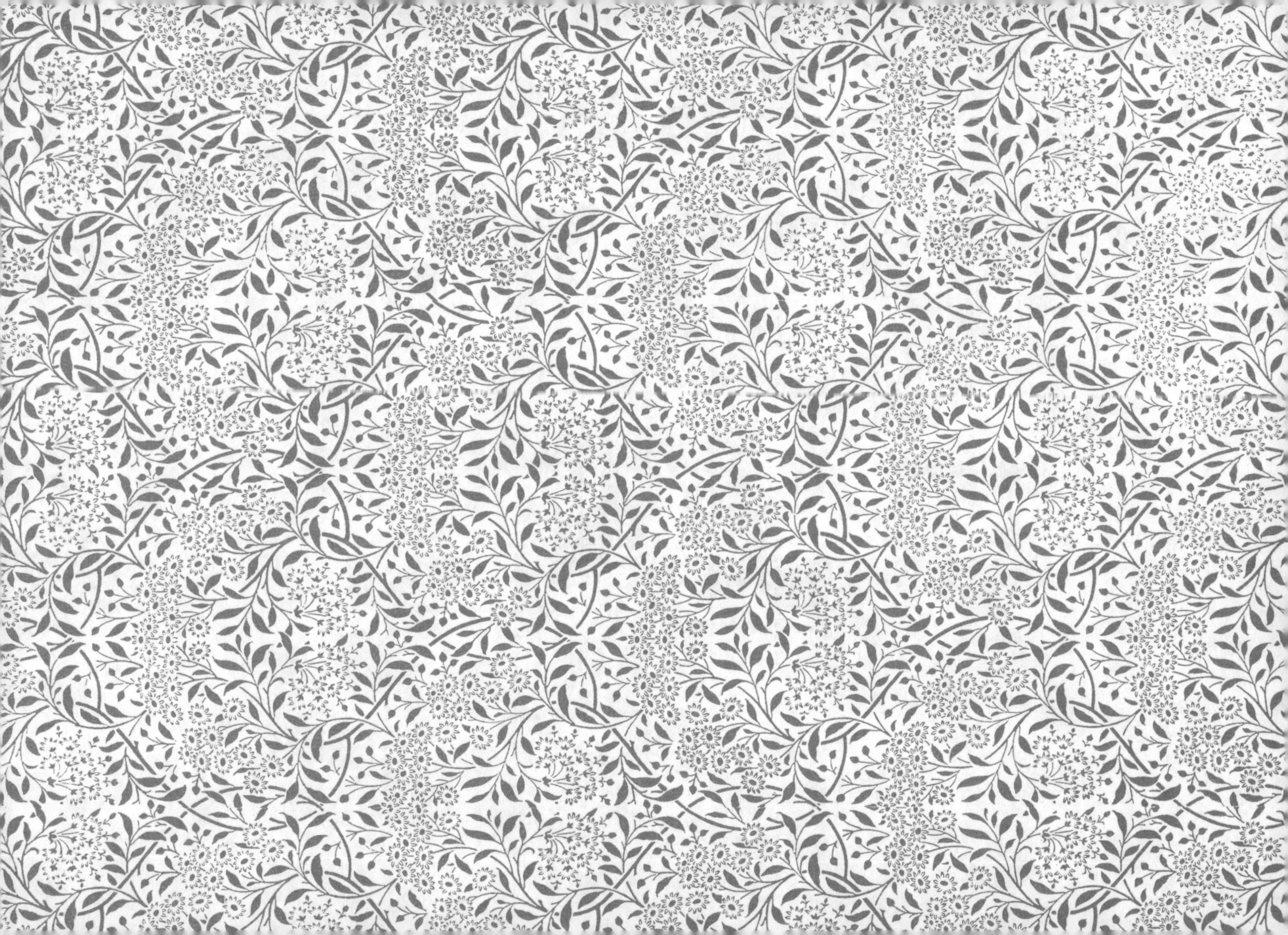

TO

FROM

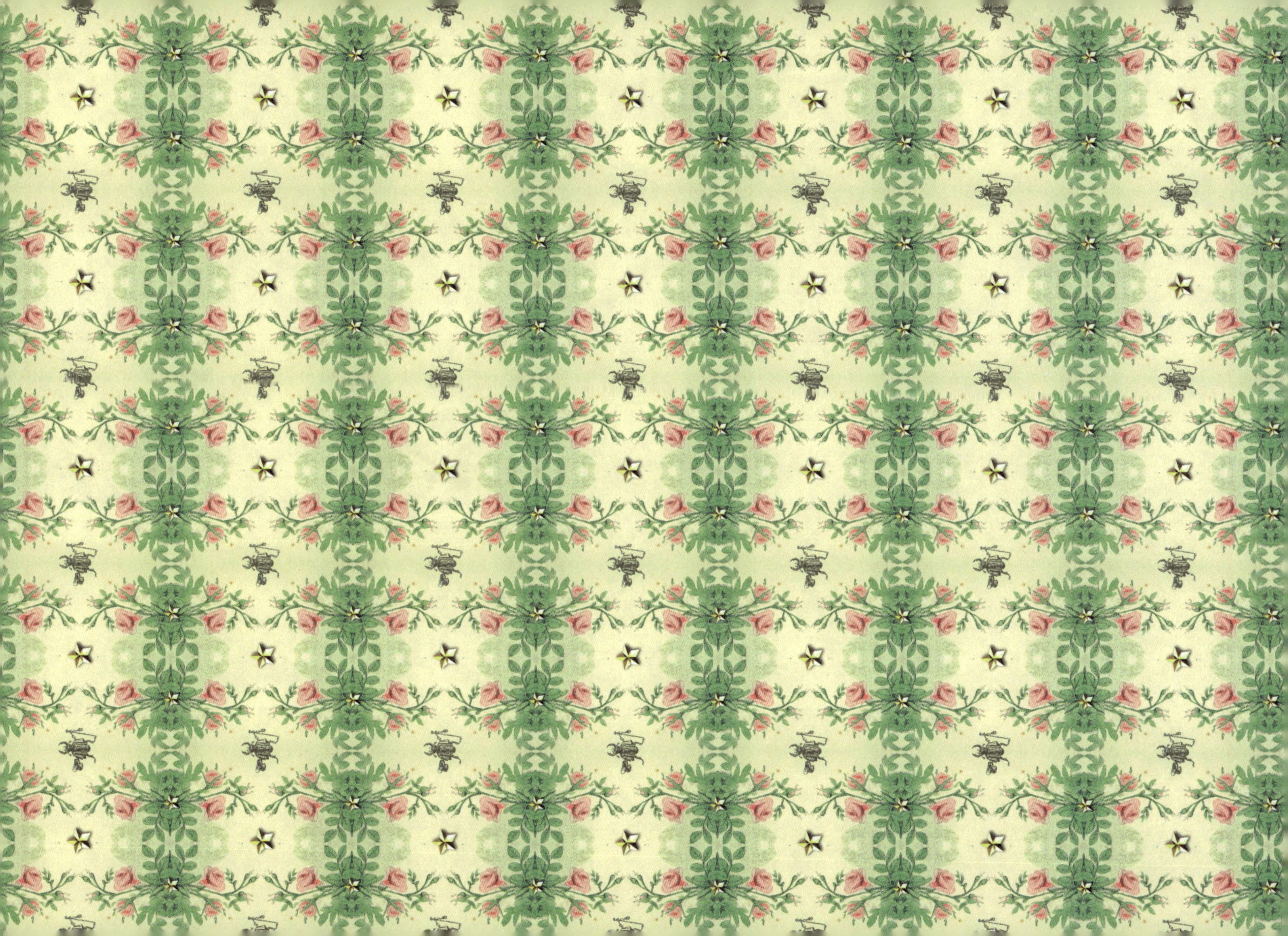

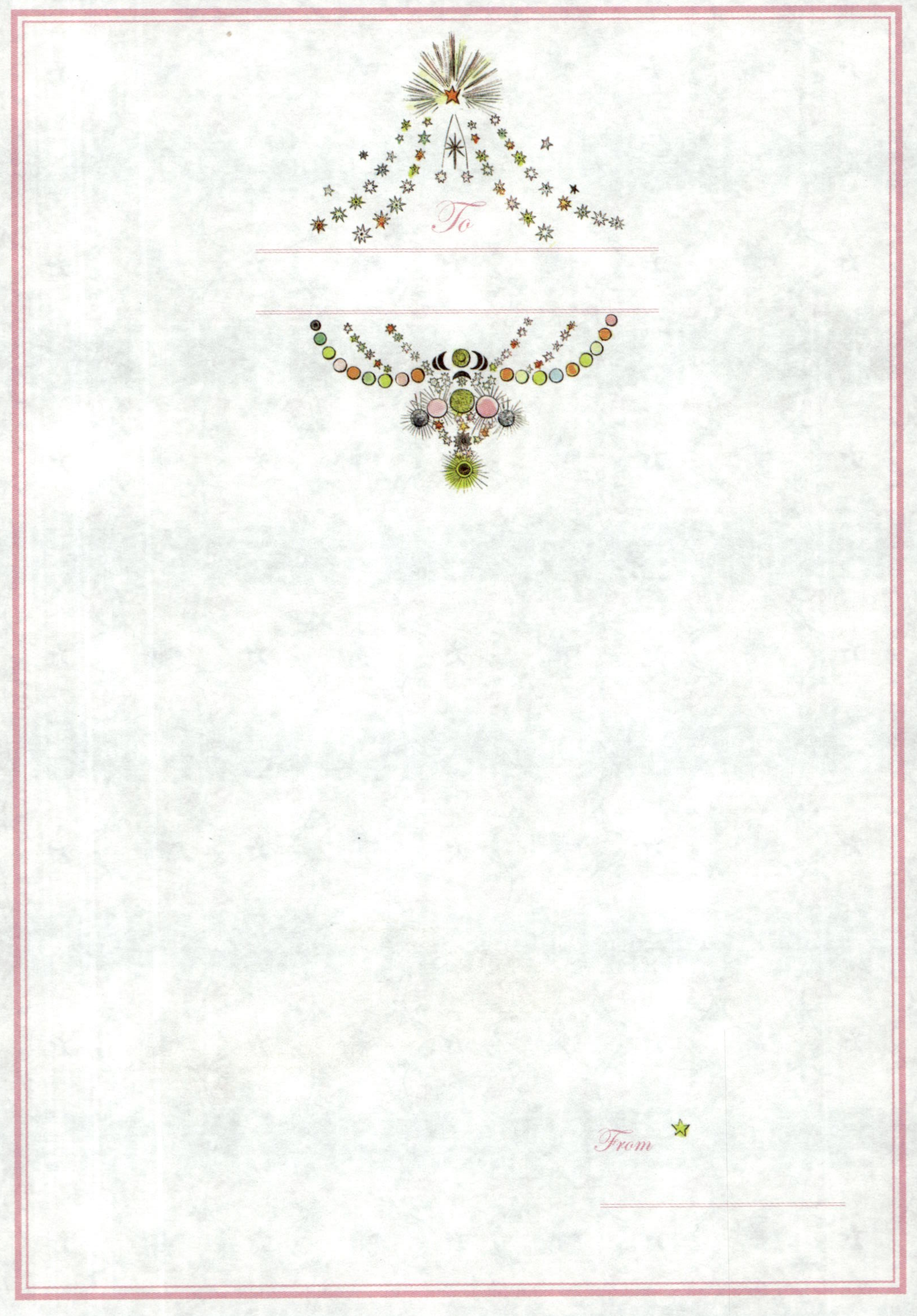
To
From

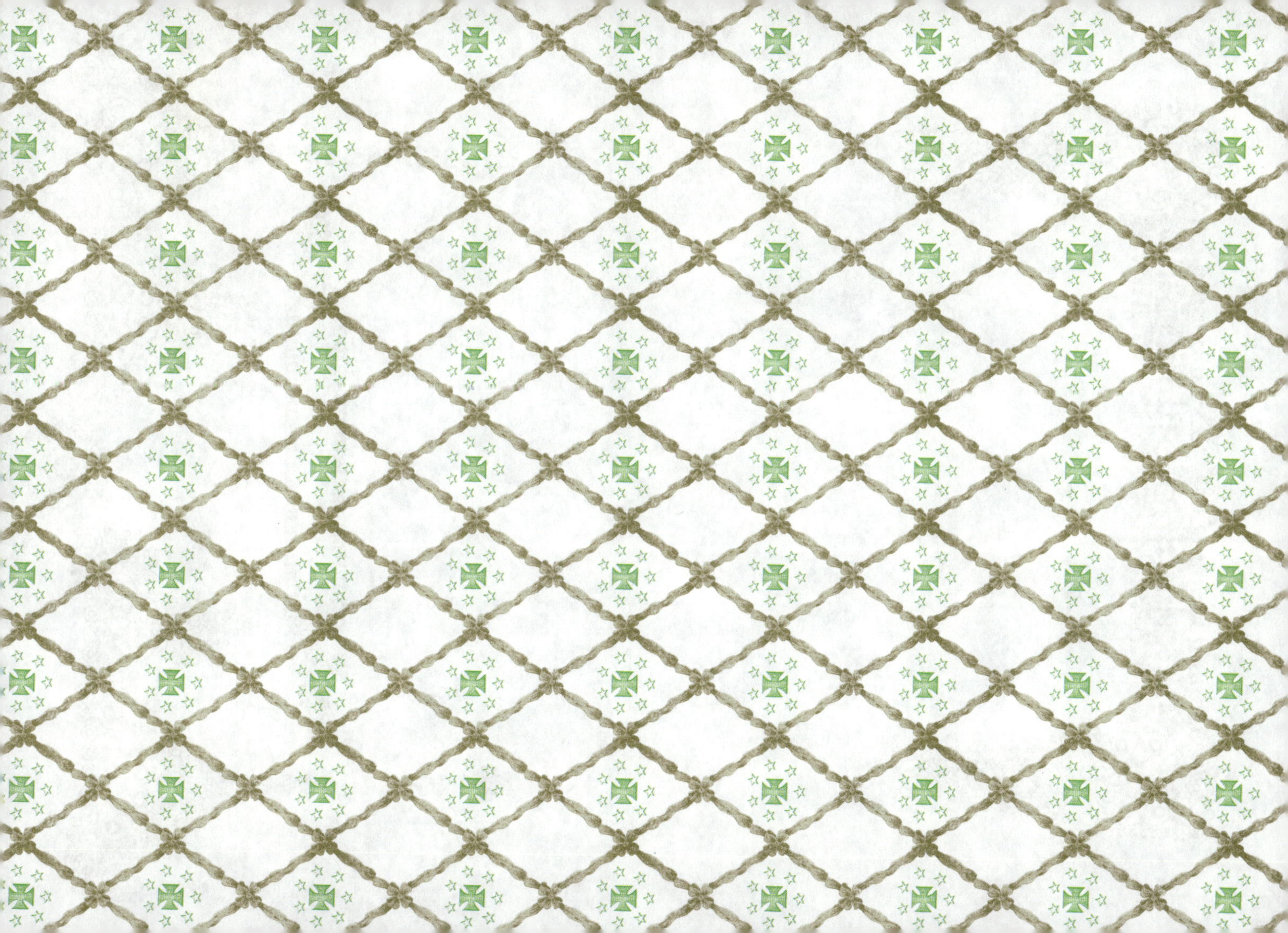

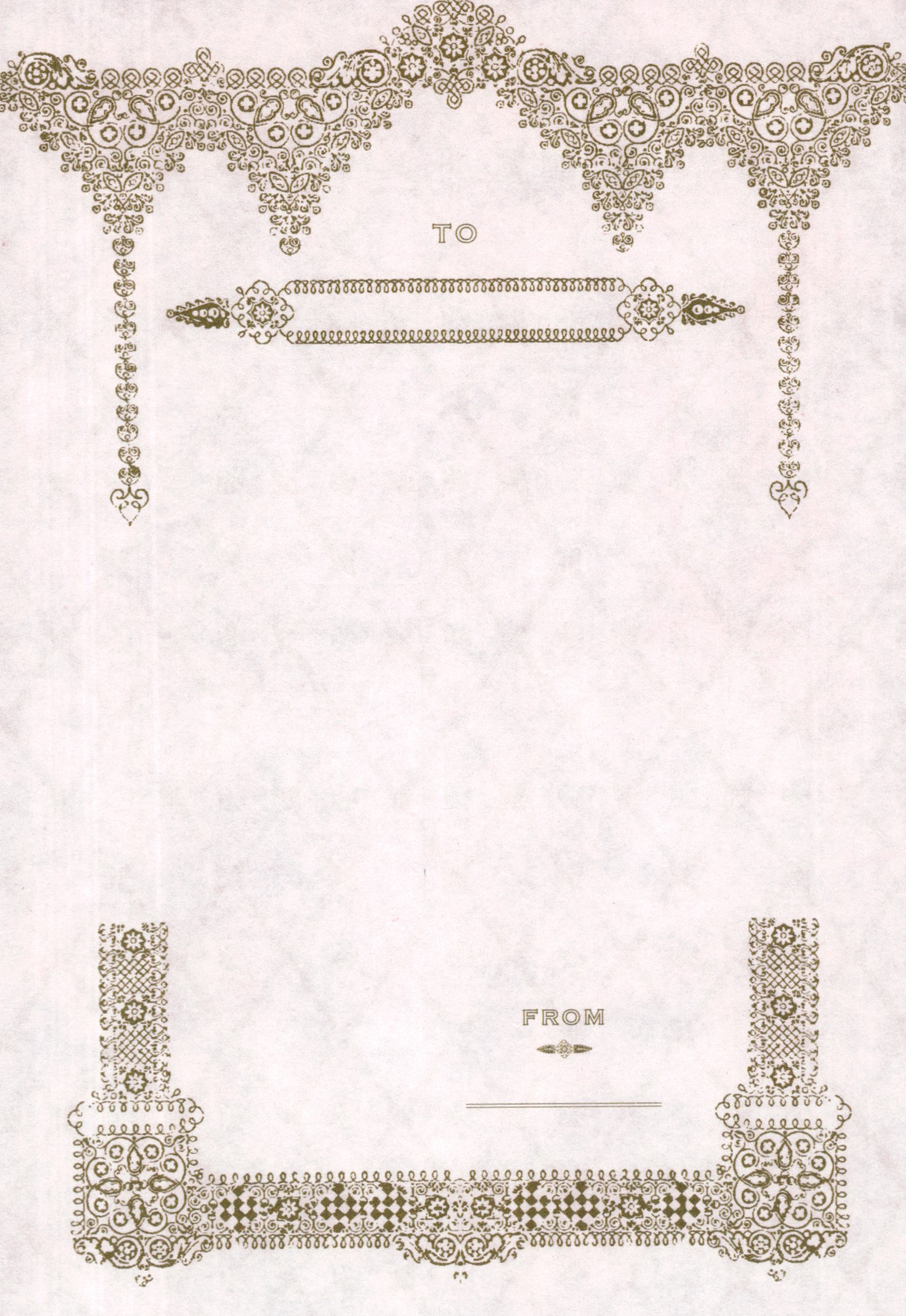

TO
FROM

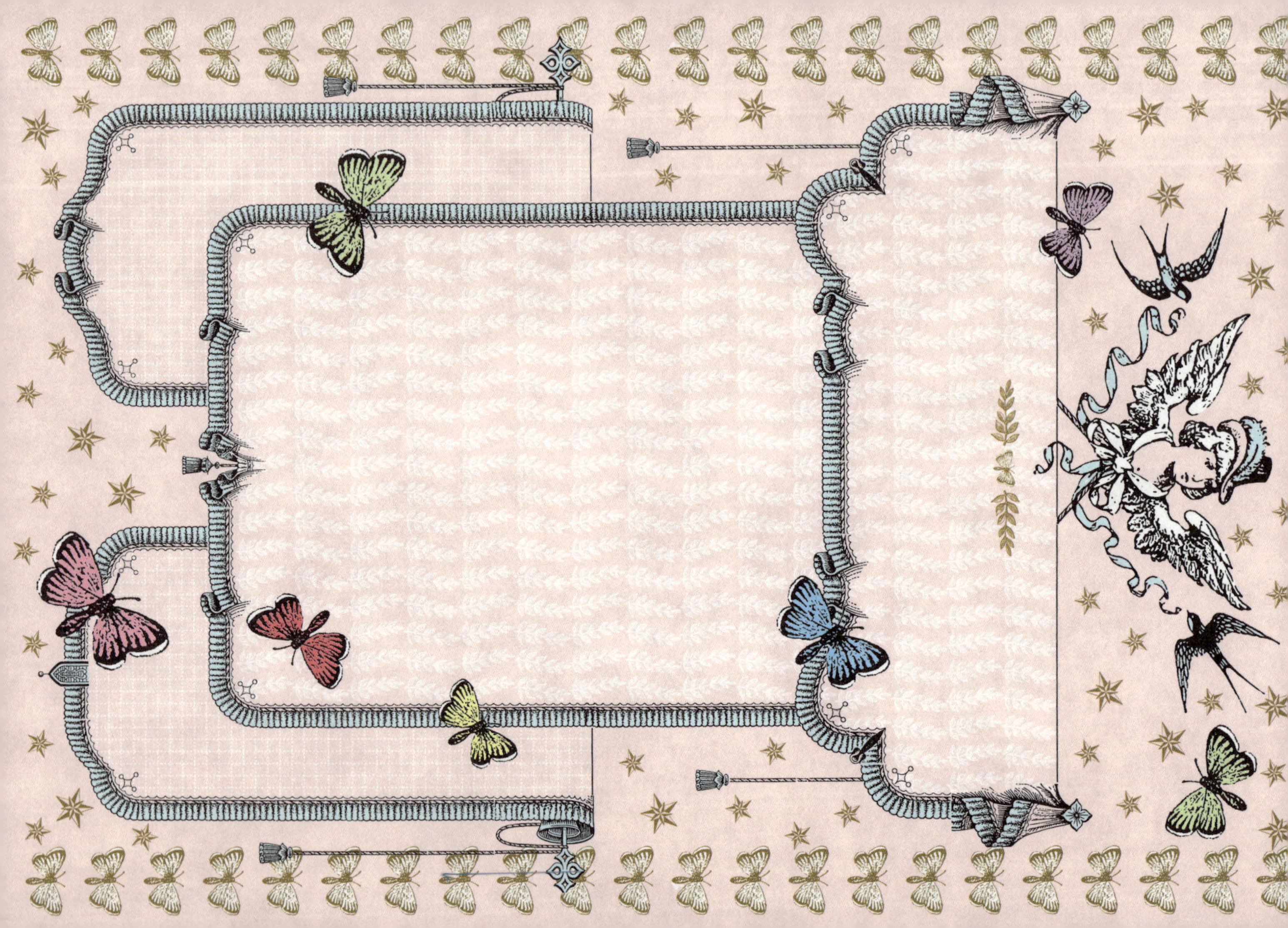

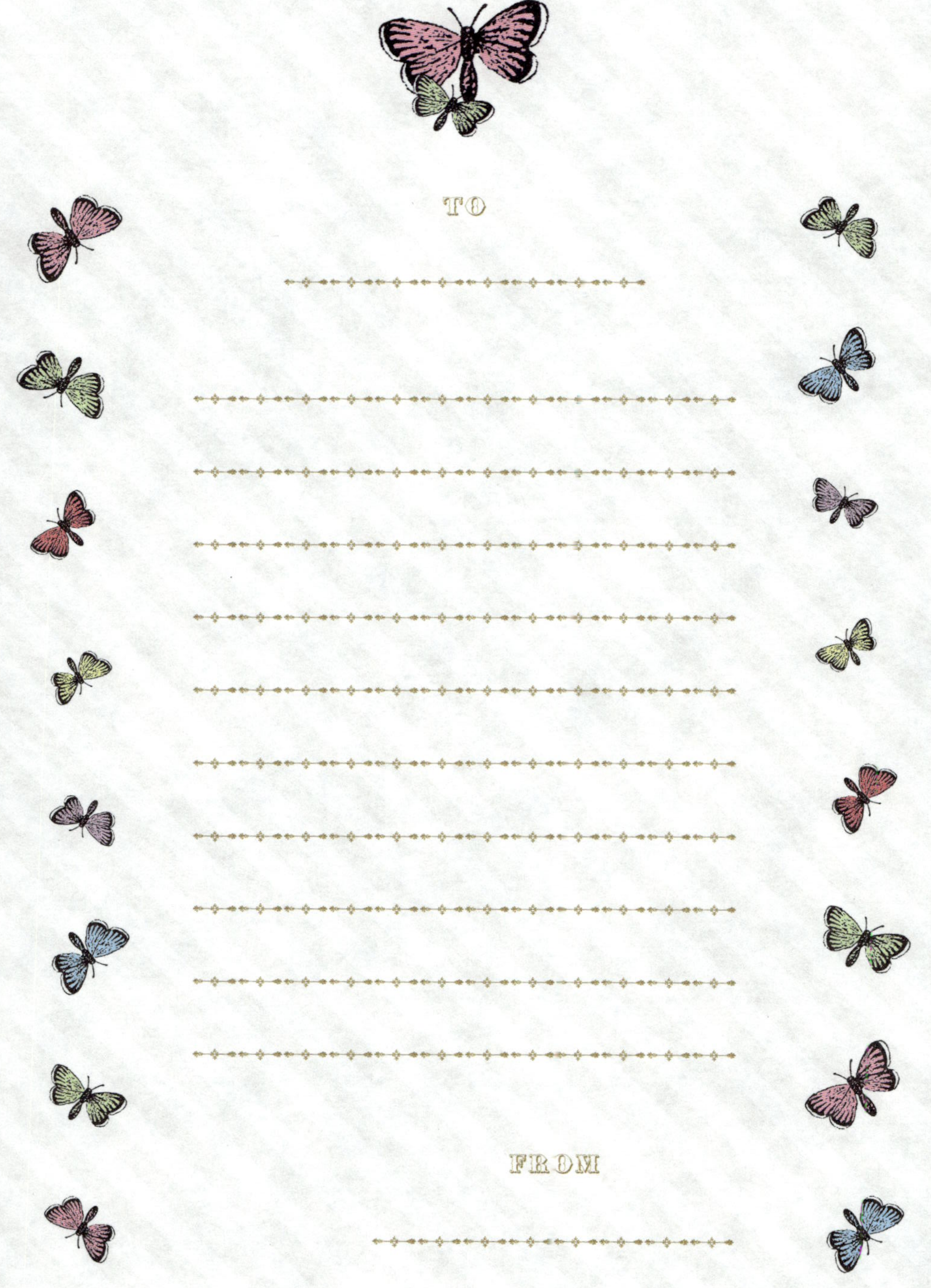

TO
FROM

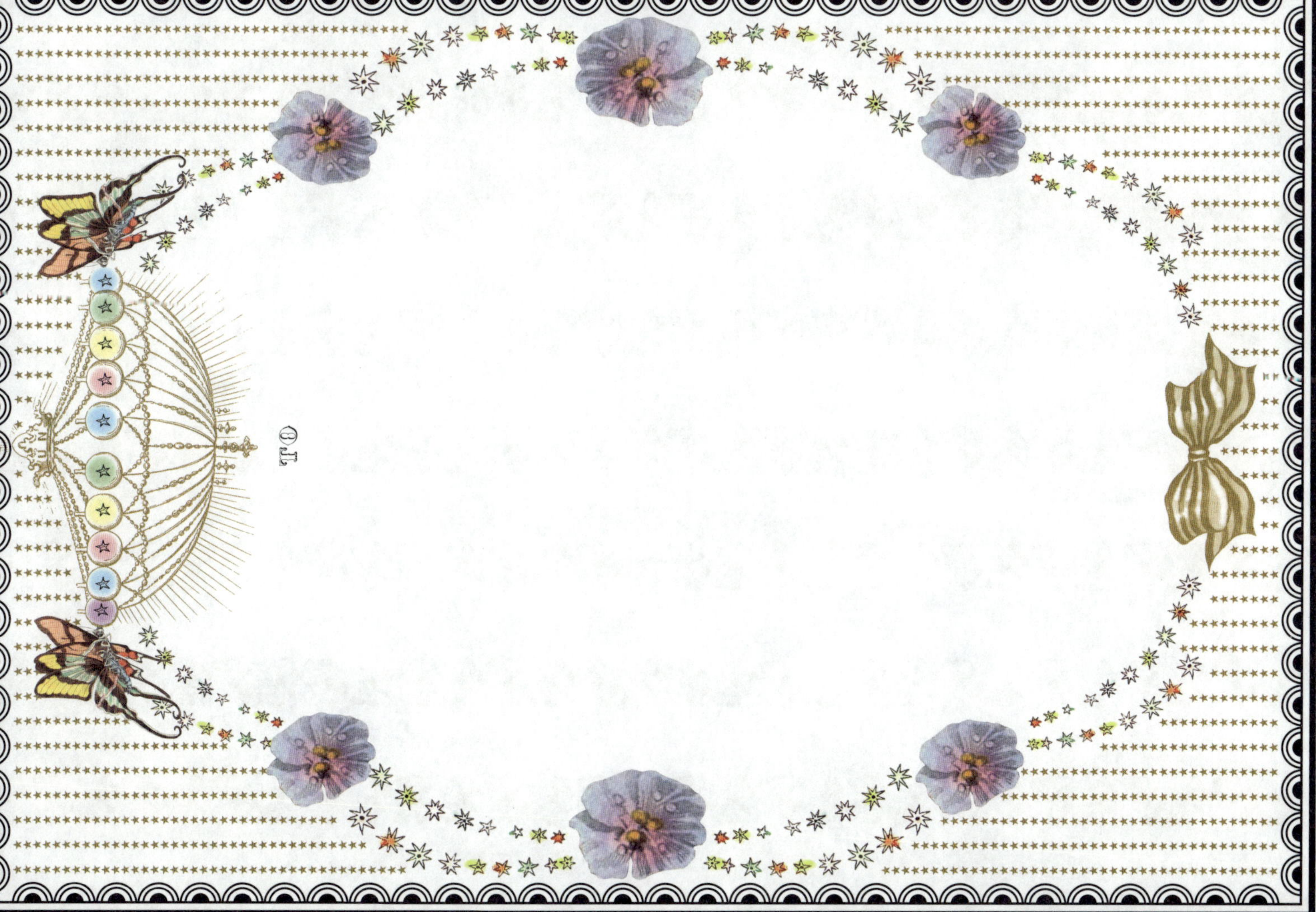

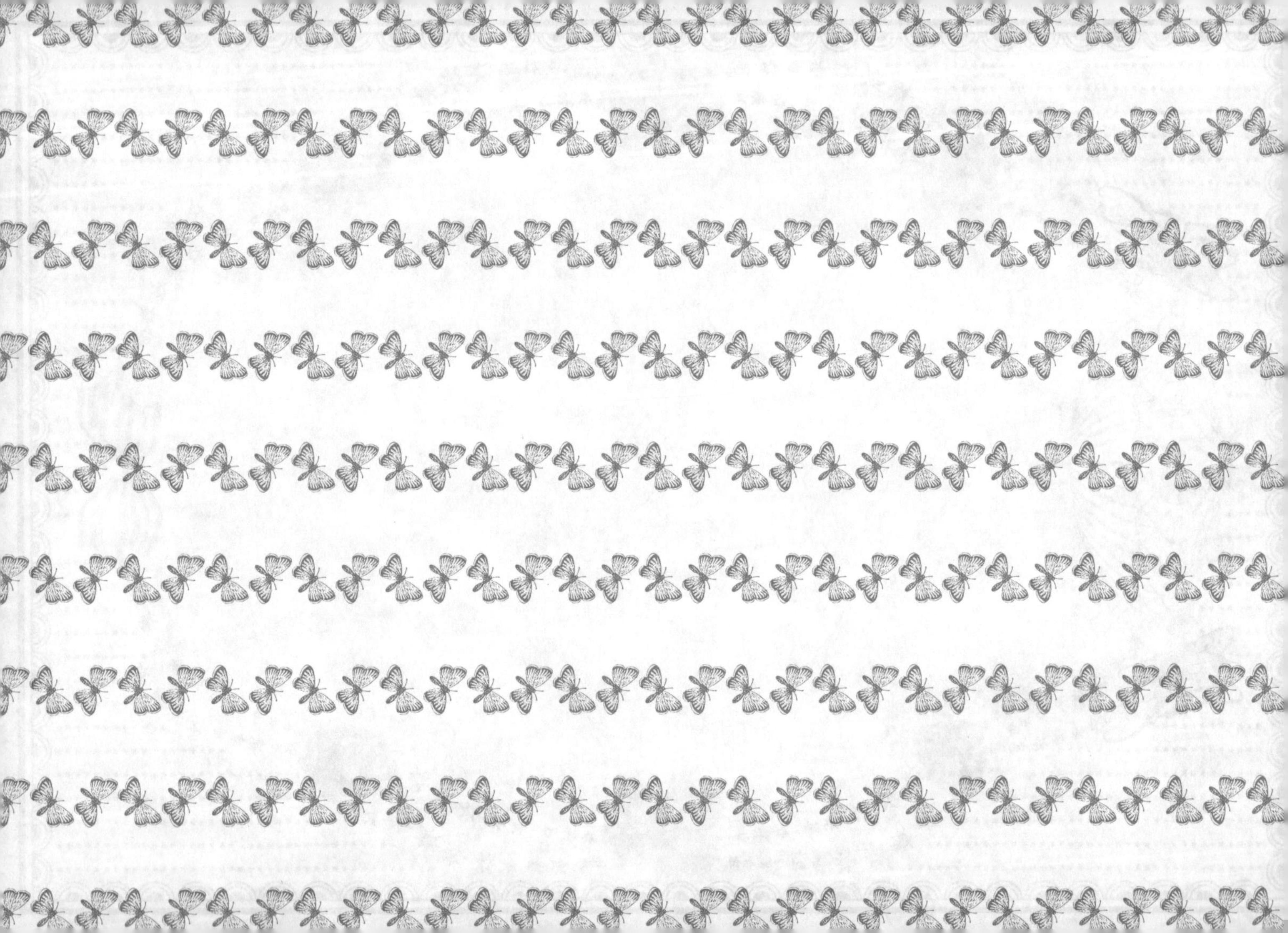

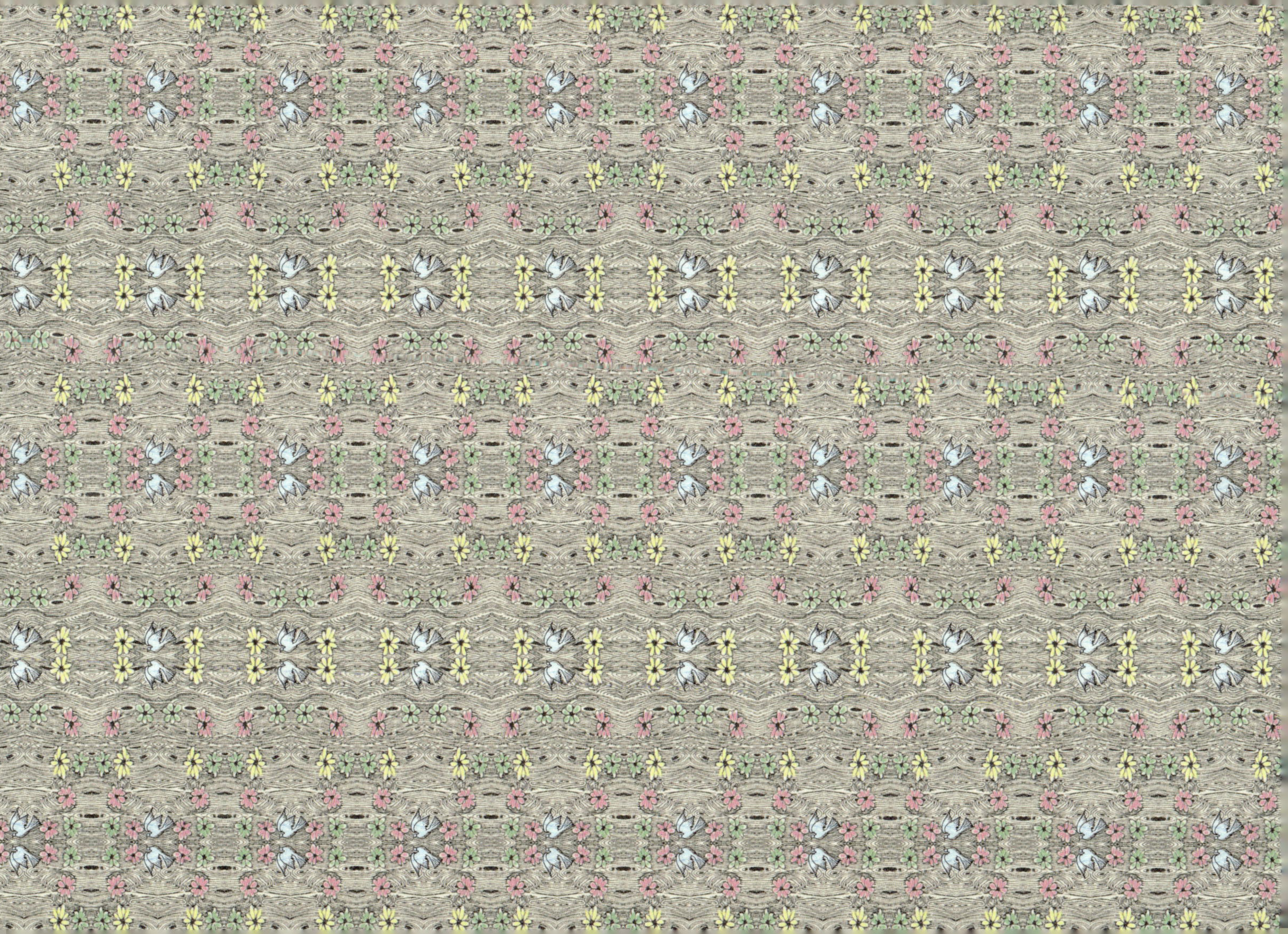

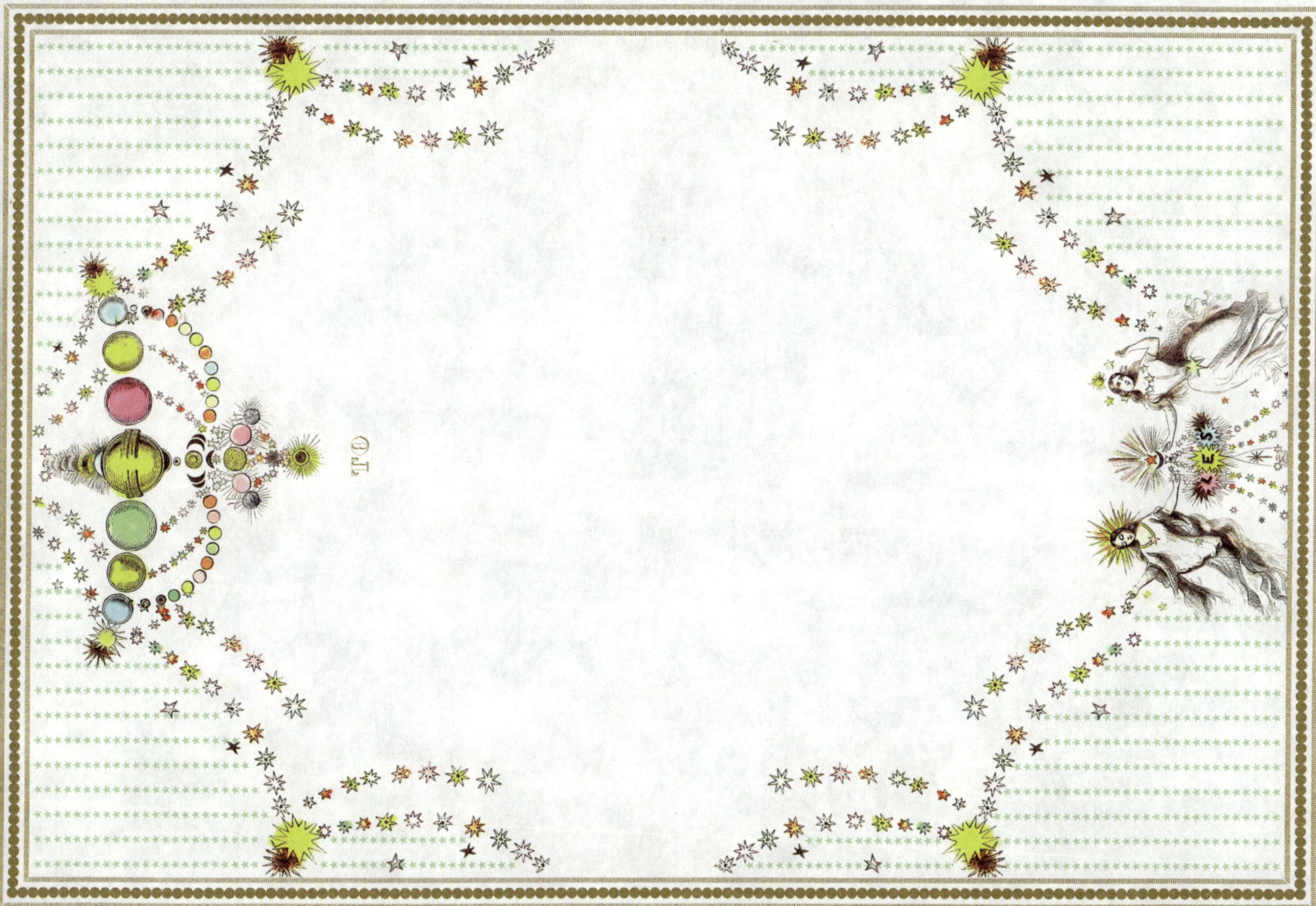

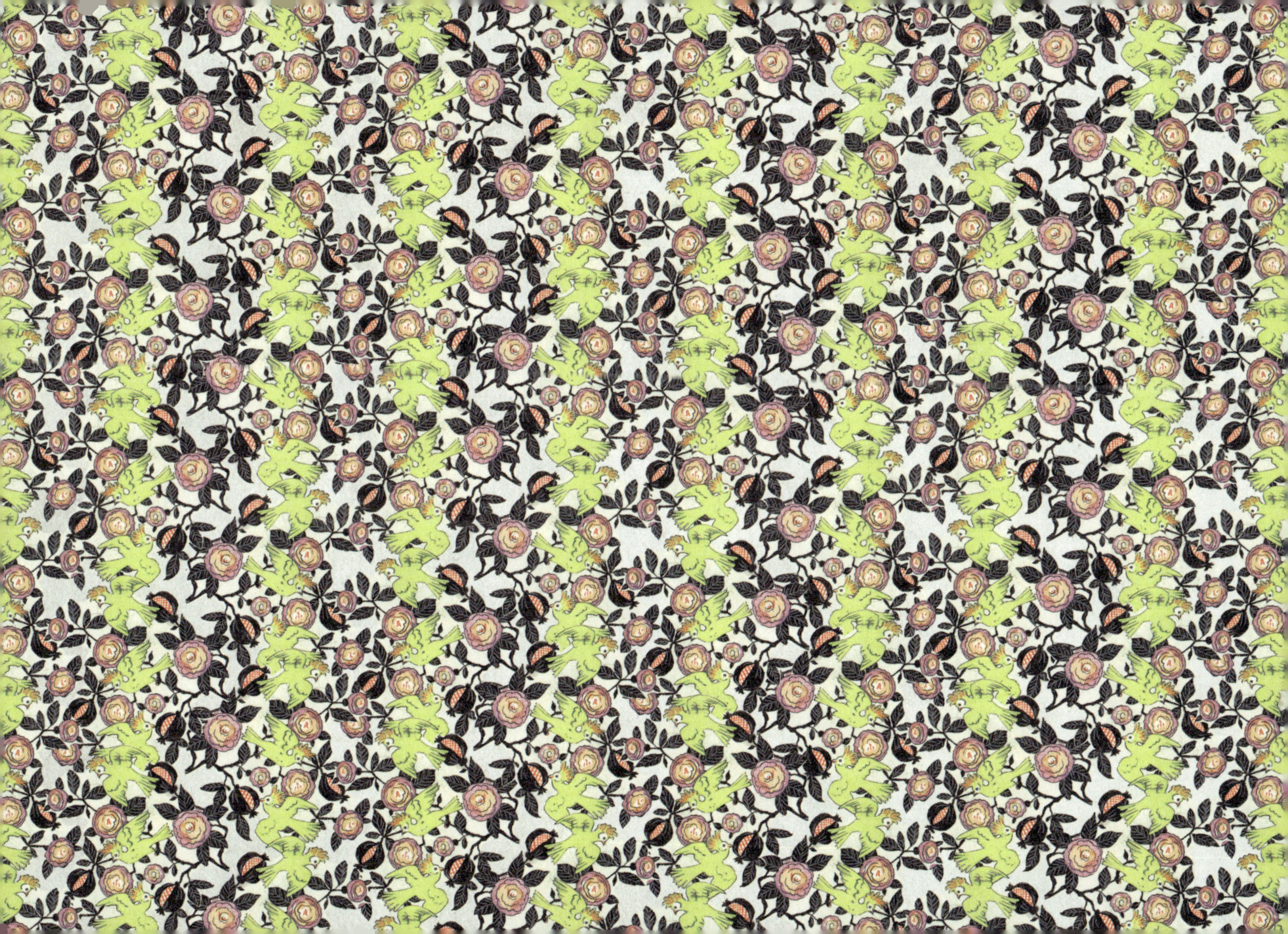

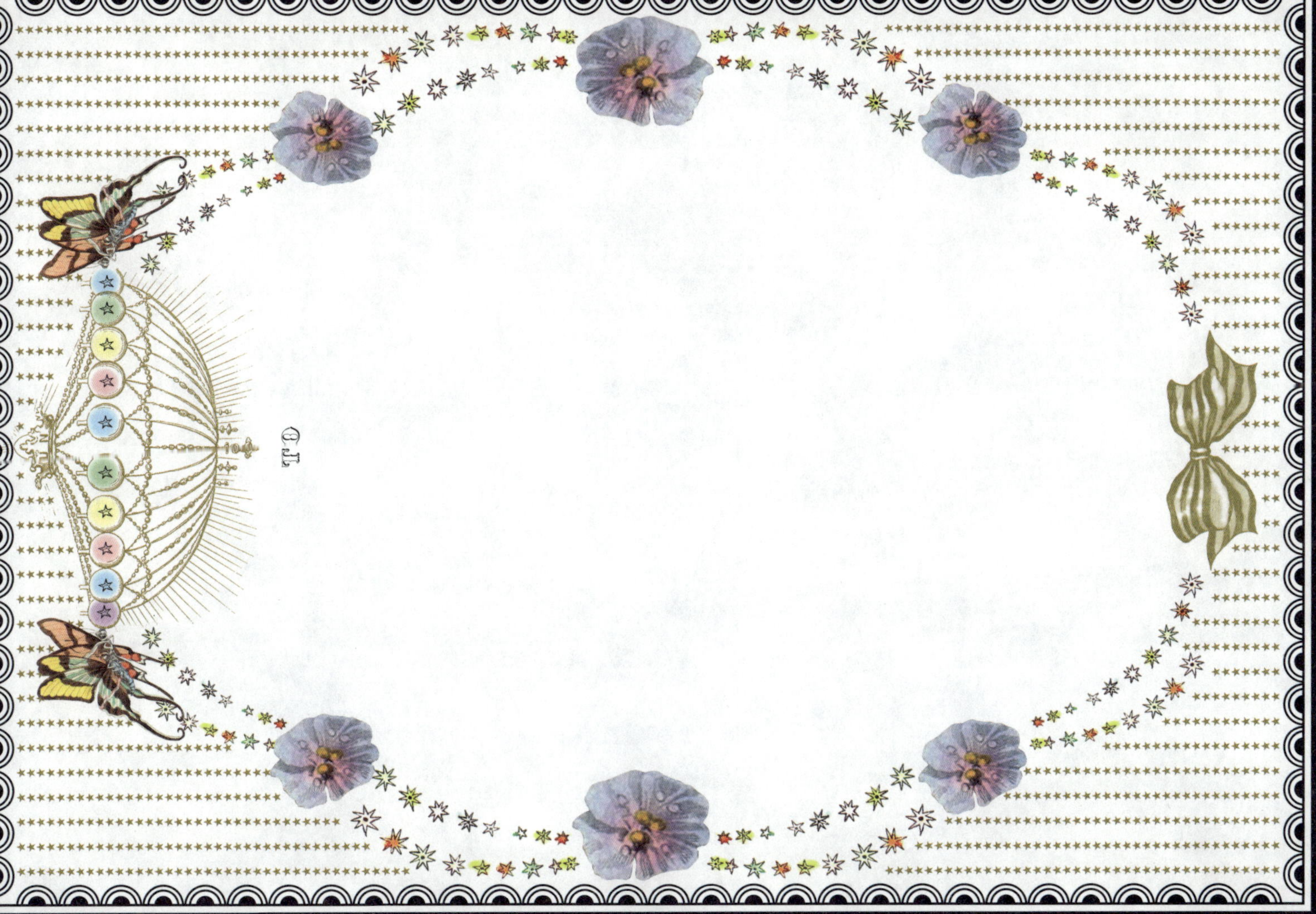

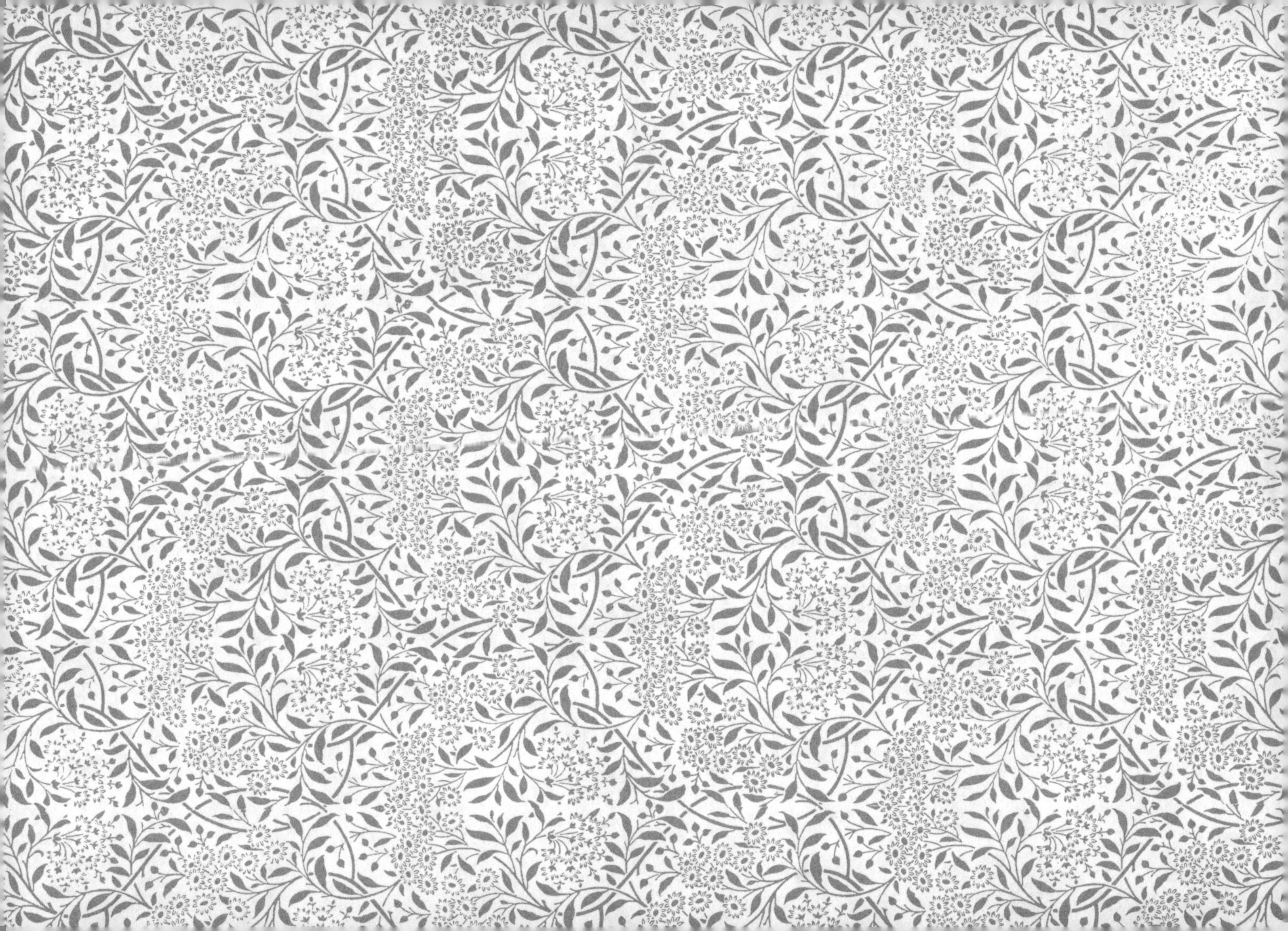

TO
FROM

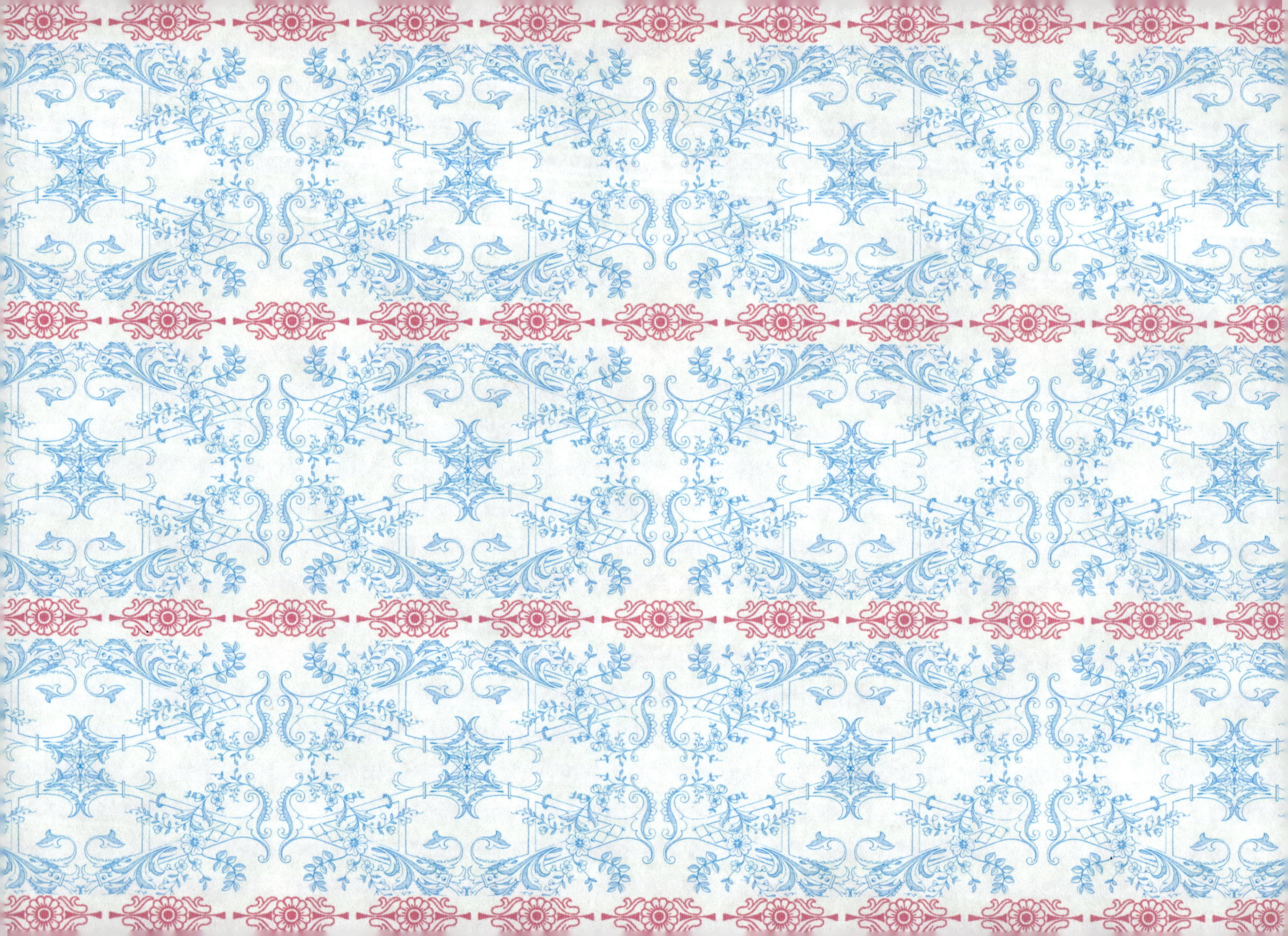

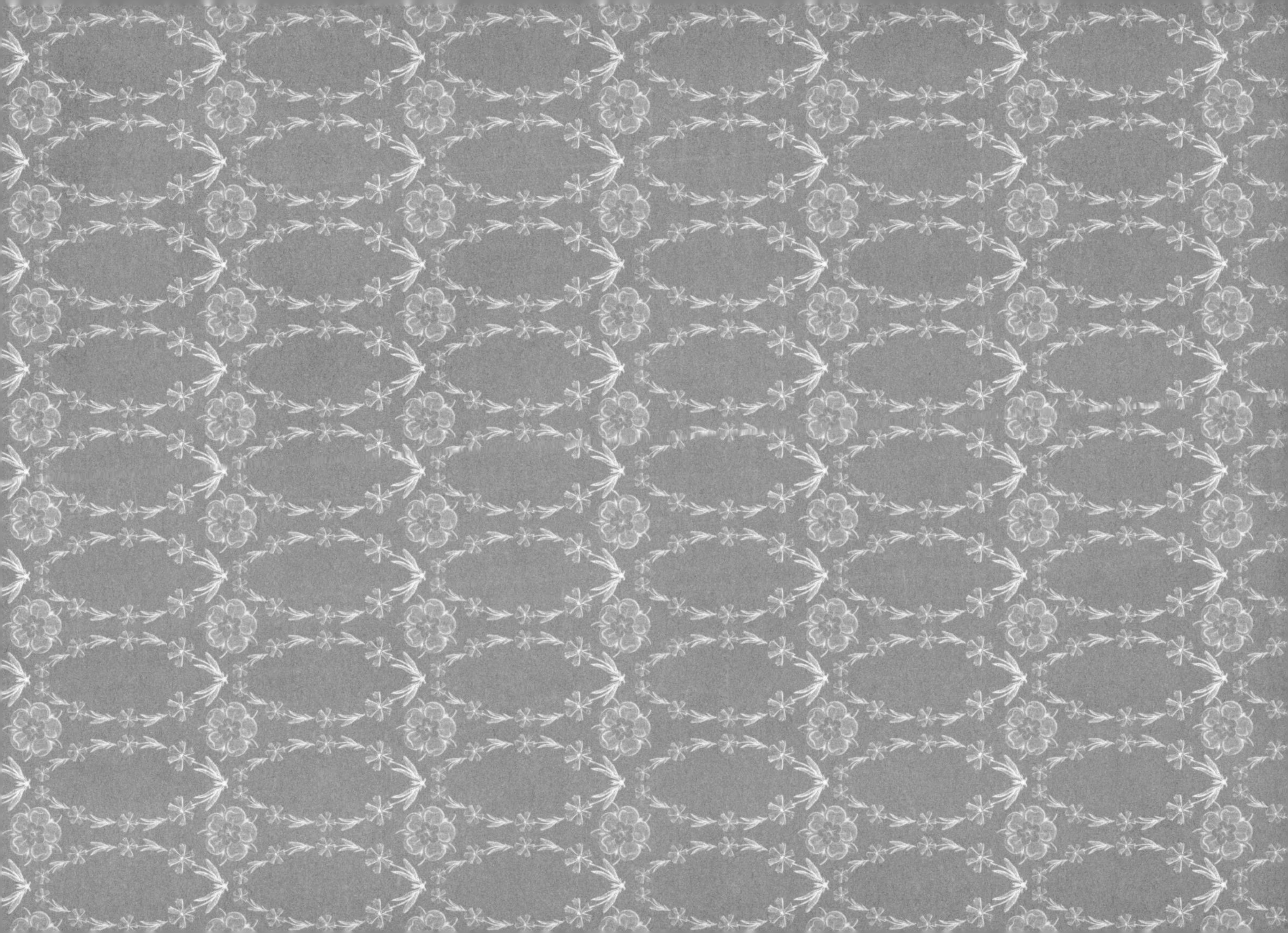

To
From

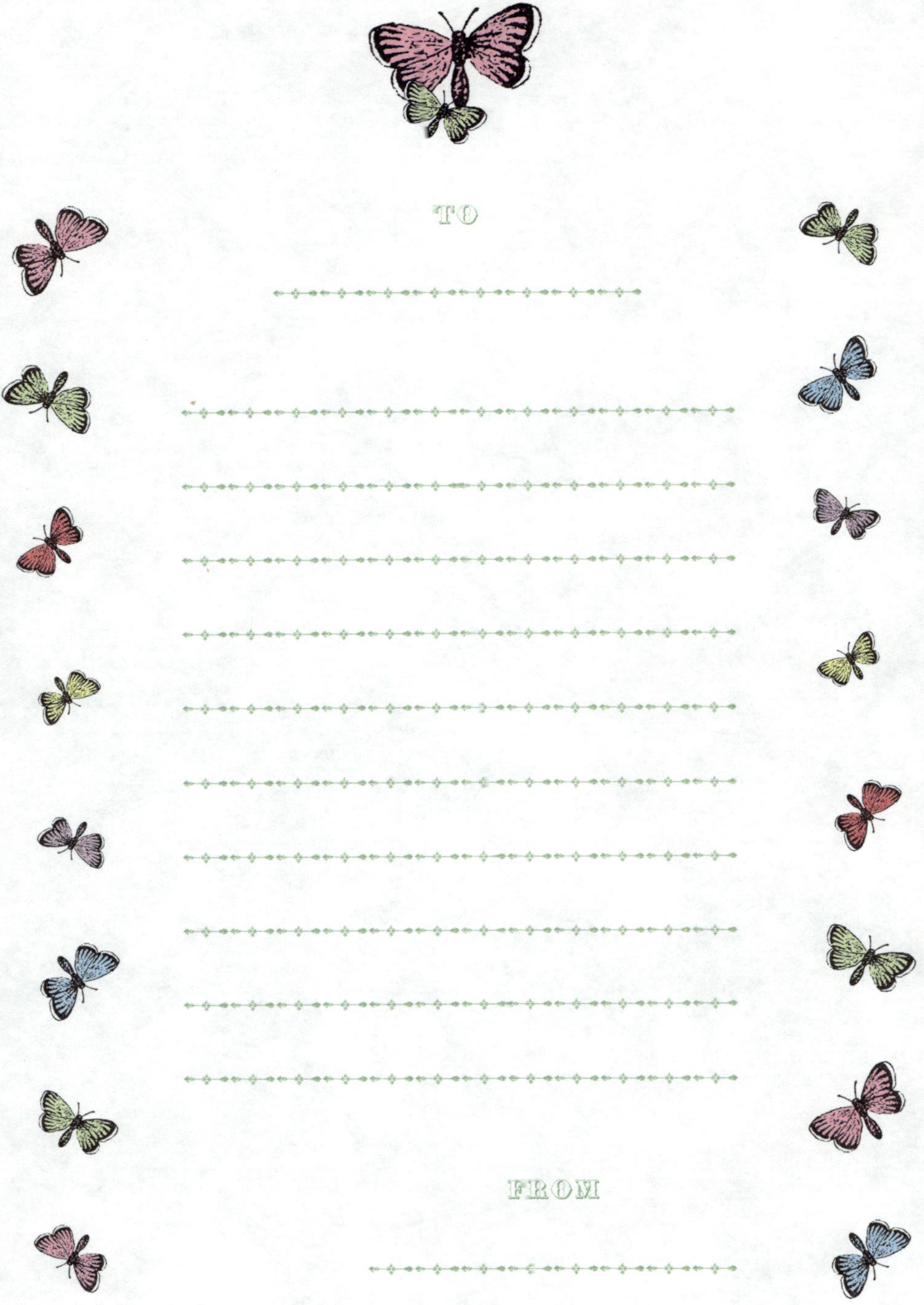
TO
FROM

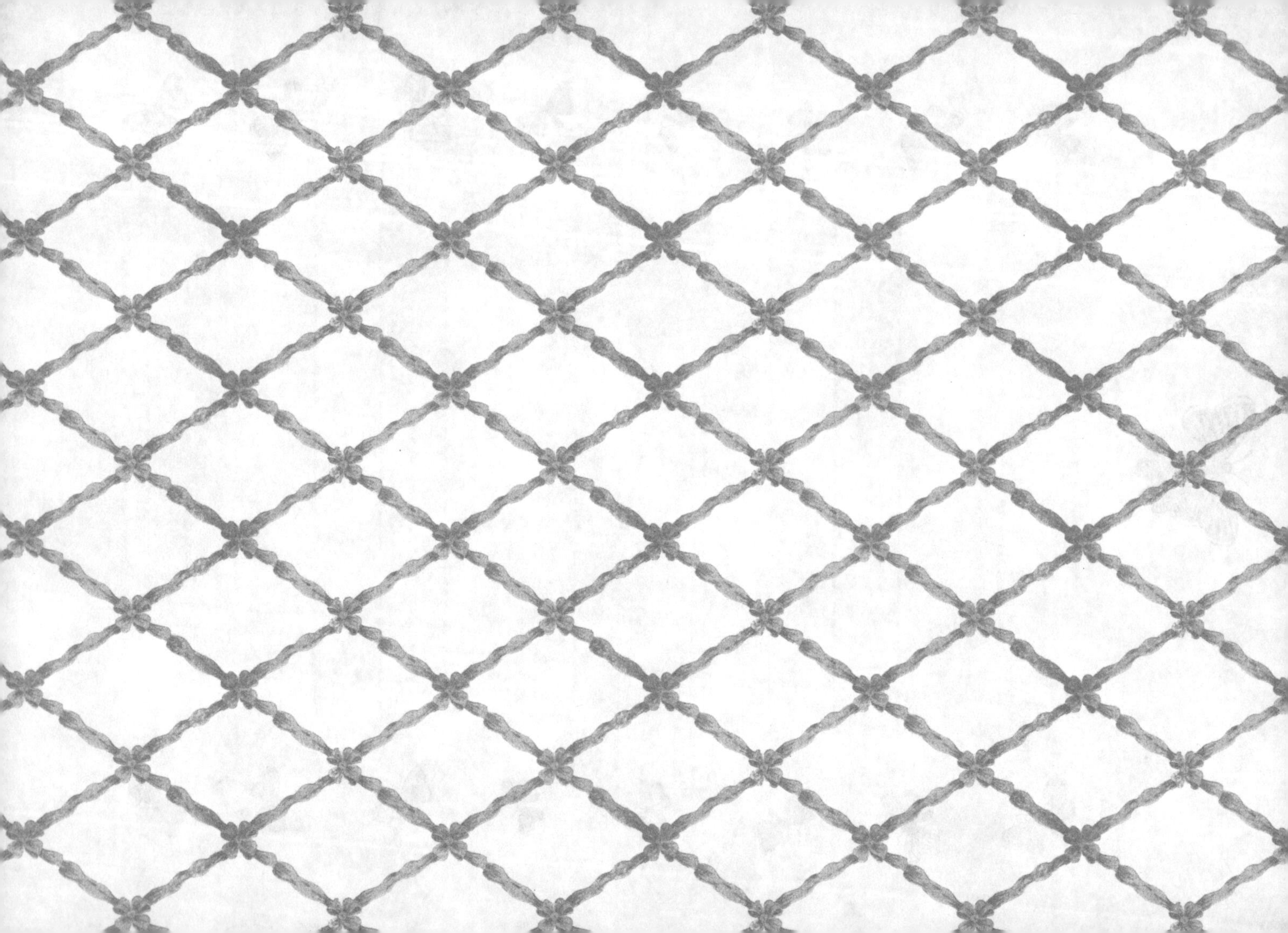

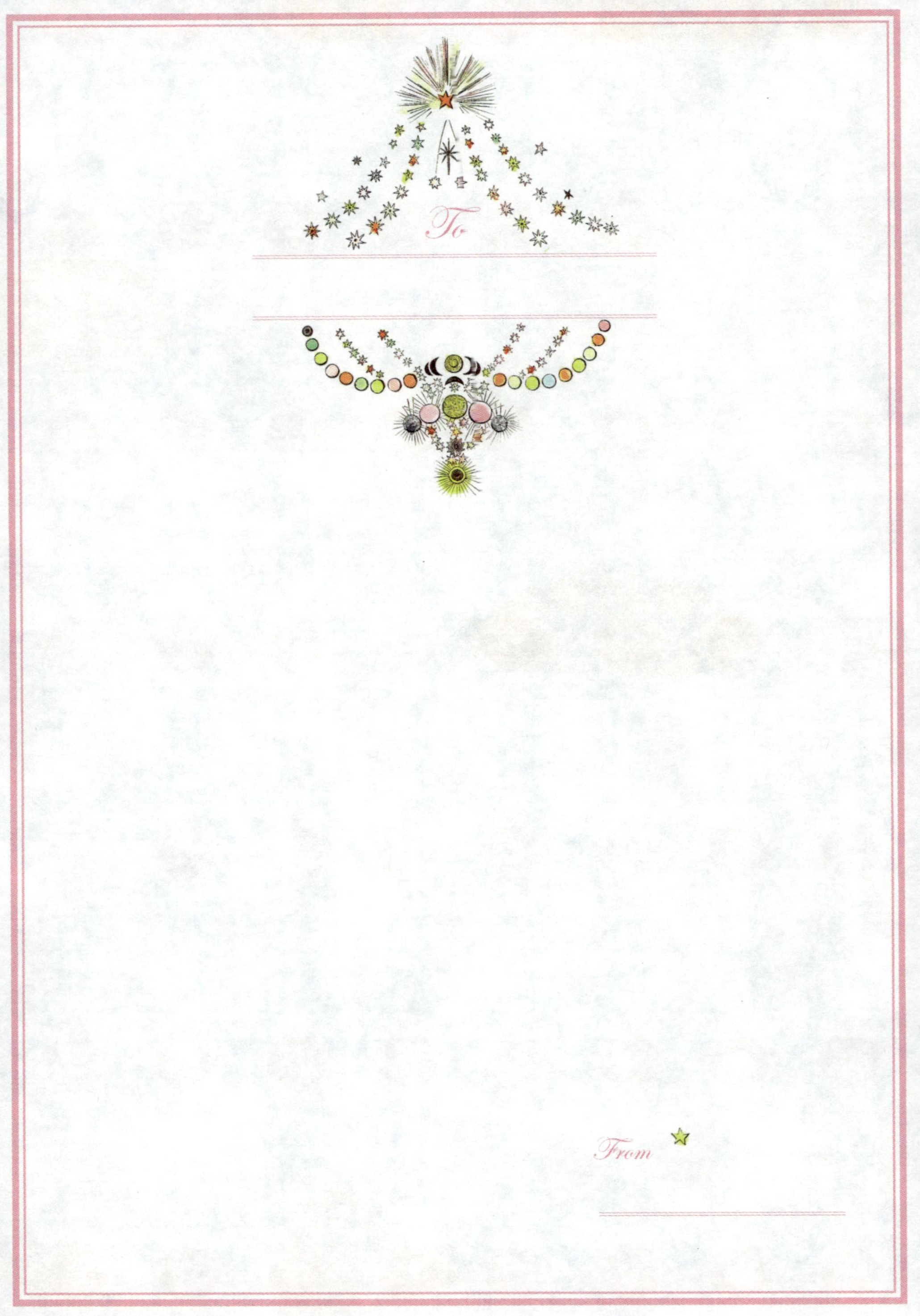
To
From

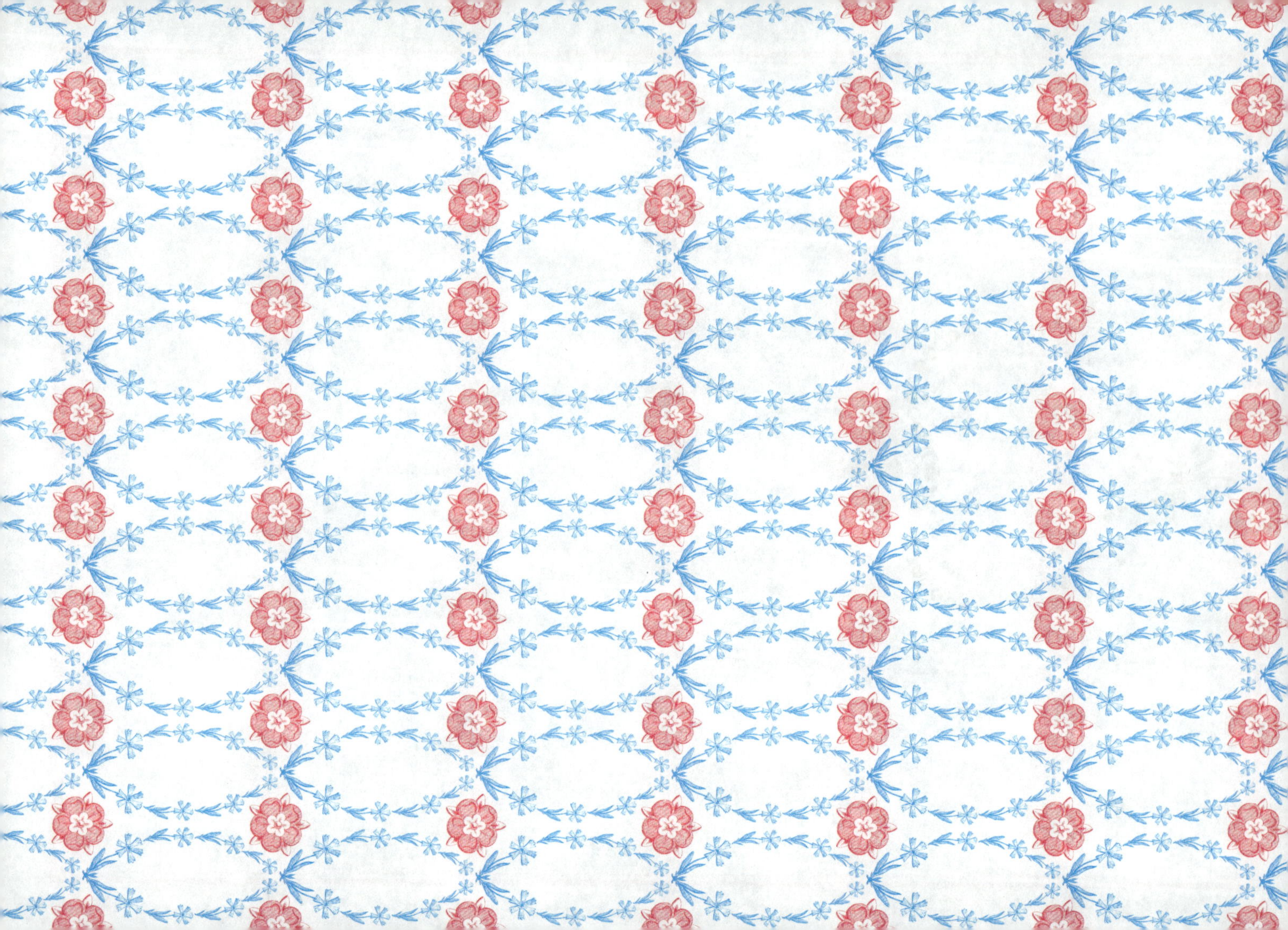

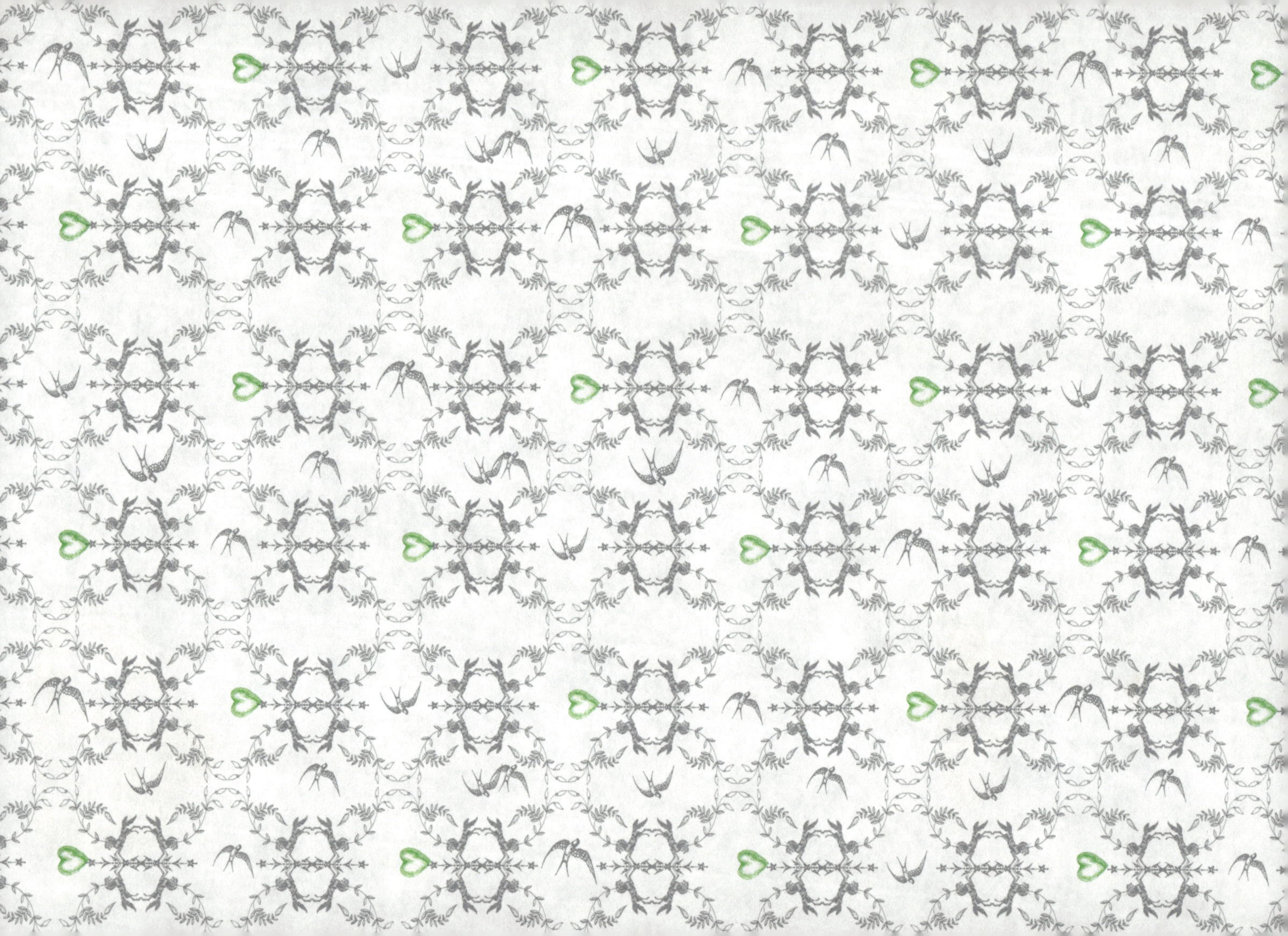

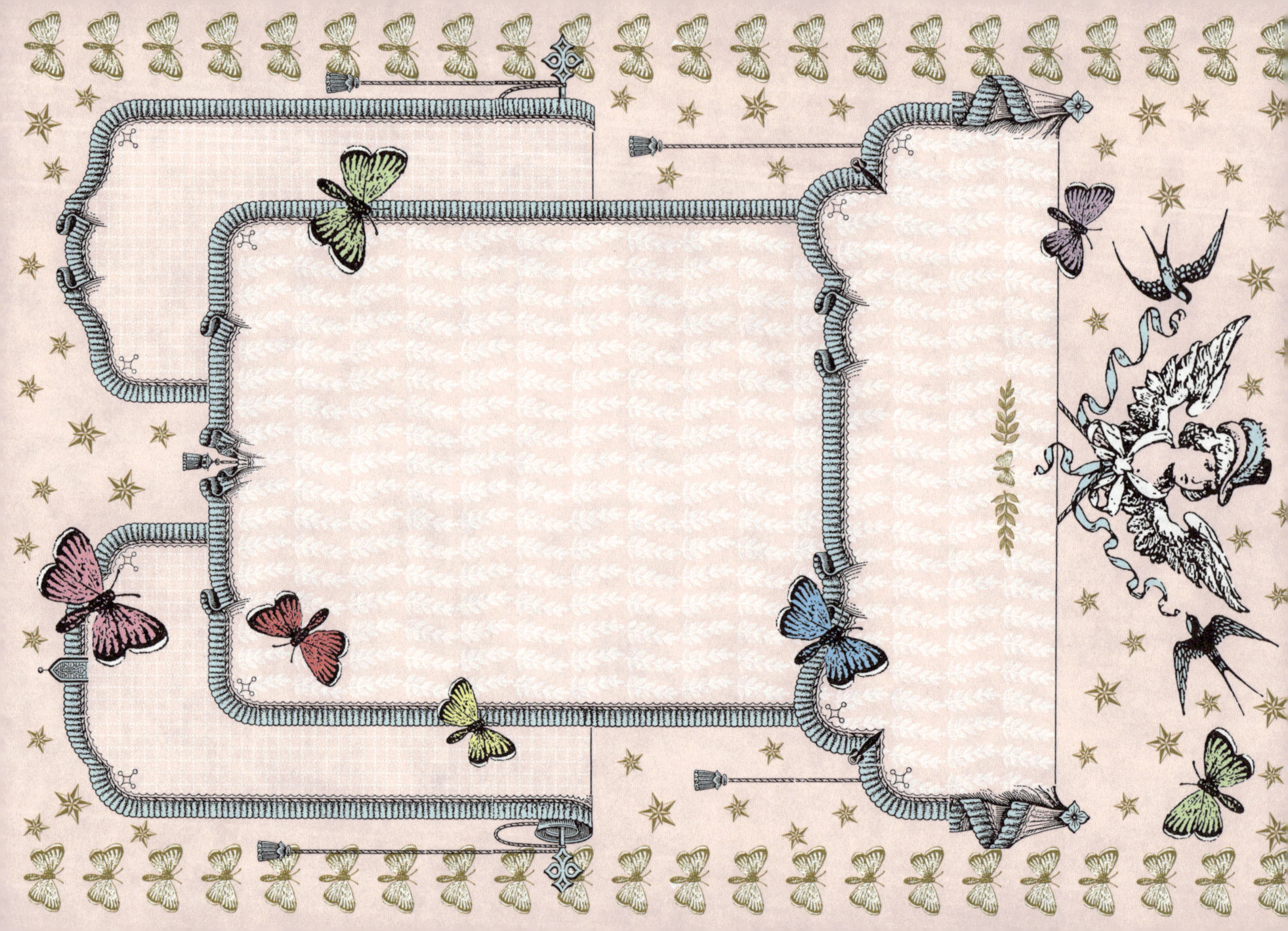

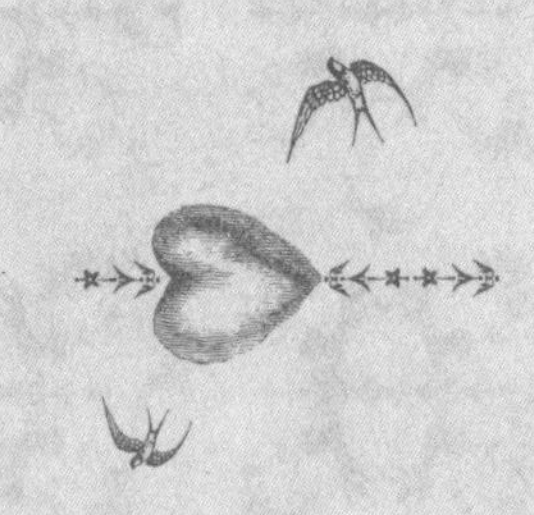

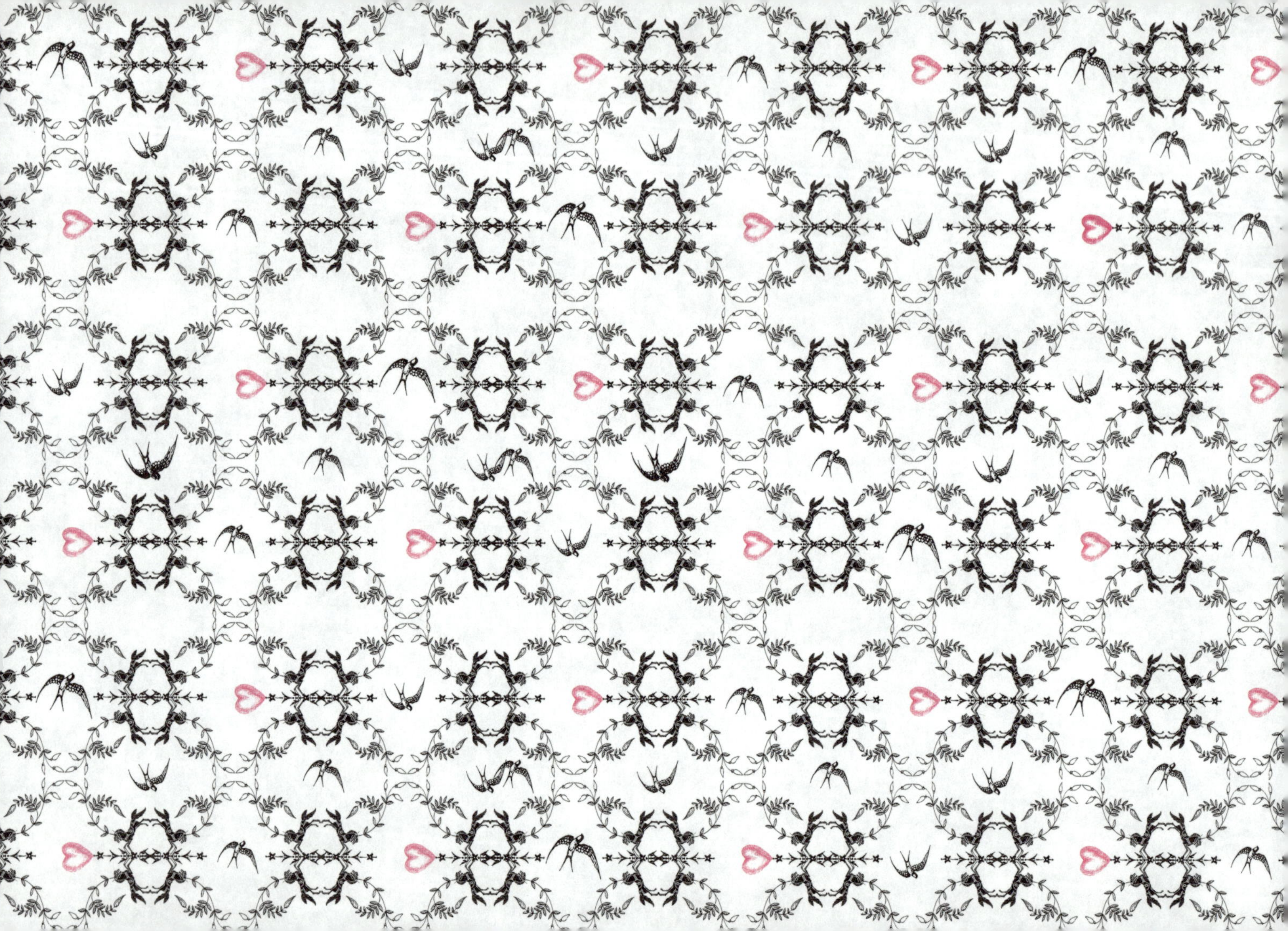

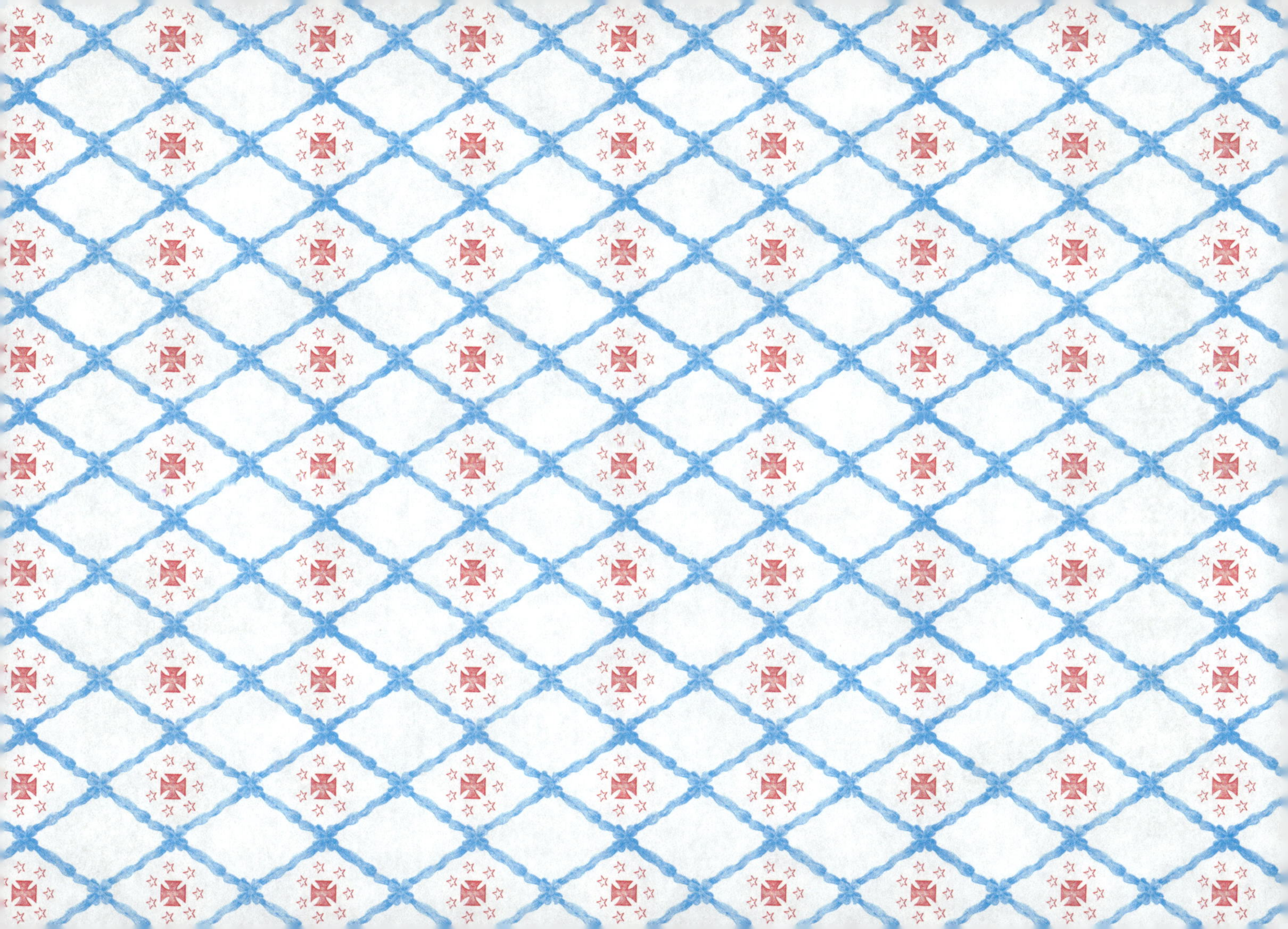

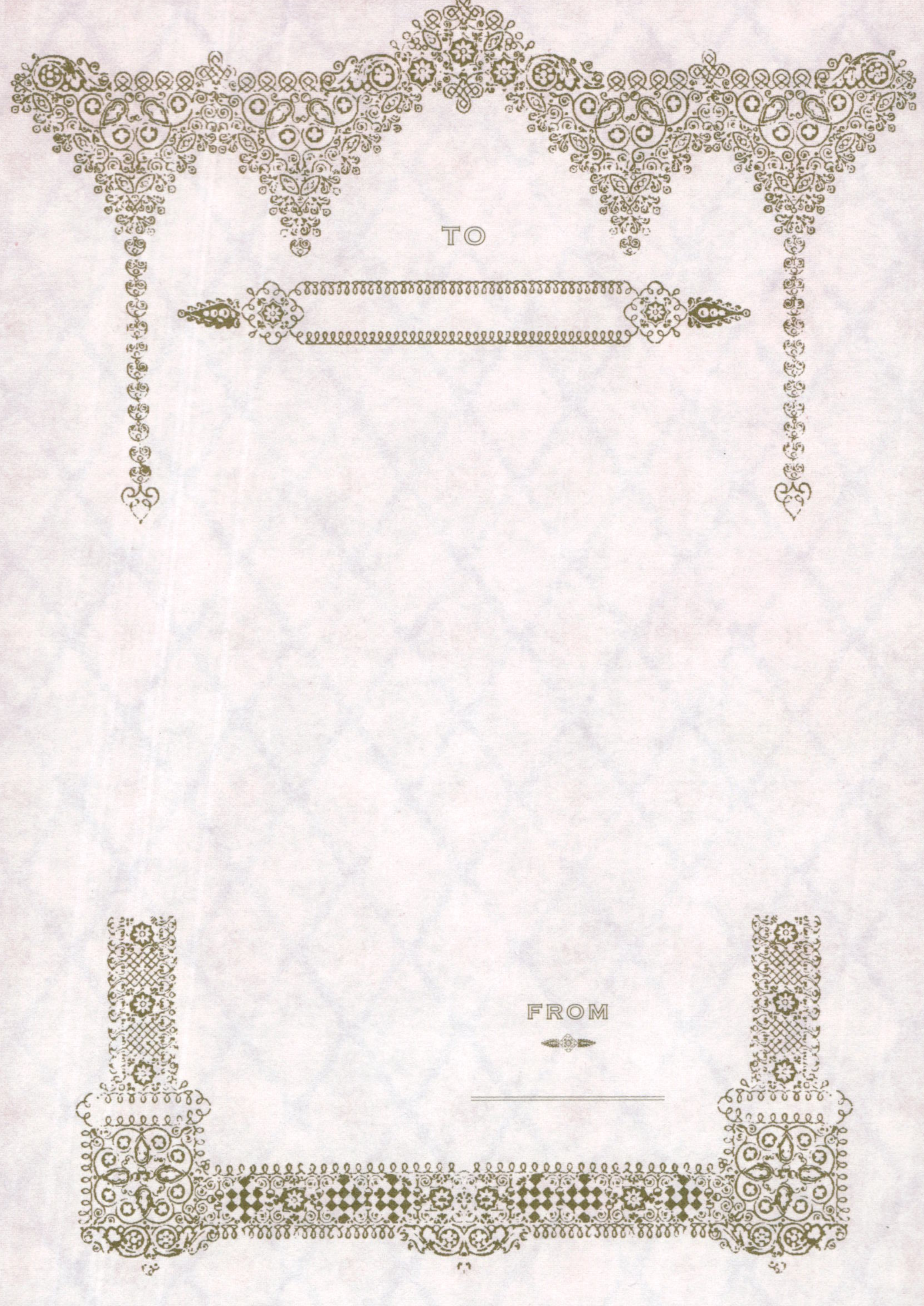

TO
FROM

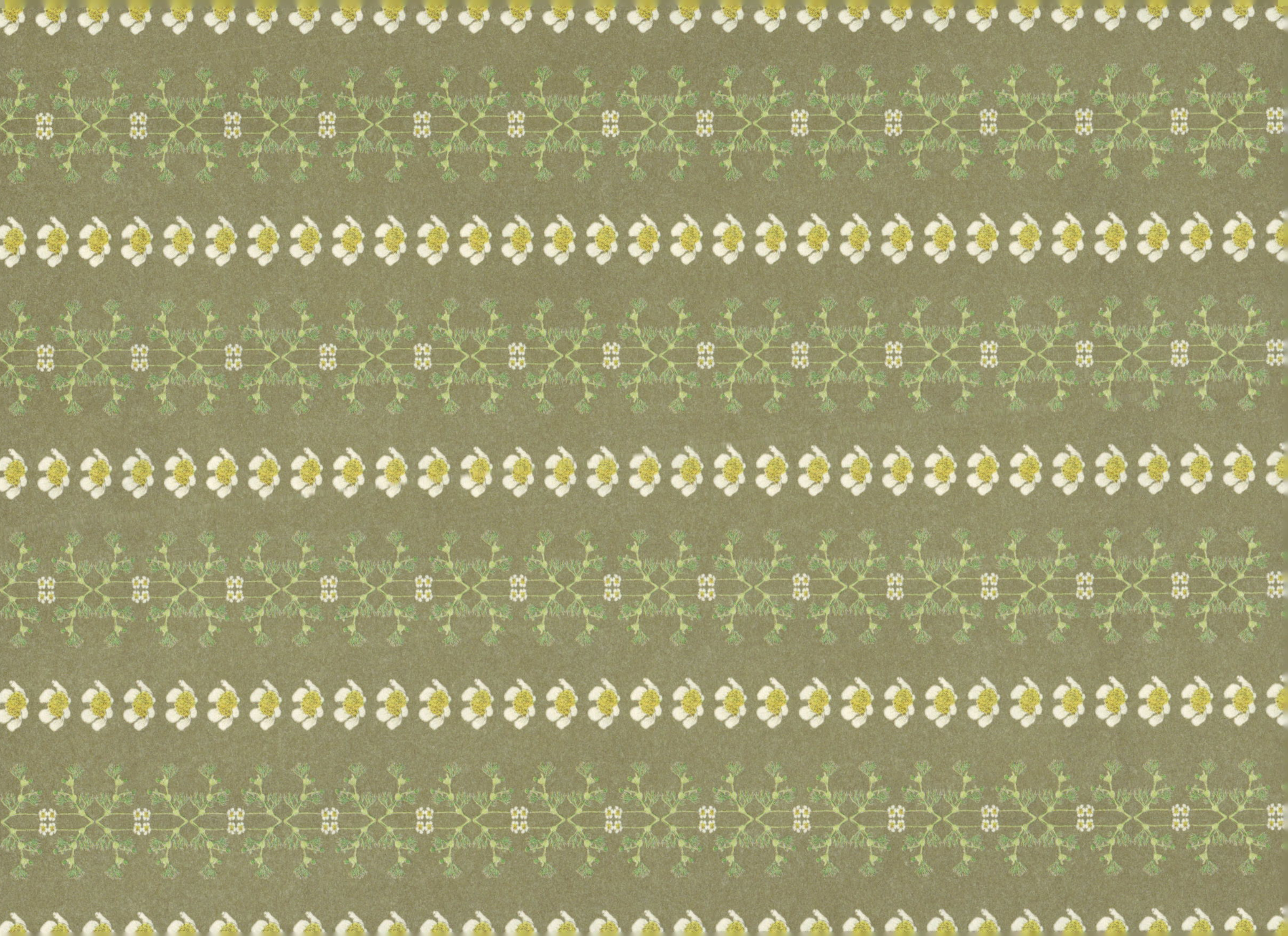

To
From

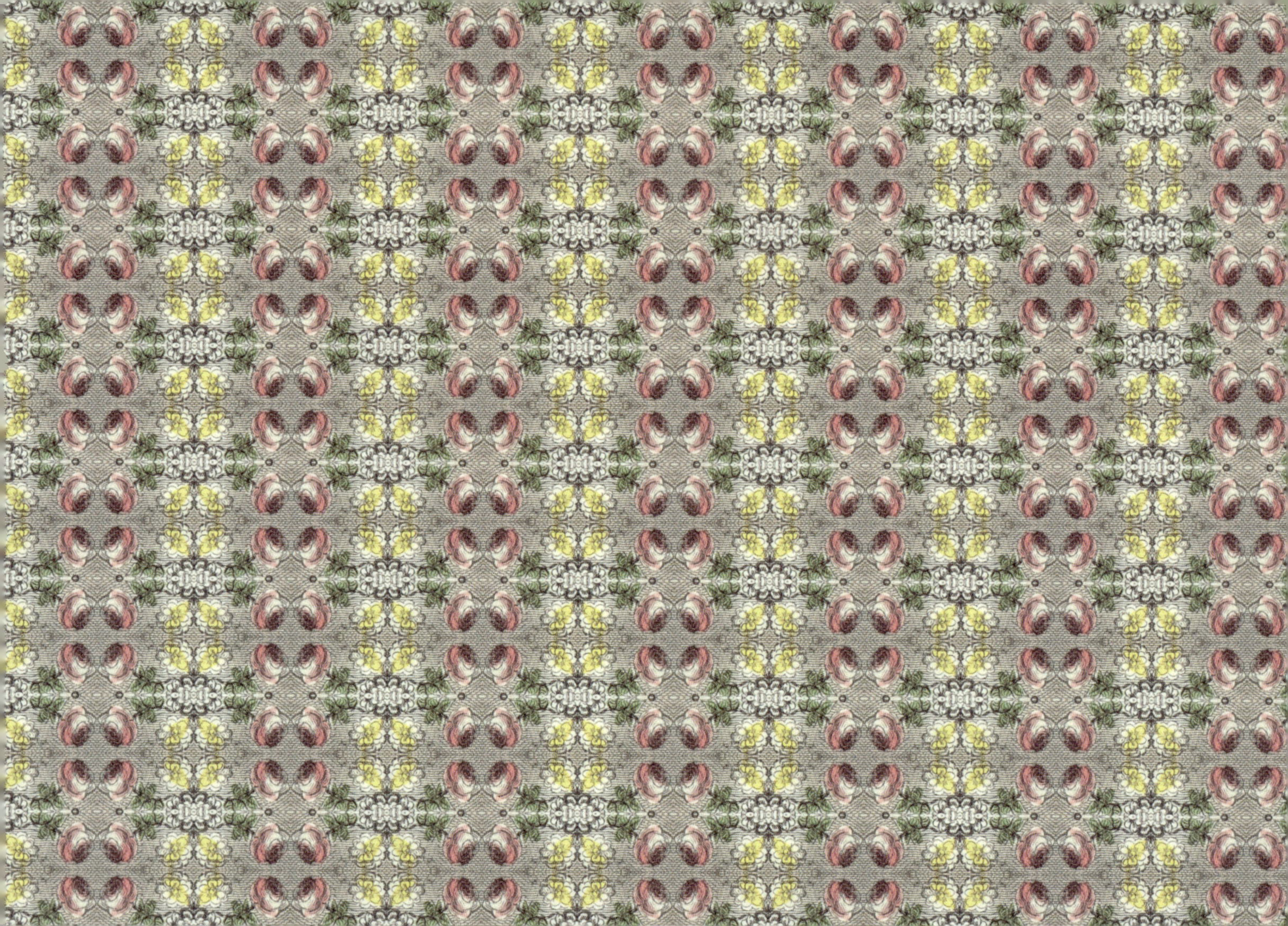